Robert Knight

Robert Knight
Reforming Editor in Victorian India

EDWIN HIRSCHMANN

OXFORD
UNIVERSITY PRESS

OXFORD
UNIVERSITY PRESS

YMCA Library Building, Jai Singh Road, New Delhi 110 001

Oxford University Press is a department of the University of Oxford.
It furthers the University's objective of excellence in research,
scholarship, and education by publishing worldwide in

Oxford   New York

Auckland   Cape Town   Dar es Salaam   Hong Kong   Karachi
Kuala Lumpur   Madrid   Melbourne   Mexico City   Nairobi
New Delhi   Shanghai   Taipei   Toronto

With offices in

Argentina   Austria   Brazil   Chile   Czech Republic   France   Greece
Guatemala   Hungary   Italy   Japan   Poland   Portugal   Singapore
South Korea   Switzerland   Thailand   Turkey   Ukraine   Vietnam

ISBN-13: 978-0-19-569622-6
ISBN-10: 0-19-569622-0

Typeset in Veljovic 10/12.4 by JoJy Philip
Printed in India at Star Print O Bind, New Delhi 110 020
Published by Oxford University Press
YMCA Library Building, Jai Singh Road, New Delhi 110 001

To Del

In appreciation of her help, encouragement, and patience

Contents

Plates

Preface

I first met Robert Knight in a journalism history which told of his creating the *Times of India* in Bombay and mentioned offhand that he later moved to Calcutta and founded the *Statesman*. Nothing further. As these were the two most prestigious newspapers in India, here was a hidden giant, a forgotten founder. Knight had been omitted from all histories of British India and all biographical dictionaries.

I soon discovered why, as I began excavating archives, the files of Knight's newspapers, and other remote sources. Knight's editorial views and their vehement and pungent style provoked the enmity of many of his Anglo-Indian countrymen, including three consecutive viceroys. He scorned the view that Indian people were a part of the booty of the buccaneering seizure of India by the East India Company; he saw them as equal citizens of Victoria's global empire and encouraged them to work for political rights, a free press, and economic justice. He applauded the formation of the Indian National Congress in 1885 and pointed the way for it.

During the course of this forty-year project, I have had the support and assistance of many many people whom I must thank. Undoubtedly the first and foremost is late B.J. Kirchner. Without Bernard Kirchner's help and his enthusiastic encouragement, I could never have undertaken this project. A retired editor of the *Statesman*, he had married into the Knight family and introduced me to them. Principal among them was Hilda (Knight) Kidd, youngest and only surviving child of Robert. She too urged me to search out the story of her father's life. She was 93 when we met; she had been fifteen when her father died and knew little of his controversies, but she remembered some crucial childhood details which enabled me to proceed.

There were Knight's grandchildren, Imogen ('Grace') de Morgan, Catherine, Lady Peake, George Knight (who thoughtfully provided a family tree), and his brother, Robert ('Ivan') Knight. And the great-grandchildren: Joan Young, Evelyn ('Eve') Knight, Michael Peake, the Rev. Canon Jeremy Peake, and, especially helpful in recent decades, Deirdre ('Sally') Godwin-Austen. One great-nephew who filled in some important blanks was Jamie R. Camplin.

I have had many years of support from my home institution, Towson University, in Maryland, USA, its Albert S. Cook Library, and my History Department colleagues, especially Karl Larew, Ronn Pineo, Patricia Romero, and Wayne McWilliams. There was financial support at various times from the American Institute of Indian Studies, National Endowment for the Humanities, and US Educational Foundation in India (and its Fulbright Program).

I am also grateful to many professional colleagues, of whom the foremost has been S.R. Mehrotra, of Shimla, who over the decades has even shared research finds with me. Also Edward S. Moulton, whose advice and encouragement have been most helpful; Norman G. Barrier, Marc Jason Gilbert, Uma Dasgupta, T.J.S. George, Aroon Tikekar, Nilufer Bharuchia, Julie Codell, and my guru of old, Robert Eric Frykenberg.

There were the libraries and other institutions which extended their cooperation and hospitality: Indian National Library, Kolkata; National Archives of India, New Delhi; the state archives of Andhra Pradesh, West Bengal, and Maharashtra; British Library, London; US Library of Congress, Washington DC; Milton S. Eisenhower Library at Johns Hopkins University; Jamia Millia Islamia, New Delhi; Nehru Memorial Museum and Library, New Delhi; Asiatic Society of Bombay; and the university libraries at University of Bombay; London School of Economics, Yale University, and University of Manchester.

There was the staff of the *Statesman* in Calcutta, headed by the late C.R. Irani, who helped the search for elusive details of their past.

There were my helpful and patient editors at Oxford University Press.

The helpers were many, but all errors of omission and commission belong to only one.

Finally a note on chapterization. I have deliberately kept the expression 'The Making...' in all the chapter titles as I feel this is the best way to show continuity in Robert Knight's life, how it remains constant, how it evolves and changes. These are not isolated episodes; they show how changing circumstances tested his beliefs in human freedom and dignity, his hatred of oppression and injustice, his faith in Christianity and private enterprise, his growing doubts about imperialism, etc. At each stage of his life he had to amalgamate new events into his existing beliefs.

Baltimore   EDWIN HIRSCHMANN

Introduction

Imperialism, the rule of one people by another, requires some combination of physical, usually military force, political skill, and popular persuasion. When the military force is weak, as in the British Indian empire, the acceptance of alien rule by most of the populace, or at least its acquiescence, is essential. Never have so few ruled so many, so easily, as in 'the Raj', the British-run Government of India. But when sufficient segments of the populace turned against it and were stirred into resistance, British rule could not be maintained. It was an 'empire of opinion', a journal warned in 1836.[1]

Control of the populace required control of public opinion, and this required control of mass communications. As long as the mass media—the newspapers—explained the news from the rulers' point of view, political events could be kept under official control. However, the empire was jeopardized when a dissident such as Robert Knight presented his view of current events, and in the process dispelled the halo of omniscience and omnipotence of the empire. The papers which Knight created— the *Times of India* in Bombay and the *Statesman* in Calcutta— vigorously criticized the Raj as long as he controlled them.

The Raj was an ill-matched hybrid of British and Indian concepts and practices. The very thin end of the wedge had been the trading operations of the East India Company, which led to the gradual takeover of political power in the subcontinent (never actually a 'conquest of India'). Even before the takeover had been completed, however, British opinion (as expressed through Parliament's charter revision acts)[2] demanded that the Raj curb its authoritarian appetites and recognize the rights of its subjects. This was implemented by officials in India in a most reluctant and dilatory manner.

One reason for these demands was the growing numbers of Britons settling in India after 1820, due to increasing security and easier transport. Some of these were independent businessmen and professionals, who felt that the Magna Carta accompanied them whenever they travelled within 'their' empire. Another reason was the view that god-fearing Englishmen, by seizing political rule, had also accepted some responsibility for the welfare of their subjects. As early as 1783, Edmund Burke had denounced the British predators in India as 'birds of prey and passage'[3] who swooped to plunder. Thomas B. Macaulay, in the bubbly benevolence of his 1835 'Minute on Indian Education', urged the Raj to thrust India into the modern world by providing English education instead of its own.[4]

The British settlers were not walled off from their Indian neighbours, and ideas and influences spread. The British interest in community news led to the first newspaper in India, Hicky's *Bengal Gazette,* in Calcutta, in 1780. It published official announcements, advertising, local gossip, and other items of local interest. It was soon shut down by authorities, but others followed.[5] Indians had their traditional networks of communication for official and local purposes,[6] but they soon saw the advantages of the new print technology, and the first Indian-run newspaper began in 1816. Like their English contemporaries, they met immediate local needs, whether these were market prices, religious discourses, or caste/community announcements. With such a fragmented audience, these early newspapers were necessarily fragile and ephemeral.[7] Only with sturdier roots could they brave the displeasure of the Raj.

Robert Knight broke the path for them. More than anyone else, he made the press a 'fourth estate' in India, a part of the political process. He was the principal founder and first real editor of both, the *Times of India* in Bombay and the *Statesman* in Calcutta, which under him grew into the foremost newspapers of western and eastern India, respectively. He often attacked and provoked the Raj, alienating most of his countrymen, but spreading ideas and critical attitudes to English-knowing Indians like ripples on a pond. Therefore, his angry challenges of official policy and conduct gave Indians a sense of grievance and purpose which helped pave the way for the development of Indian nationalism in the years which followed. Personally, it cost him dearly.

This study of Knight shows the reactions of a young Englishman with a head full of liberal ideals when he encountered the realities of India. One can see a true believer in the mission and benevolence of British rule gradually sinking into disillusion and even despair. Knight worked to improve the newspaper press of India and develop it into a sturdier and more respected part of the political scene, despite the obstructions he faced. Yet, a study of his life shows how this idealistic man caught in a double-bind grappled again and again with the puzzle of whether imperial rule of one nation by another is *ever* justified. In fact, his writings led to the exposure of 'scandals of empire' in those times, rather than in historical hindsight.

British rule peaked from the Great Rebellion of 1857 through the early years of the nationalist movement, into the late 1880s. Knight was probably the only Anglo-Indian journalist who spanned this peak period and exposed its failures to the public.

Recent studies in mass communications in India ignore the mundane daily newspaper and focus on specialized periodicals and the stereotypes which they promulgate, or else on communication links between India and Britain and how Indian issues were handled by the British press.[8] Benedict Anderson's revisionist study of nationalism states that 'national consciousness' can be traced to a common written language, promoted by the publication and promotion of books and journals in that language (which he calls 'print-capitalism').[9]

However, a case could also be made that 'national consciousness' grows from common information on the events which impact a community and the common perception of those events. A new tax, a restrictive law, a war, an insurrection, a struggle for power—such events affect all, and the way in which people learn of them—through word of mouth, public speakers, or newspaper headline—helps to determine their reception and response. Robert Knight fought for a free press which could fully and candidly inform the people of public affairs. This is the crux of his controversial life and his perceptions of the British Raj at the peak of its power.

The events of Indian history from 1857 through 1890, Knight's editorial responses, and his personal life are intertwined in this biographical study. By tracing it chronologically, we can see how the principles learned in his youth remained as his guidelines, but also how he modified their use in changing situations. As always he demanded justice for the people of India. The consecutive chapters examine the consecutive segments of his life: his London background and start in Bombay, the first editorship and creation of the *Times of India*, the ill-fated move to Calcutta, the launching of the the *Statesman*, the London venture, and finally the mature editor coming to terms with the empire.

ABOUT SOURCES

Robert Knight, despite his importance, fell into obscurity and has been ignored by history. He appeared neither in the original *Dictionary of National Biography*, or in the *Dictionary of Indian Biography* or *Who's Who* nor any other biographical compilation until the entry by the present author in the recent *Oxford Dictionary of National Biography*. In the *Statesman* office in Kolkata, there is a bust of him in the board room. In the *Times of India* office in Mumbai he is a name in the dim and dusty archives. Apparently Anglo-Indians[10] chose to ignore a man whom many considered a renegade, while most Indians preferred to honour their own.

The only previous effort at a biography of Knight was a series of articles by S.C. Sanial, a Calcutta barrister, which appeared irregularly in the *Calcutta Review*.[11] The sources which Sanial used are also obscure. Although he attached no documentation, he cited some unpublished memoirs by Knight, memoirs which apparently no longer exist. There must be a presumption of credibility in them.

In 1950 the *Statesman* published a Souvenir Edition to mark its 75th anniversary which included several episodes from the life of its founder, Robert Knight, but they were at times inaccurate and unreliable. Printed as *A Brief History of the Statesman*, it was compiled by the then-editor, Ian Stephens, and his secretary,

H. St Clair Maidment. Instead of painstaking research they relied on random information and office traditions. When the present author requested permission to consult the old archives of the *Statesman,* he was told that they had no information and that all had been destroyed.[12]

Knight's private papers and other family records were destroyed according to directives in the will of Paul Knight, Robert's eldest son, upon his death in 1949.[13] One can only speculate whether Paul wished to suppress certain information or was just seeking family privacy. Either way, he was successful, and the unpublished memoirs which Sanial had used were probably among the '24 boxes' of papers burnt.[14]

On the other hand, surviving members of the Knight family were cooperative and candid with the author, including Robert's youngest child, Hilda (Knight) Kidd, until her death in 1974 at the age 99. Without their recollections, dredged from memories of things long past, the present work could not have been written.

The principal sources, obviously, were Knight's newspapers. This author has read a significant portion, including a cross-section from each year, enough to ascertain Knight's views on the major issues of the day. Daily newspaper page references were omitted as unnecessary; at that time they were only four, six, or eight pages, and the editorial leaders and most important news items generally appeared on the second page. Finally, it might be questioned that unsigned editorials should be attributed to Knight. In those days of small budgets and tiny staffs, the editor was personally responsible for the leaders. If he did not always write them himself, he supervised and directed a colleague who did so. Occasional personal references and a distinctive slashing style confirm the Knight touch.

NOTES

1. The *Friend of India,* a Serampore weekly, quoted by C.A. Bayley, *Empire and Information, Intelligence Gathering and Social Communication in India, 1780–1870* (Cambridge: Cambridge University Press, 1996), p. 218.

2. Charter Acts of 1813 and 1833, 55 George III, chapter 155, and 3 and 4 William IV, chapter 85.

3. *Mr. Burke's Speech on 1st December 1783....on Mr. Fox's East India Bill* (Dublin: L. White, 1784), p. 31.
4. *Speeches by Lord Macaulay, with his Minute on Indian Education* (London: Oxford University Press, 1935), pp. 345–61. This model of ludicrous ethnocentrism sounds somewhat less so in its entirety instead of the usual brief excerpts.
5. S(waminath) Natarajan, *A History of the Press in India* (Bombay: Asia Publishing House, 1962), pp. 14–19.
6. Bayley, *Empire and Information*, pp. 10–13.
7. Most, that is, but not all. The *Mumbai* (or Bombay) *Samachar*, begun in 1822, was still publishing, at last look.
8. Examples are Chandrika Kaul, *Reporting the Raj: The British Press and India* (Manchester: Manchester University Press, 2003), and David Finkelstein and Douglas M. Peers, *Negotiating India in the Nineteenth Century Media* (Basingstoke: Macmillan, 2000).
9. Benedict Anderson, *Imagined Communities, Reflections on the Origins and Spread of Nationalism,* rev. edn (London: Verso, 2006), pp. 44–6 and 138.
10. 'Anglo-Indians' is used in its nineteenth-century sense, meaning an English person residing in India.
11. The first was published as a part of Sanial's overall 'History of Journalism in India', *Calcutta Review* (henceforth *CR*), vol. 127 (July 1908). Two more chapters were entitled 'History of the Press in India' and appeared in vol. 130 (April 1910) and vol. 131 (July 1910). After sixteen years, three further articles were published under the title 'The Father of Indian Journalism', vol. 19 of the 3rd series (May–June, 1926), vol. 20 of the 3rd series, vol. 1 (July 1926) and vol. 20 of the 3rd series, vol. 2 (August 1926). Although the Calcutta years of Knight's life were not covered, apparently no further articles appeared.
12. P.T. Dustoor, business manager of the *Statesman*, to the author, dated 15 June 1968 and 15 July 1968; H. St Clair Maidment to the author, dated 13 July 1968, all in possession of the author.
13. Joan Young to the author, dated 10 February 1969, in possession of the author. Mrs Young was a great-granddaughter of Robert Knight, and other members of the family confirmed this account.
14. Ibid.

1

The Making of a Reformer, 1825–56

A NEW MAN FOR A NEW AGE

'Mr Knight, merchant', landed at Bombay on 8 October 1847, carried there from Suez by the East India Company steamship *Victoria*.[1] Bombay in 1847 was such a remote and quiet outpost in that company's far-flung empire that the arrival of a European, any European, was worth noting in the annual directory. But that was about to change dramatically. The development of the steamship led to the switch of Indo-European traffic from around Africa to the route through Egypt and the Red Sea during the 1830s and 1840s, making Bombay the natural gateway to and from India. Within decades it would be a major metropolis, commercial centre, and world seaport.

Young Mr Knight (Plate I)—he was then 22—brought with him the ideas of a new age, ideas of reform, of free enterprise, of an empire run for the mutual benefit of rulers and subjects, as judged by the values of that new age. These were a far cry from the buccaneer ethics of Robert Clive and his associates, founders of the British Indian empire during the eighteenth century, and the new ideas from the West would jolt India even more than the steam engine.

Robert Knight was born in Lambeth, a modest South Bank neighbourhood of London, on 13 March 1825, the son of William and Anna Maria (Coombs) Knight.[2] William was a banker's clerk who, according to family belief, worked fifty years with Gosling and Sharpe, bankers, at 19 Fleet Street, near the Strand. He played

Plate I: Robert Knight. Courtesy the Knight family

cricket and was described as good-humoured and high-spirited. He was a widower with two children when he married Anna Maria Coombs, from Frome, Somerset. She was the daughter of James Coombs, a schoolmaster and musician who became land steward for the Marquis of Bath and later a building contractor in London.[3] William and Anna Maria had nine children who grew to maturity (and at least two who died in childhood). Robert grew up with three older sisters, Anna Maria, Theresa, and Sarah Ann;

one slightly older brother, James; two younger sisters, Emma and Esther, and, finally, two more brothers, Henry and Edward.[4]

The Borough of Lambeth had grown back from the south bank of the Thames, where it had been characterized by riverfront occupations, decrepit housing, and the odiferous river itself. It was distinguished only by the vast estate of Lambeth Palace, the London residence of the Archbishop of Canterbury. Lambeth in 1820 was described by one observer as 'mean and rickety', with tottering shacks teeming with ragged children.[5] However, Robert Knight was not a child of the slums. During Georgian times a number of substantial blocks of brick houses had been built back from the river, behind Lambeth Palace. The opening of Westminster Bridge in 1750 (replacing a ferry) and Waterloo Bridge in 1817 made Lambeth a commuting suburb, with many stagecoaches providing easy transport to the city.[6] William probably took them to his work in Fleet Street.

When Robert was born, the family probably lived on Vauxhall Walk, which it clearly continued to do four years later, in 1829.[7] The 1836 Electors' Registrar shows William Knight at 4 Canterbury Place, as does the 1841 census and the 1855 Post Office Directory.[8] Those houses and streets no longer exist. The Lambeth Road area, which included Canterbury Place, was badly damaged in the World War II blitz, and the remains were swept away in postwar redevelopment, including 'old Georgian houses on the south side of Lambeth Road'.[9] However, a block of Georgian houses still stand at nearby Pratt Walk, solid brick with plenty of windows. It apparently looks much as it had in Robert Knight's day, and the houses of Canterbury Place were probably similar.[10] One social critic, the Chartist Francis Place, visited Lambeth in 1824 and found even then substantial houses with sash windows and curtains, and people dressed like gentlefolk. 'Could this change in manners take place without a corresponding change in morals?' he asked.[11]

Little is known of Robert's youth and upbringing, but some influences may be inferred. The Knight family members including Robert were traditionally and devoutly religious, and were communicants of the Church of England. (In fact, some of his descendants thought William Knight had been a missionary.) From 1820 to 1846 the rector at St Mary's, the

Lambeth parish church where Robert was baptized, was the Rev. Dr George D'Oyley. Dr D'Oyley was a noted theologian (two volumes of sermons published), evangelist (thirteen places of worship opened in his parish), and educator (one of the principal founders of King's College, London).[12] King's College had a 'Lower Department' for secondary education which opened in 1832 and included Anglican religious instruction. No records have survived to show Robert Knight's matriculation, but it seems unlikely that such a zealous educator would have neglected a bright and idealistic lad among his parishioners. (Since there was no system of state-run schools in the 1830s, the schools of that day were endowed by philanthropists or associations and/ or were church-sponsored.)

No records show any university attendance. His later prose was that of an educated man, but it did not drip Latin and Greek phrases. Many years later, Knight disparaged English universities as opponents of all reforms, which, he said, must rise from the middle classes.[13] As a reformer he did not identify with the universities.

Robert reportedly intended to enter the church but was too independent-minded and non-conformist. Another career had to be found, and his father approached a family friend, Major General Sir Archibald Galloway. Galloway had retired from a military career in India and was a director of the East India Company; he arranged a job for the young man as Bombay agent for the wine-importing firm of Cutler, Palmer, and Company, a London company whose Bombay office had been opened in 1842.[14] And so Robert left for India and an intended business career, but his luggage included ideas of Christian evangelism and liberal political and economic reform.

IMPERIAL IDEOLOGY AND THE WAVE OF REFORM

In 1832, when Robert Knight was seven, Britain was swept by a tidal wave of reform, a wave which was to carry around the world to India and other parts of the British Empire. The Parliamentary reform act which launched it was truly revolutionary. Since 1689 Britain had been run essentially by Parliament, and Parliament had been run essentially by the landed aristocracy and gentry. In 1832, faced with growing popular demand for democracy and other 'radical' measures, the conservative elite increased by about 50 per cent the number of electors for the House of Commons and transferred 56 seats from underpopulated 'rotten boroughs' to burgeoning industrial and commercial areas, including Lambeth, where William Knight could vote for the first time.[15]

The election of a more liberal Commons opened the door to an entire programme of reforms, pressures for which had been building for decades. Some reformers were secular and liberal, such as the Utilitarians, who wanted to rebuild society along practical and efficient lines. Others were evangelical Christians, heirs of the great religious revival of the late eighteenth century. These reformers did not always agree, but one issue on which they did was the abolition of slavery in the British Empire. They overcame resistance by the planting interests, and slavery was ended in 1833. Another measure with a global impact was the Durham Report and its proposal of responsible government for Canada through an elected legislature, which the Parliament enacted in 1840. Having accepted the principle of colonial home rule, the Parliament soon enacted similar legislation for New Zealand and Australia. Politicians and editors elsewhere in the empire, including India, observed these events with much interest.

The great popular protest of the 1840s opposed the Corn Laws, which artificially raised the prices of imported grains. Reformers saw this as not only inflating the price of bread but as a glaring example of class favouritism, the large landowners being the favoured class. After 1820, the commercial classes were converted to the virtues of 'free trade' and during the 1840s the entire body of old mercantilist restrictions and protective tariffs, Corn Laws included, was swept away.

Lambeth was clearly on the crest of this wave of reform, from its first enfranchisement in 1832. One history reported:

In Lambeth there was much excitement, and the newly-created electors scanned the printed lists with interest. When the day of election came they spoke with no uncertain voice, and since that day none but Liberal members have represented the Borough in Parliament.[16]

By 1841 Lambeth was known as a 'Radical stronghold', and its MP's were outspoken enemies of the Corn Laws.[17]

There is no evidence that William Knight or any of his family was personally involved in politics, but this was the atmosphere in which Robert spent his formative years, and it impressed him. The ideals of that wave of reform—free trade, abolition of slavery, home rule, elected representatives, just and effective government—would reverberate through thirty years of Knight's editorials.

In this temper of the new times, the old East India Company stood out like the fossil remains of some prehistoric monster. Of the many chartered trading companies from the mercantilist age, it was one of the last survivors. In 1600, this company of London merchants had received a monopoly of British trade with half the world, and with it the right to found trading settlements. Later charters added the power to defend those settlements by raising troops, declaring war, and judging and punishing its servants and other residents.[18] The company took control of more and more of the Indian subcontinent, but as it did so, a more vigilant Parliament reasserted more and more of its own authority. The company's charter was due to expire in 1833, and the reformers and free traders fought against its renewal.

However, the company's defence was spearheaded by James Mill, the eminent Utilitarian philosopher and economist, who had become the chief examiner in the company's head office. Mill, regarded in Britain as the greatest India expert of his day, told Parliament that what the people of India really wanted was governance 'well and cheaply performed' and the East India Company, by supplying it, had reversed the 'moral deterioration' caused by tyrannical rulers of the past.[19] Parliament therefore accepted a compromise: the charter was renewed, but the company was ordered to conclude all commercial activities and to administer India 'in trust for the Crown'. The company survived, but only by presenting itself as the protector and guardian of the Indian people, a commitment for which it would soon have to answer.

CLASSICAL ECONOMICS AND INDIAN REVENUES: THE LAND TITLE TANGLE

The reformers of the 1830s and 1840s made less impact in India than they had expected. The reformers, including Mill had been misled by some palpable misinformation about India, and the traditional societies and lifestyles of India proved hardier and more durable than expected. Moreover, most British responsible for controlling India scoffed at reformers and considered their ideas foolish if not downright dangerous.[20] For all their bravado, the wiser Englishmen knew how flimsy their Raj was. Several thousand of them, aided by Indian soldiers and servants, and about 500 princes whom they were protecting, were stretched thin, trying to maintain law and order among perhaps two hundred millions of Indians. The last thing they wanted was interfering busybodies such as reformers, educators, missionaries, or journalists, stirring up people. That was why the company had barred missionaries from its territories until 1813, when it had lost the power to do so.

Mill was the most prestigious purveyor of misinformation. By the time of his 1831 testimony he had written the first and only (supposedly) comprehensive history of India. His *History of British India* (which included far more) was first published in 1818 and made a deep impression; it was reprinted in 1820 and 1826. It got Mill his position with the East India Company, which used it as a textbook for its training college at Haileybury.[21] For the generation of young Robert Knight, the influence of James Mill was inescapable.

However, Mill, who never saw India for himself, relied on impressionistic travellers' accounts and translations of classical treatises, notably the Manu's *Dharmashastra*. Mill's Book II, 'Of the Hindoos', is sprinkled with references to 'The Laws of Menu' [*sic*], which he took to be literally and universally applied in Hindu India, like the common law in England.

One of the principal drawbacks to Indian progress, in Mill's opinion, was the alleged ownership of all land by the state, which usually meant the monarch.[22] This complex and tangled question was to befog and bedevil administrators and others (such as Robert Knight) throughout the era of the British Raj. The young men influenced by Mill accepted his views and served in India with that premise. Later scholars such as Karl Marx and Max Weber also accepted it. Nevertheless, more recent and more painstaking scholarship has shown that Indian monarchs generally respected traditional tenurial roles of the occupants of the land as long as the land revenue was paid, and that the royal 'ownership' was essentially symbolic or at best nominal.[23] Certainly it was not ownership in the western sense.

The status of the land determined the status of the land revenue. Traditionally a substantial part of the harvest was paid to royal agents as the 'raja's share'. But was this payment rent to a landlord or taxes to a government? To Indians the question was meaningless, but to the British it was quite significant. Malthus and Ricardo had developed the doctrine of 'rent theory', the idea that the peasant deserves only the amount of money for his crops which he needs for family subsistence. If he gets more, it is because of the accident of his working on better soil, not because of his greater effort. This, therefore, is an 'unearned increment' which the landlord is entitled to take. In the case of India, if the state was the landlord of all, the state was entitled to the entire harvest beyond what the *ryot* (cultivator) needed for survival. However, later writers considered Indians among the lightest-taxed people in the world: because the hefty portion which the state took was called 'rent' instead of 'taxes'.

Robert Knight was clearly a disciple of these classical economists. He claimed it at least once, in a dispute over a question of currency: 'We believe we have read every production of Ricardo upon the subject of currency, and confidently defy these Calcutta critics to point out any difference between what we have advanced and Mr. Ricardo's views.'[24] The land revenue, he declared, was rent, and therefore lowering it would not reduce the price of food.[25] Many times he urged the rigorous assessment and collection of the land revenue; if this were done, he said, not only would more food be shipped to market, but there would be no need for levies such as tariffs or an income tax, measures harmful to commerce (see p. 57).

The East India Company, guided by Mill, felt entitled to that land revenue, and it certainly needed the funds to feed its expanding administration. But it sought the traditional system in a land of many local traditions and very little system. In Bengal, the first large province to come under British rule, the governor general in 1793, Lord Cornwallis, recognized as landowners the zamindars, local strongmen who had served as intermediaries between Mughal officials and village notables. This zamindari system assured the company of its much-needed revenue, but it also froze the rates permanently and stripped the ryots of whatever tenurial rights they had had. Provincial officials in Madras and Bombay presidencies opposed the extension of this 'permanent settlement' and persuaded the company to make its revenue settlements directly with the ryots, thus recognizing their titles.[26] This also gave the British settlement officers the massive job of visiting every field on a thirty-year cycle to estimate its yield.

The Bombay Presidency had no large *mufassil* (rural hinterland) until the end of the Third Anglo-Maratha War in 1818, when the lands ruled by the Maratha *peshwa* (prime minister) were annexed. The land revenue survey of the 'Bombay Deccan' was begun in 1824, but badly. The assessment system was too elaborate and confusing, the survey personnel untrained and sometimes unreliable. Mill, who was in England, ordered 55 per cent of the harvest collected, which proved impossible, even with the (later reported) use of torture.[27] It impoverished many of the ryots and even caused some to abandon their fields. The survey was halted in 1828, then resumed in 1835 under Henry E. Goldsmid and a young officer of the Bombay engineers, Lieutenant (later Sir) George Wingate. They devised a less elaborate and more pragmatic system. Wingate, who became supervisor in 1838, accepted Mill's directions, but he also tried to protect the ryots; they were entitled to their lands, he argued, not as proprietors but as 'occupancy tenants'.[28] The new system proved more practical, and Wingate's 'moderation and leniency' helped to make it work.[29] The survey culminated with a joint report in 1847, setting out the rules to be followed in the anticipated thirty-year reassessments.

In that same year Wingate took into his home a young lodger, newly-arrived from England: Robert Knight.[30] Wingate became Knight's guide and mentor during his early years in Bombay, especially on Indian economics. The latter wrote in his memoirs: 'No man in our day has exercised such powerful influence indirectly upon Indian affairs as Sir George Wingate. We sat at his feet very early and have but reflected in popular form in our writings the doctrines we learned thereat....'[31] Knight also lauded Wingate in his newspapers from time to time and praised him generously in a speech twenty years later: 'Few men ever possessed equal insight into the conditions of the material prosperity of the people of India....I hold in my hand his pamphlet upon the subject, which first powerfully directed my own mind to its investigation....'[32]

BOMBAY AS A RISING CITY

The Bombay which greeted Knight in October of 1847 had just found the path to its fortune as metropolis, commercial centre, and world seaport, a fortune to which he would contribute significantly. Of the three British 'presidency towns' in India, Bombay had lagged well behind Madras and Calcutta in development. It had begun as a series of islands—actually, two parallel ridges of the Western Ghats, off India's west coast. When the Portuguese dealt the islands to the British in 1661, they contained several villages of fishermen and palm tree tappers, and a few Portuguese estates.

The main island, also called Bombay, was then shaped like a crude 'H', and the British built their fortified settlement on the southern part of the eastern spur. The Indian bazaar or 'native town' developed to the north of the Fort. The parallel ridge consisted of Malabar and Cumbala Hills, with Girgaum as the saddle linking them to the Fort and the bazaar. Separating Cumbala Hill from the ridge-island of Worli to its north was the inlet called 'Breach Candy', through which flowed the Arabian Sea. The other islands were less defined, and inlets and marshlands spread wide.[33] Bombay, lacking an accessible commercial or territorial hinterland, had the further handicap of deadly tropical diseases; one early visitor was warned that 'two mussouns [monsoons] are the age of a man.'[34]

The rise of Bombay required physical improvements, political gains, and a new economic role. Physically, the East India Company had built its fort and harbour along the east side of the island, the landward side, which protected ships from the annual monsoons. The biggest improvement was the closing of the breach between Cumballa Hill and Worli, done finally by construction of the great double seawall called the Hornby Vellard, in the 1770s. Without the regular flushing by the tidal seas, the marshlands could be drained and filled in, uniting the islands.[35]

Militarily, Bombay was under constant threat from the bellicose Marathas until their fractious leadership gradually dissolved their power. The Bombay Council intervened in Maratha politics in 1774 and seized Salsette, the large island to the north of Bombay. In 1802, the peshwa fled to Pune, his capital, and sought the protection of Bombay from his own menacing chieftains. The resulting war broke Maratha power. A third Anglo-Maratha war in 1817–18 ended in the annexation of the peshwa's lands. Those small, near-empty islands thus became the capital of western India.

Meanwhile, the pluralistic business leadership, both Indian and European, gradually migrated south to Bombay from Surat, which had been the leading world port of the Mughal Empire. However, the European populace of Bombay remained sparse, mostly the company's military and civil employees. As late as 1785 the unofficial European population of Bombay was tallied at 72.[36] This would be changed by the recasting of global shipping patterns. From the days of Vasco da Gama, Europeans had reached India by sailing around Africa, a dangerous and uncomfortable trip which took four to eight months, depending on the weather. The time and risks could be reduced sharply by the development and use of the steamship in the early nineteenth century, but the costs of a sufficient coal supply and the space to hold it, both aboard and on shore, ate up the profits. A new scheme surfaced: Europe-to-India travel through Egypt, cutting thousands of miles from the trip, with a steamship run between Bombay and Suez. Egypt was ruled by the autocratic Muhammed Ali, who sought European-type improvements for Egypt and would cooperate. Bombay, nearly a thousand miles nearer Suez than Calcutta or Madras, would become the inevitable gateway.

The Bombay government and business community saw their opportunity and seized it. In 1829 they launched their own steamship and sent it to Suez and back. The East India Company lent its support by sending two steamers for the new route in 1837 and, despite delays, rivalries, and opposition from Calcutta merchant houses, the route to Bombay was established. The award of a government mail contract in 1845 confirmed it.[37] The passage through Egypt, from Alexandria to Suez, was haphazard and uncomfortable in those days, but by the 1840s improvements had begun.[38] The construction of railroads in the 1850s eased the trip through Egypt, though the Arabian Sea passage remained crude.[39]

Even before Bombay began its rapid growth, the European community burst through the walls of the Fort and built spacious homes in scattered suburbs. The governor joined the trend, moving the Government House to a former Jesuit church and convent in Parel, in north-central Bombay, in 1829.[40] Some Europeans moved to Mazagaon, on the mid-island eastern waterfront, and a map sketched in 1846 shows the 'native town' developed to what became Grant Road.[41]

Commercially, Bombay began shipping bales of raw cotton for the factories of Britain. Chests of opium were sent the other way, to China.[42] Bombay founded a chamber of commerce in 1836, with a feature most rare for its day: racial integration, with fifteen European and ten Indian business firms as original members and three Indians on the first committee.[43] Churches and schools arose, and the handsome Town Hall opened in 1838.[44]

How did this burgeoning Bombay impress the 22-year-old Robert Knight, upon his arrival in 1847? Few of his reactions have survived, but some may be inferred from the impressions of other western visitors of that time. Almost all nineteenth-century visitors admired the beauty of the verdant Bombay harbour and noted the wide mix of languages and ethnic types within that one city. Passenger ships then docked at Apollo Bunder, the 'new bunder' to the south of the Fort (the area dominated in the twentieth–twenty-first centuries by the Gateway of India and the Taj Hotel).

Lady Amelia Falkland, wife of the governor, found on her arrival in 1848, society limited to dinners, balls, and an occasional picnic, with concerts rare and theatre absent.[45] Emma Roberts, a literary lady who arrived in 1839, also lamented the lack of concerts and public life, except for the Town Hall library. She added: 'It is certainly very pleasing to see the numbers of native gentlemen of all religious persuasions, who enter into the private society of Bombay....'[46] Dr J. Berncastle, a physician, visited in 1850. He explored the several islands and was impressed by the botanical gardens at Mazagaon and the Sir Jamshedji Jeejeebhoy Native Hospital. The doctor recommended that the climate be fought by pith helmet, mosquito netting, ice (shipped in bulk from Boston), and not too much 'brandy-pani'.[47] Bayard Taylor, the American travel writer, spent several amiable days in 1853, but found the Fort area crowded and dirty.[48]

The writer probably closest to Knight in background and acerbic outlook was Sidney Terry. Terry, a small businessman like Knight, griped about the trip from Egypt in 1844 and then griped about life in Bombay. Like Knight he had to stretch his modest means to support the lifestyle required of a *pukka sahib* (respected sir). He wrote to his wife:

The system of keeping so many servants is very ridiculous, but the only answer I can ever get to my remarks is, you are obliged to do so, every one does, because one servant will only do one thing. It all has originated from the indolence of the English residents, some of whom have Servants to put on their Stockings. I am only surprised that they do not keep men to masticate their food for them. The following is the list of servants generally kept in a modest establishment, a Butler, a man for each individual of the family, a Cook, a groom for each horse, a Man for the Carriage, a man to sweep and dust furniture, a man to light and keep the lamps in order and clean boots and a Man to bring water and fill your bath.[49]

Terry's family joined him in 1845, but he remained bitter and depressed, as can be judged from his letters. He died in 1847.[50]

YOUNG MR KNIGHT MEETS THE PRESS

One of Knight's impressions-on-arrival is known. He was appalled to find, attached to the walls of the Fort, posters vilifying John Connon, editor of the *Bombay Gazette,* one of three local English weeklies. But Connon would fire abuse right back at his rival of the *Telegraph and Courier,* and Knight recalled in his memoir:

We well remember one of these amenities in which he opened his attack upon 'the spirit of a jackass that dwells in our flunky contemporary.' George Craig took over the *Telegraph and Courier* and made it too hot for Connon, who complained about the 'ruffianly degradation of the Bombay Press by Mr. Craig.' As a fact, the ruffianism of the Bombay Press for several years was certainly unprecedented.[51]

Early newspapers in India were, as mentioned, fragile, often personal, and sometimes sharply partisan. Their tiny budgets could only afford the simplest of equipment: handset type and manpowered flatbed presses, while the editorial staff might consist of a single editor and occasional friends. News from other cities and abroad came from *their* newspapers, freely copied, and letters from correspondents of varying talents and reliability. With such puny resources these newspapers tried to inform their small circles of readers—perhaps a hundred or a few thousand—of the news of the day.

Bombay's first newspaper was the weekly *Bombay Herald*, founded in 1789, followed by the *Bombay Courier* in 1790, and the *Gazette* in 1791. In 1792, the *Gazette* absorbed the *Herald* and became the paper of government patronage, a vital matter in those days of little private advertising. An itinerant journalist who arrived in 1822 gibed:

There were but two papers extant at the time, and comical things they were. The *Bombay Courier* and the *Gazette,* composed entirely of selections from English papers and an occasional law report; the pen of the editor seldom found nobler occupation than the record of a ball and supper or a laudatory notice of an amateur performance.[52]

Editors had the further problem of living under the heavy hand of the East India Company, whose officials disliked critical or independent voices and who at times seized presses, imprisoned editors, and even shipped them back to England. As a later editor observed: 'Journals in those circumstances were either official, safe, and dull, or they were written with an eye to the scandals of the community, in which case their life was apt to be short.'[53]

When the company was stripped of near-total control of its settlements by the charter renewal of 1813, its officials had to endure a (somewhat) free press in India. In the burgeoning Bombay of 1838, business leaders from the new chamber of commerce supported a new and weightier newspaper, the *Bombay Times and Journal of Commerce*. Its first editor, J.E. Brennan, died after a few months, and the proprietors engaged a Scotsman of literary and scientific renown, Dr George Buist.[54] As the demand for timely information rose, the *Gazette* switched to daily publication in 1843, followed by the *Courier* (by then the *Telegraph and Courier*) in 1847, and the *Times* in 1850.

Knight had gone to Bombay as a merchant, not as a journalist. He took over the Bombay branch of the London wine importer,

Cutler, Palmer, and Company.[55] That branch soon closed, and Knight became the local manager for Zorn and Company, booksellers.[56] He next formed the partnership of Cleverly, Knight and Company (business unspecified), then was employed by Robert Frith and Company, auctioneers. In 1852 he was engaged by Waghorn and Company, shipping agents; the enthusiastic

Plate II: Catherine (Hannah Payne) Knight. Courtesy the Knight family

Lieutanent Thomas Waghorn had been the pioneering promoter of the Egyptian shipping route.[57] This apparently lasted into 1856, after which he worked as a freight broker.[58] The particulars are obscure, but clearly these were difficult years; Knight later admitted having declared bankruptcy.[59]

On the other hand, Knight's first decade in India was highly successful domestically. On 2 November 1854, he married Catherine Hannah Payne (Plate II), daughter of William Hugh and Johanna Payne, in a ceremony at St Thomas's Church in the Fort.[60] Payne had settled in India in 1830 and was, like Knight, one of the modest middle-class Europeans there. Though listed as a schoolmaster, he had been appointed to the uncovenanted civil service in 1838, and in 1846 was working as an assistant collector of continental customs.[61]

Catherine had been born at Colaba, the southern appendage of Bombay, on 4 May 1837, and thus was seventeen at the time of her marriage, twelve years younger than her husband. Her family remembered her as 'a beautiful woman with a lovely singing voice, and was a good amateur pianist.'[62] From all indications the marriage was singularly successful. Certainly it was most fruitful. A daughter, Alice Catherine, was born in 1856; she would be the first of twelve children, ten of whom survived their father.[63]

William Knight, father of Robert, died on 3 November 1855, at the age of 69 at his London home, still 8 Canterbury Place. The death certificate states that William had suffered from stomach cancer for six months, and that his son Henry was present.[64] Care of their mother would be an additional responsibility for Robert and his brothers.

Knight's first decade in India coincided with the administration of that most developmental of governors general, the Marquess of Dalhousie (1848–56). Under the dynamic Dalhousie the first Department of Public Works was created in India, the first public postal system was established, the electric telegraph linked India's major cities, plans for a nationwide railway system were approved, and its first segments built.[65] No conquest or annexation, no political or ideological movement did more to end local isolation and create a nation-state than these measures. No city would be as transformed by them as Bombay, and no enterprise more than the press.

The Government of India built a short experimental telegraph line in 1851 and began a national network in 1853. By 1857 its wires linked Bombay to Madras, Calcutta, Agra, and Peshawar.[66] The manual telegraphers and their dot-and-dash Morse code were elementary, but their journalistic impact was immediate. Editors cut into leisurely Victorian-era essays for terse news bulletins 'via the electric telegraph'.

Construction of railroads was costlier, riskier, more complicated, and even greater in impact, but the Dalhousie regime tackled it with similar vigour and success. Contracts were let to British companies, lured by guarantees of five per cent annual profits. Bombay officials and investors, who had been planning a railway since 1845, formed the Great Indian Peninsula Railway Company.[67] It began construction in 1850; the first segment, twenty-one miles from Bombay to Thana (the adjoining district town), began operating in 1853, amidst much celebration. A further forty-three miles had been opened by 1857.[68]

Bombay progressed in other areas. In 1856 a Parsi businessman, Cowasji N. Davar, opened India's first steam-powered factory, a cotton mill.[69] The charter to create the University of Bombay was being finalized as 1857 began. One resident wrote later: 'Everything was showing new life, and even the press became vivacious....so successful was one paper that its sixteen shares of Rs. 800 each rose in five years to be worth Rs 6,000 each.'[70] Buist, the *Bombay Times and Journal of Commerce* editor, left for Britain on 'home leave'. His replacement as acting editor was an articulate man who had written some impressive freelance articles on Indian economics, Robert Knight.[71] Yes, 1857 would be a memorable year for Bombay and for India, but for unexpected reasons.

NOTES

1. *Bombay Calendar and General Directory for the Year 1848* (Bombay: Courier Press, 1848), p. xv.
2. Baptismal certificate found in the 1826 ledger of the Lambeth parish church, St Mary's. The church has since been closed, and its archives are presumably preserved in the central facilities of the Church of England.

3. From a note dated 1915 by Jack Zorn, a nephew of Robert Knight, and kept in the family. It is now held by Michael Peake, a great-grandson of Robert. Some details are confirmed by the baptismal certificate cited above.

4. Ibid.; Great Britain, *Census of 1841,* Parish of Lambeth, and *Census of 1851,* Parish of Lambeth; Great Britain, *Post Office Directory for London,* 1853, p. 266. In later life Sarah became Mrs Riddle, Emma Mrs Burnside, and Esther Mrs Zorn.

5. Sir Walter Besant, *South London* (New York: Frederick Stokes, 1898), p. 112.

6. H.J. Dyos, *Victorian Suburb: A Study of the Growth of Camberwell* (Leicester: University Press, 1977), p. 37.

7. Borough of Lambeth, *Poor Rate List for Parish of Lambeth*, 1829.

8. Ibid., rate books and electors' registers cited; Great Britain, *Census of 1841,* microfilm reel #1057; *Census of 1851,* vol. 1571, p. 313; *Post Office Directory for London,* 1855, p. 2164.

9. Harold P. Clunn, *The Face of London* (London: Spring Books, approximately (ap.) 1960), p. 333. The author visited the area. An entirely new shopping centre had been built on the spot, and the old streets had been obliterated.

10. The author wishes to thank especially Jamie R. Camplin and Jill Barrett for research assistance on this section. Mr Camplin is a grandson of Edward Knight and therefore a great-nephew of Robert.

11. Francis Place Papers, British Library, Add. MSS 27827, pp. 52-3.

12. *Dictionary of National Biography* (hereafter *DNB*) 1921-2 edn, vol. 5, p. 1324.

13. *Star of India* (Bombay), 4 July 1871.

14. *DNB,* vol. 7, pp. 824-5; S.C. Sanial, 'The Father of Indian Journalism—I', *Calcutta Review* (hereafter *CR*), vol. 19 of 3rd series (May–June, 1926), pp. 289-90. Sanial was apparently using Knight's unpublished memoirs; see 'Introduction' on sources.

15. *Electors' Registry for 1837,* Borough of Lambeth Archives.

16. George Hill, *The Electoral History of the Borough of Lambeth Since the Enfranchisement in 1832* (London: Stanford , 1879), p. 16.

17. Ibid., pp. 17 and 63.

18. Courtenay Ilbert, *The Government of India, Being a Digest of the Statute Law Relating Thereto* (Oxford: Clarendon Press, 1907), pp. 5, 9, 14, 19, and 33.

19. Evidence of James Mill, Parliamentary Papers, 1831, vol. 5, pp. 335 and 396.

20. This scorn of reformers was a repeated theme of Kipling late in the century. See for instance his poem 'Pagett M.P.', In *The Sahib*

Edition of Rudyard Kipling (New York: P.F. Collier and Son, n.d.), vol. 10, pp. 231–3.

21. C.H. Philips, 'James Mill, Mountstuart Elphinstone, and the History of India', in C.H. Philips, ed., *Historians of India, Pakistan, and Ceylon* (London: Oxford University Press, 1961), pp. 219–26.

22. Mill, Book II, pp. 209–14. For recent evaluations of Mill, see Ronald Inden, *Imagining India* (Oxford: Blackwell, 1990), p. 45, and Nicholas B. Dirks, *Castes of Mind, Colonialism and the Making of Modern India* (Princeton: Princeton University Press, 2001), p. 32.

23. John W. Spellman, *Political Theory of Ancient India* (Oxford: Clarendon Press, 1964), pp. 206–10; R.N. Saletore, *Early Indian Economic History* (London: Curzon Press, 1973), pp. 458–75.

24. *Bombay Times and Standard*, 8 March 1860.

25. Ibid., 17 April 1860. Classical economists believed that a peasant would only work for immediate subsistence. Therefore, a lower rent would mean less work and lower productivity, thus reducing market supplies and raising prices. Knight's views on land revenue are further articulated below (see p. 106).

26. E.J. Hobsbawm is mistaken when he calls this 'virtual nationalization of the land' (*The Age of Revolution, 1789–1848* Mentor, ed., New American Library, 1962, p. 196). There were never any collective farms or state-run plantations in British India (except some cinchona plantations in Bengal and Madras).

27. India, *General Report on the Administration of the Bombay Presidency for the year 1872–73* (Bombay: Government Central Press, 1874), pp. 41–2.

28. Ibid., Eric Stokes, *The English Utilitarians and India* (Oxford: Clarendon Press, 1959), p.122. British officials continued to praise and defend the 'rent theory' which they dared not enforce literally; it would have beggared much of the peasantry. Stokes, an authoritative scholar in this area, denied 'the possibility of official hypocrisy', but admitted receiving 'the impression of double-think and double-speak' on the enforcement question. *The Peasant and the Raj, Studies in Agrarian Society and Peasant Rebellion in Colonial India* (Cambridge: Cambridge University Press, 1978), pp. 46–7.

29. Romesh Dutt, *The Economic History of India Under Early British Rule* (London: Routledge and Kegan Paul, 8th impression, 1956 [1901], p. 377. For a more recent and thorough study of the ideology of the Bombay survey, see Michelle Burge McAlpin, 'Economic Policy and the True Believer: The Use of Ricardian Rent Theory in the Bombay Survey and Settlement System', *Journal of Economic History*, 44 (2), June 1984, pp. 421–7.

30. Sanial, 'The Father of Indian Journalism—I', *CR*, p. 290. Sanial says Knight carried an introduction to Wingate, but he does not say from whom. Perhaps it was the helpful General Galloway again.

31. Ibid.

32. Speech to the East India Association, London, 3 March 1868, and published as 'India: A Review of England's Financial Relations Therewith', *Journal of the East India Association*, vol. 2, p. 233.

33. Probably the most thorough account of Bombay's natural setting and early history is Stephen Meredith Edwardes, *District Gazetteer of Bombay City and Island* (Bombay: Times Press, 1909).

34. J. Ovington, *A Voyage to Surat in the year 1689,* H.G. Rawlinson, ed., (London: Oxford University Press, 1926), p. 87.

35. Edwardes, *The Rise of Bombay, A Perspective* (Bombay: Times of India Press, 1902; reprinted from 10 of *Census of India* Series, 1901), pp. 204–5.

36. Percival Spear, *The Nabobs, A Study of the Social Life of the English in Eighteenth Century India* (London: Oxford University Press, 1963, 1st edn 1932), p. 23.

37. *Bombay Calendar and Almanac for 1856* (Bombay: Bombay Times Press, 1856), pp. 149–63; Daniel Thorner, *Investment in Empire, British Railway and Steam Shipping Enterprise in India* (Philadelphia: University of Pennsylvania Press, 1950), pp. 25–36.

38. Douglas Dewar, *Bygone Days in India* (London: John Lane the Bodley Head, 1922), pp. 4–8; Sarah Searight, *Steaming East, The Forging of Steamship and Rail Links Between Europe and Asia* (London: Bodley Head, 1991), pp. 43, 45, and 79.

39. James Douglas, *Round About Bombay* (Bombay: Bombay Gazette Steam Press, 1886), pp.131–9.

40. Samuel T. Sheppard, *Bombay* (Bombay: The Times of India Press, 1932), p. 113.

41. James Douglas, *Bombay and Western India* (London: Sampson, Low, Marston, 1893), vol. 1, pp. 176 and 189.

42. Lakshmi Subramanian, *Indigenous Capital and Imperial Expansion in Bombay, Surat and the West Coast* (New Delhi: Oxford University Press, 1996), p. 271.

43. Christine Dobbin, *Urban Leadership in Western India* (London: Oxford University Press, 1972), p. 22.

44. Edwardes, *Rise of Bombay*, pp. 250–2. Today that Town Hall houses two libraries.

45. Lady Falkland (Amelia Cary), *Chow-Chow, A Journal Kept in India, Egypt, and Syria* (London: Eric Partridge, 1930), pp. 4–7 and 36–8.

46. Emma Roberts, *Notes of an Overland Journey Through France and Egypt to Bombay* (London: W.H. Allen, 1841), pp. 257–9.

47. J. Berncastle, *A Voyage to China, Including Bombay Presidency* (London: William Shobeil, 1850), vol. 1, pp. 92–104 and 132.

48. Bayard Taylor, *A Visit to India, China, and Japan in the Year 1853* (New York: G.P. Putnam's Sons, 1874), pp. 35–44.

49. Sidney Terry, *Letters,* MSS Eur. C250, p. 93. On the same subject, see Berncastle, pp. 91–2.

50. Terry, *Letters,* pp. 197–200.

51. S.C. Sanial, 'History of the Press in India—II', *CR,* 130 (2), April, 1910, pp. 111–18.

52. J.H. Stocqueler [Joachim Siddons], *Memoirs of a Journalist* (Bombay: The Times of India, 1873), pp. 46–7.

53. Alfred H. Watson, 'Origin and Growth of Journalism Among Europeans', *The Annals* [of the American Academy of Political and Social Science], 115 (2), September 1929, p. 169.

54. Sanial, 'The Father of Indian Journalism—I', *CR,* p. 299.

55. Ibid., p. 299n.

56. From Knight's obituary in the *Bombay Gazette,* 28 January 1890.

57. C.E. Buckland, *Dictionary of Indian Biography* (London: Swan Sonnenschein, 1906), p. 438; Searight, pp. 30 and 35.

58. *Bombay Almanac and Book of Direction for 1850 (Bombay: Gazette Press, 1850),* p. 275; *Almanac and Directory for 1851,* p. 932; *...for 1852,* p. 579; *...for 1853,* p. 594; *...for 1854,* p. 519; *...for 1855,* p. 215; *...for 1856,* p. 472; *...for 1857,* p. 618. However, Sanial, 'The Father of Indian Journalism—I', pp. 299–300, reported that from 1850 to 1857 Knight edited the biweekly *Poona Observer.* It is unlikely that he held both jobs simultaneously since a commute between Bombay and Pune (Poona) would have been too difficult in the 1850s.

59. *Times of India* (Bombay), 18 August 1863.

60. *Bombay Almanac and Directory for 1855,* p. 620.

61. *Bombay Calendar and General Directory for the Year 1846* (Bombay: Courier Press, 1846), p. 407; *Times of India Calendar and Directory* (Bombay: Press Exchange, 1864), pp. 404 and 561.

62. George H. Knight (a grandson) to the author, 28 November 1982 (though mistakenly dated 1972), in possession of the author.

63. Bombay, *Register of Baptisms, Marriages, and Burials,* India Office Records, 30, p. 399 and *seq.,* and Bengal, *Register of Baptisms, Marriages, and Burials,* vol. 30, p. 399. Later births were also found in the Bombay and Bengal registers.

64. Great Britain, Death Certificates, 1D, p. 176.

65. Particulars may be found in any account of the 1850s in India. One such is Suresh Chandra Ghosh, *Dalhousie in India, 1848–56* (New Delhi: Munshiram Manohar, 1975), pp. 57–126.

66. Ibid., pp. 93–105.
67. Edwardes, *District Gazetteer,* p. 342. They opted for the steam locomotive over the horse on the assumption that it would not exceed ten miles per hour.
68. India, *History of Indian Railways, Constructed and In Progress* (Simla: Govt of India Press, 1924), n.p.
69. Morris D. Morris, 'The Growth of Large-Scale Industry to 1947', in Dharma Kumar (ed.), *The Cambridge Economic History of India,* (Hyderabad: Orient Longman, 1984 [1982]), vol. 2, p. 574.
70. Douglas, *Round About Bombay,* p.149.
71. Sanial, 'The Father of Indian Journalism—I', p. 299.

2

The Making of an Editor, 1857–63

CONSTRUCTION OF A PLATFORM

From the start, Robert Knight's *Bombay Times* took an outspoken and often defiant editorial stance. In his (presumed) first issue, that of 1 January 1857, he sharply criticized 'forward' strategists in official and journalistic circles who wanted British forces to occupy Herat in south-western Afghanistan, which the Persians had just vacated under British pressure. Such a move, he wrote, would betray treaty obligations and offend and alarm Dost Muhammad, the amir of Kabul, whose friendship the British needed.[1]

Knight, throughout his long editorial career, always ridiculed the fear of a Russian invasion of India through the mountain passes of the north-west and the itch for pre-emptive British intervention in frontier politics. A modern army, he wrote, would require a large baggage train for its munitions and other necessities, and feeding the horses or camels during the long and dangerous passage of the Bolan or Khyber Pass, in bleak and often hostile territory, would present a great problem.[2]

He also opposed on moral grounds the war with Persia which had resulted in the occupation of the Persian Gulf port of Bushire by British troops several months earlier. He denounced the 'shameless profligacy and dishonesty' of British policy and asserted: 'We have been charged with want of patriotism in these statements. If it be patriotic to call our statesmen honest when they are profligate, and wise men when they are fools, we make no pretensions to virtue.'[3]

By 10 April 1857, Knight was indignant enough to accuse the British public of supporting a war about which they knew nothing, and favouring the shedding of blood as long as it was Persian blood. He preached:

Do our countrymen know what war is, when they dare permit such ready recourse to it? Do they know the guilt of an unjust war?... Why it is downright murder for men to draw their swords in a quarrel of which they know nothing, and to such frightful issues does my Lord Palmerston's conduct of foreign affairs commit us.[4]

War was never a 'great game' to him.

However, Knight had his own version of the 'white man's burden'. He claimed that the only two 'truly civilized' nations, Britain and the United States, were obliged to spread their ideas of liberty and progress over the earth. But the best way to reform a people, he said, was to teach them to reform themselves, and this was what Britain should do in India. It would be a slow process and antagonistic to their old systems, but it was 'the way in which Britain is fulfilling her mission in introducing and establishing the true system of popular rights in India....'[5]

Another enduring theme was India's economic need for public improvements and the large capital investments to provide them. Whether these investments were private, state, or state-guaranteed private seemed irrelevant. Knight's first issue called for an extension of the budding railroads (with their five per cent annual profit guarantee) and improvement of the city's water system. Three months later he warned: 'Bombay is again threatened with a water famine, and we have been compelled, to drive all cattle off the island, and refuse to allow the shipping access to our wells....'[6] Then he called for a road improvement scheme and urged the Bombay government to fight 'Leadenhall Street' (headquarters of the East India Company in London) for it because of the urgent need.[7]

Three months later Knight made a proposal that was far ahead of its time: that the government borrow enough money to develop India's rural resources through the construction of roads and irrigation facilities. If British millowners want Indian cotton, he wrote, let them offer the Government of India a loan of five million sterling for roads and irrigation works in the cotton districts of Bombay Presidency. The government would not take the lead; it lacked the courage. He appealed to Britain:

We [emphasis mine] are a poor people, miserably poor. There is no seeking capital in India to find investment in the improvement of the land....We are a nation of peasant cultivators, living hand to mouth; and taking just what the land spontaneously produces, without the expenditure of an anna to increase its powers. Our cotton fields are parched with drought, because we have not the means to store the floods which annually deluge them. We are so distant from the market where you gentlemen buy, that we are compelled to sell for almost nothing on the spot....[8]

Like most Victorian Englishmen, Knight was suspicious of India's Muslim minority. All Muslims, he wrote, belonged to 'a great confederacy bound together by the strongest ties and imbued with the historic conviction that its destiny is to rule and not to obey.'[9] A Muslim soldier 'cannot be loyal to a power which is antagonistic to the Koran'. However, he never crusaded against Muslims, and he later showed more sympathy for them (see p. 217).

Knight's resentment of the 'home charges'—bills run up by officials in Britain but charged to the Government of India and its taxpayers (see pp. 54–5)—was expressed early, often, and vigorously. India supposedly had a favourable balance of trade, but Knight figured that it had actually been a 'frightful drain' of £6 million a year during the previous decade because of East India Company drafts, private remittances, and transfers of property to Britain.[10] As a moral man he disliked the opium trade with China, but he saw no way those home charges could be paid without the three million sterling which the government derived each year from its opium excises.[11]

This, then, was Knight's enduring platform as editor: just and peaceful relations with India's neighbours, European-type modernization and self-government, economic development, and removal of unjust fiscal burdens from Britain.

The editor had never served in the army, but he always maintained a lively interest in military matters. In the 21 March editorial cited above, he warned of the danger of a mutiny because of the understaffing of British officers with Indian sepoy regiments. A little later he urged Bombay not to copy the recruiting pattern of the Bengal Army[12] (which garrisoned northern as well as eastern India) 'at the very moment when mutiny is rife from Calcutta to Lahore'.[13]

It was an astounding preview. Knight probably wrote it on Saturday, 9 May, for the issue of Monday morning, 11 May. However, while the ink was still wet, on the evening of 10 May, two regiments mutinied in their camp at Meerut, near Delhi, and began shooting their officers and other Europeans. The Great Rebellion had begun.

EDITING DURING THE REBELLION[14]

The newspapers of 1857 are a valuable primary source for events of that year, but they are limited and haphazard. Even prestigious papers such as the *Bombay Times* had meager news staffs, and the day of the news agency and the press relations officer had not yet reached India. Constructive editing of dispatches and attractive makeup of pages were unknown, so the papers had a scattershot appearance. Telegraphed bulletins were usually strung verbatim down a column or two of the main news page. The scope of the coverage, therefore, was mostly restricted to fragmentary accounts, rumours, and snap judgments on this most widespread and significant challenge to British rule until its final years.

The *Bombay Times* first informed its readers of the uprising in its issue of 12 May, reporting the revolt of the Third Light Cavalry at Meerut. Inquiries began immediately (and continue yet) on the causes of the rebellion and appropriate responses. One correspondent declared the dissatisfaction in the Bengal Army was due to its Brahman dominance and their fear of the white man's religion. Editor Knight added a note that the army must serve the state and not caste; if there were to be a fight between Christianity and Brahmanism, it should be fought, not in the army, but in the schools and villages.[15]

As reports arrived of rebel takeovers, mob rule, and murder of Europeans, Knight acknowledged that more than army reform was needed. But unlike many Anglo-Indian journalists, he refused to castigate the Indian people as a whole for the rash and bloody deeds of a few, nor to call for an equally rash and bloody vengeance. In the issue of 19 May, with the insurrection scarcely a week old, Knight denounced 'the cowardly massacre of the defenceless women and children', but concluded: 'Let the thought of bloody retaliation, which invariably arises in every one's mind, give place to the memory that these men know not what they do', and that Britain's mission in India 'is to civilize and not destroy her'.[16]

The insurrection was soon confined and limited. Although the mutineers from Meerut seized Delhi and persuaded Mughal emperor Bahadur Shah Zafar to lead the revolt, neither he nor local rebel leaders could create an effective state or a coordinated strategy. They never approached the centres of British power, Bombay and Calcutta. The British, recovering from their shock, gathered their people in such centres as Lucknow and Cawnpore (Kanpur) and moved in loyal forces from the Punjab. By July, Anglo-Indians (that is, British residents of India) were demanding the recapture of Delhi and punishment of the rebels.

In Bombay, Knight was already hatching post-mutiny plans. He had already proposed a scheme for the development of the Indian *mufassil* (countryside).[17] Future progress should include tutelage in popular government: 'The best way for a foreign power to seek the reformation of a people is to teach them to reform themselves....'[18] Such talk outraged many Anglo-Indians, and Knight later recalled enduring 'a torrent of obloquy such perhaps as no Englishman ever before encountered from his countrymen. We knew we were right in that terrible crisis, and it was that alone that gave us the courage to face the storm.'[19]

George Buist heard of his paper's radical policies, and he hastened back from Britain and resumed charge on 6 October. Its editorial policy changed suddenly and drastically. It now stated that 'vengeance must be had at any price' and 'those who have eaten our salt and ought to have been civilized by our society, that have acted the tiger—that the habits of the wild beast have been brought with them from the jungle.' And 'we have for a century been living in a den of wild beasts.' And 'The natives of India are incapable of combination for other purposes than those of mischief. They have no truth in them....'[20] All Indians were implicated in the barbarities of the rebellion; the stereotypes about their cultures had so condemned them.

However, the wrathful Buist overlooked or ignored the fact that the controlling interest in the *Bombay Times and Journal of Commerce* had been purchased the previous April by local Indian businessmen, who were offended by his remarks. Led by a Parsi businessman, Furdoonji Naoroji, they convened a special meeting on 23 December 1857. Furdoonji called those editorials 'absolutely unjust and debasing'.[21] When Buist refused to take the proprietors' orders on his editorial policies, he was dismissed and the editorship offered to Robert Knight. Knight was caught in a dilemma. He disapproved of proprietary interference in editorial policies, but he agreed that Buist's comments were intolerable. He wrote:

The native proprietors, goaded by severe and incessant invective into interference with the editor...and ill-advised enough to go beyond the occasion and attempt to dictate the policy of the journal...has rendered our succession to the office a singularly infelicitous and undesirable appointment. With the frankest acknowledgement of the great natural abilities and extensive acquirements of the late editor, we are unable to approve for one moment his violent and indiscriminating attacks, made day after day in this journal, upon the whole native population of this country.[22]

In accepting the editorship, Knight also violated one of the cardinal rules of imperialism: a European was not supposed to take a subaltern position by accepting employment from 'natives'. The *Bombay Times* had already been called 'an organ of native interests'. Knight, in his letter of acceptance of 2 January 1858, warned that he could never accept the position under those terms. In reply, the paper's manager, Dosabhoy Framjee, wrote: 'The wish of the proprietors is that the *Bombay Times* shall represent no class interest whatsoever, but that its advocacy should be given to the promotion of the wellbeing of all of Her Majesty's subjects in India.'[23] Knight, he promised, would be 'absolutely unfettered in the Editorial charge'.

The proprietors kept their word during 1858, Knight wrote, but the jibes of the other Anglo-Indian papers must have discomfited him.[24] Therefore, the Indian proprietors agreed in 1859 to sell their shares to Knight for Rs 18,000.

Meanwhile, the arrival of British reinforcements, the recapture of Delhi, and the seizure of its ruler, Bahadur Shah, had sealed the fate of the insurrection, and 1858 was given over to crushing the remaining resistance, mopping up, and reconstruction. Knight denounced the demand for summary execution of all mutineers, pointing out that would mean the massacre of thousands of prisoners, and he praised the governor general, Lord Canning, for his calm and moderate policies.[25]

Knight may have been the first Englishman to sympathize with the Rani of Jhansi, killed while leading her troops in battle against the British. The rani, he pointed out, had been goaded into rebellion by the arbitrary annexation of her state by Lord Dalhousie, who had rejected the Hindu practice of adoption of an heir by the childless royal couple.[26]

He was surely the first, perhaps the only Englishman to propose that Britain pay reparations for the damages of the rebellion, since India, 'probably the very poorest civilized country in the world,' had remitted to England about £200 million since the beginning of the nineteenth century.[27]

Knight never excused the uprising, despite the misreadings of some agitated readers. Instead, he attributed it to exploitive and bullying British rule; the desperation of Indian poverty, and aggressive missionary efforts. (Knight, though a devout Christian, opposed the tactics of other devout Christians for pressured conversions.) He shunned the notion that India was a prize, to be milked to benefit the victorious English: 'it is only a trust in our hands, to be administered for the welfare of its people.'[28] By this standard, British rule had thus far been a failure. According to Knight, the Rebellion had revealed the oppressions and miseries suffered by the Indian people, and so why did Britain feel she deserved their loyalty? He concluded grandiloquently that British rule was to blame for this popular disaffection, and so, 'instead of heaping invective upon the people, a truer wisdom would lead us to concentrate all our energies upon the future. We believe, without a moment's falter, in the mission which England has to accomplish in the East....'[29]

The idea of the empire was noble; only its execution had been bungled. So wrote Knight in 1859.

THE FIRST CRUSADE: THE INIQUITOUS INAM
COMMISSION

The Rebellion still raged and preoccupied Anglo-India in 1858, but Robert Knight turned his major attention to a far different subject, one in which he was defending the rights of Indian peasantry against alleged misdeeds of British officials. It was an angry and tenacious crusade against the Revenue Alienations or Inam Commission of the Bombay government. It became such a fixation during late 1858 and 1859 that Knight at times gave his entire editorial page to the attack.[30]

As mentioned (see p. 15), the lands previously ruled by the peshwa in the Maratha state were annexed to the Bombay Presidency after the Third Anglo-Maratha War, 1818–19. The Bombay government decided to make a ryotwari land settlement, that is, a revenue settlement with each landholder which recognized the cultivator's right to occupy the land, and set his payments for the next thirty years. This system (contrasting with the zamindari settlement in Bengal) required revenue officials to visit each field, determine its legitimate occupant, estimate its expected yield, and assess the anticipated revenue. This difficult and tedious survey was worsened by land titles which were at times disputed, garbled, vague, or even unwritten. The peshwa's administration in the more remote areas had gradually deteriorated into impotence during its last twenty or so years, and even the land records in Pune (its capital) had not been maintained.[31]

When Henry Goldsmid became superintendent of the revenue survey in the 'Southern Mahratta' lands in 1835, he was startled to find many landholders—perhaps a fourth or a third—claiming exemption from revenue demands because of *inam* grants.[32] A monarch might, according to Indian tradition, grant a tax exemption for land dedicated to a religious body, for military heroics, for hereditary village officials (*watan* grants),[33] or even personal services to the monarch. It might be granted in perpetuity or it might expire with the grantee. A 'perpetual' grant might lapse if the holder produced no sons, but here another Hindu tradition intervened: the easy adoption of male heirs. An adopted son might be a distant family member or a complete stranger; he need not even be an orphan. British officials were dubious when such alleged adoptions prevented the forfeiture of inam grants, and they demanded firm burdens of proof.

To handle this problem, Act XI of 1852 empowered inam commissioners to examine and judge these claims. Supervised by Captain T.A. Cowper after 1856, their quasi-judicial role included the power to compel testimony and punish false witnesses, but the commissioners were not judges and were not bound by judicial regulations. An aggrieved landholder could not appeal to the courts, but only to the remote Governor of Bombay in Council.[34] One critic (not Knight) depicted the dread scenario:

From one village to another passed the appalling news that the Commissioner had appeared, had called for titles that could not be produced, and that nothing but a general confiscation of property was likely to result....Each day, it has been said, produced its list of victims.... the pangs of the crowd who came forth from the shearing house, shorn to the skin, unable to work, ashamed to beg, condemned to penury....[35]

Knight saw the commission's records and was shocked at what he called 'unprecedented scoundrelism'; he doubted that there had ever been 'a grosser oppression practiced anywhere in the world, than the investigation of landed titles in this presidency....'[36] He said that Cowper, the Revenue Commissioner of Alienations, was alienating many of the Deccan peasantry and driving them to join the Rebellion.[37]

More specifically, it was a travesty of judicial procedures. One commissioner, he said, boasted that he alone had decided 638 cases in less than six months, which Knight figured as one-and-a-half hours per case. He continued:

The commissioner himself is at once the plaintiff, the judge, and virtually the last court of appeals. The proceedings of his court are conducted with closed doors, and absolute secresy [sic]; the proprietors whose titles are impeached, not being allowed copies even of the documentary evidence, upon which the case against their title rests; and this farce is enacted in the name of justice....[38]

Moreover, the burden of proof of title legitimacy was placed on the *inamdar* (holder of the inam), who faced stringent legal criteria: first, a traditional Indian title might be upset if it did not follow 'the circumlocutions of English parchments'[39]; second, unless the *sanad* (charter) explicitly stated that the title was to be hereditary, it was assumed that it was not; third, the commissioner had to be satisfied that the grant came from a competent authority; and fourth, proof was needed of an unimpeded succession from father to son for a hundred years; if that proof lay in the peshwa's records in Pune, the inamdar had no access to it.[40] During this year-plus campaign, Knight also accused Cowper and his predecessor, William Hart, of dishonesty, falsifying minutes, misconstruing memos, hiding a decision overrule from England, and systematically vilifying all critics.[41]

Captain Cowper responded with a memo to the Governor of Bombay which called such accusations 'a public evil of the greatest magnitude'. Knight's articles were appearing in translation in Indian newspapers throughout the Presidency and thus teaching the people 'discontent and sedition', he said. It would make the governing of India 'impossible', and he stood ready to prosecute the editor for libel. The governor, Lord John Elphinstone, agreed the articles were 'an unqualified evil', but feared that a libel suit would probably fail.[42]

The Inam Commission and its acts preoccupied Knight more than any single issue ever would again. The *Bombay Times* issue of 15 November 1858 had as its entire editorial page a series of essays on that topic. The issue of 17 November had just one long leader on it. In 1859 Knight wrote, published and distributed in England a booklet entitled *The Inam Commission Unmasked*. After a reprint of several *Bombay Times* articles, it told British readers that 'the author of this pamphlet is probably the only man in the Bombay Presidency who, from a long study of its recorded minutes, [knows] of the profound misrepresentations upon which its proceedings have been based.'[43] He urged abolition of the commission; otherwise 'you must follow it up with an army, and will hold the lands you have unjustly confiscated no longer than the people are helpless to wrest them from you.' He added: 'The tendency of our rule to reduce all classes to a dead level of pauperism is truly sickening to contemplate.'[44]

Perhaps because of Knight, reports of protests against land seizures in India were reaching the British public. Lord Stanley, Secretary of State for India, assured the Parliament on 14 February 1859 that the purpose of the inquiry was to confirm legitimate titles, not void them. The government did not want to seize a landed estate because of some flaw in the title, he said, and it placed little value on reversions due to failure of heirs.[45] When Knight read this, he exulted: 'The fate of the Inam Commission is no longer doubtful, and its agents may close their books.'[46]

Four months later, Stanley rejected a ruling from Bombay that one inam grant be revoked because of an endorsement omitted thirty-two years earlier; voiding the grant would be 'both impolitic and unjust at this distance in time' he wrote. The Bombay government kept this embarrassing overruling a secret, but Knight revealed it. Consequently, eight members of the secretariat were reportedly suspended for leaking Stanley's letter to him.[47] (Knight and other journalists relied heavily on 'whistle-blowers,' that is, confidential informants.)

In 1860 another commissioner deprived a landholder of his long-settled title because of a defect which he was not allowed to examine. Such a proceeding, said Knight, would be 'laughed out of any court in the world, but that of Captain Cowper.'[48]

The next year the Bombay government, probably wearying of these fractious and sometimes embarrassing exchanges, proposed a compromise: any inamdar who would agree to pay one-fourth of a disputed revenue assessment would be excused from further inquiry into his title. This was embodied in two Summary Settlement Acts of 1863. In 1864 it was decreed that 'terminable' grants, instead of being promptly terminated, would be phased out over the next four generations.[49] With these measures, the inam issue faded from sight. Knight had struck a sharp blow against the Raj's arbitrary and contemptuous handling of peasant land titles.

DEFENDER OF MAHARAJAS

It is ironic that Robert Knight, an idealistic liberal, reformer, and progressive, with his London lower-middle class background, should have become a conspicuous defender of Indian princes, but so it was. His standards were honesty, legitimacy, and fairness, which he frequently accused the British Indian government of violating.

This 'Raj' was actually a conglomerate which included almost six hundred Indian states, great and small, and their traditional princes. Called 'native states' or 'princely states', they covered about two-fifths of the subcontinent and held about a third of its people. A few of these states were as substantial as European nations, while others were minute and puny, like some post-medieval European duchies.

The status of these states and their princes was a matter of dispute up to the day the British left India. The British had relied on the help of Indian chieftains (or would-be chieftains) since their first footholds in India, but as the British grip strengthened, the role of these allies shrivelled. They were persuaded to enter defensive alliances with the East India Company which included a ban on the princes entering any external relationship without the company's approval, the stationing of a 'protective' force on or near their territory, to be financed by the princes, and the posting of a company agent at the court as a resident 'advisor'.

Only forty-some states had formal treaties with the British. Most of those treaties did not mention 'paramount power' or 'subsidiary' status, though these became common British parlance.[50] A prince, therefore, might have failed to realize that with such an 'alliance' he had signed away the independence of his state. He was soon disabused. The force sent for his 'protection' became a virtual army of occupation, and the resident sent to 'advise' him a petty tyrant whose approval and goodwill became essential to the prince. Disputes were settled unilaterally and sometimes peremptorily by the autocratic British.[51] A dissatisfied prince had few weapons available if the resident and his boss, the governor general, proved unsympathetic. One of these few was to engage an agent who could present the prince's case to the-powers-that-be in London. This provided a lucrative retirement income for an unknown number of the company's military and civil officers. One such was retired Major T. Evans Bell, of the Madras Army, whose influential friends included the editor of the *Bombay Times*, Robert Knight.

Thomas Evans Bell, son of a London merchant, was educated at King's College School, Wandsworth. He was appointed a cadet in the Second Regiment of Madras European Infantry (of the East India Company), commissioned as an ensign in 1842 and rose to the rank of major on the Madras Staff Corps.[52]

Dalhousie believed that Indian states should be annexed and ruled directly whenever a plausible reason could be found, for the benefit of both the empire and the subject population.[53] In 1853, the Bhonsle raja of Nagpur, one of the major states of central India, died unexpectedly, before adopting an heir. His rani then did so, but Dalhousie refused to recognize the adoptee as the legitimate heir, declared that the royal line had lapsed, and annexed the state—and its treasury—over bitter protests.[54]

Evans Bell was appointed assistant commissioner at Nagpur in 1855, but he came to sympathize with the displaced royal family. He defended them in an 1859 book, *The English in India*, but he lost his appointment in 1860 for 'insubordination to the Chief Commissioner in advocating the claims of the dispossessed ruling family....'[55] He retired from the army in 1863.

Bell then became a London agent of the maharaja of Mysore. Mysore had been a major south Indian power under the usurper Hyder Ali, but the British finally subdued it in 1798 and restored its hereditary ruler. However, they were so displeased by this maharaja's inept governance that in 1831 the administration was taken from the prince and given to a British commission. The ruler pleaded until his death in 1867 for restoration of his authority, but futilely. Bell presented his case in his book, *The Mysore Reversion.* [56]

Bell and Knight were linked by their political views and their friendship over the years; Bell was described as a 'true comrade' of Knight.[57] In fact, Bell claimed in an 1884 letter that he was writing editorials in Knight's *Statesman*: 'These are all my writing—though sometimes Mr. Knight takes a few of my sentences and frames them in one of his own articles.'[58]

A question that arises here is whether Knight was also being paid by princes, directly or through Bell. There was an occasion in 1879 (see pp. 173–5), but no earlier evidence. It is a fact that Knight had financial difficulties most of his life. Newspapers in India, as mentioned, were not moneymakers in the nineteenth century, and Knight's other financial ventures seem to have been uniformly unsuccessful. At the same time he had to maintain the lifestyle of a proper Victorian gentleman and provide for his rapidly-growing family. Bell may have helped; but there is no evidence.

Knight often wrote about the perceived injustices of Dalhousie's 'Doctrine of Lapse'. It had swallowed the state of Jhansi, he noted, goading its rani into revolt.[59] There was the case of the raja of Tanjore, whose small but historic state in south-eastern India *was* annexed because of the lack of a legitimate heir, though he was survived by 'his Ranee and other wives, two legitimate daughters, six natural sons, and ninety collateral heirs.'[60] The annexed state of Nagpur had seen no economic development, and the people were not 'one whit better' for it. [61]

Knight rejoiced, therefore, when Queen Victoria proclaimed, on the crown's assumption of the Government of India from the East India Company on 1 November 1858, that no extension of crown territory was desired, all treaties and engagements with the princes would be 'scrupulously maintained' and 'due regard' would be paid to 'the ancient rights, usages, and customs of India.'[62] If the hopes thus awakened are fulfilled, he responded, this proclamation would become 'the Great Charter of the nation's rights, reversing twenty years' policy on annexations, adoptions, and alienations.'[63] Similarly, when Lord Stanley told the Parliament that the princes' help in suppressing the Rebellion showed 'the importance of keeping up the independence and dignity of these Native States', the editor said he could have wept 'tears of joy'.[64]

An elated Knight called for an entirely new relationship between the empire and the princes, starting with a legal delineation of the rights and roles of princes and residents. He proposed that instead of reducing the princes to puppets in the hands of domineering residents, Britain should regenerate them by giving the empire a federal structure, with an imperial diet meeting annually to represent the princes. Then, 'withdrawing the Resident from the invidious and false position in which he stands, let the diet be the medium of communicating all recommendations to the individual State....'[65] The powers-that-were ignored this proposal, but some of its spirit may be seen in the appointment of several princes or their dewans (prime ministers) to the Legislative Councils created in 1861 and the later launching of a Chamber of Princes by the Government of India Act of 1921.

In another visionary editorial, Knight wrote that instead of annexing more territory, British India should start dismantling an empire which future revolts would make untenable:

The substitution of European, for native administrative machinery, throughout a country numbering two hundred millions of people, is one of those marvels of audacity [similar to] the feats of a tight rope dancer; a very interesting, but by no means satisfactory, spectacle, and one suggestive of a tragic ending.[66]

Ruling India through a military occupation was 'the dream of a fool', he wrote.[67]

Despite the new approach promised by the queen's proclamation, the same imperial officials retained the same hostile attitudes toward the Indian princes. The viceroy, Lord Canning, did nothing to help the Bhonsle family of Nagpur, which Knight said had been reduced to beggary by seizure of the royal estates.[68] Moreover, Canning maintained the discretionary power to accept or reject a royal adoption; he did reject a number of adoptions, though he was thrice overruled by Sir Charles Wood as Secretary of State.[69]

Even more reprehensible, in Knight's eyes, was Dalhousie's 1856 annexation of Oudh (or Awadh), a major north Indian state, not for failure of heirs, but on grounds of misgovernment. 'All the public and private faults of the royal family of Oude cannot justify the extinction of sovereignty, the seizure of territories and revenue, and a confiscation of a great part of the private property of our faithful ally', he wrote. Dalhousie's policy 'was one of destroying the confidence of our friends, justifying the distrust of our worst enemies, converting loyal submission into mere imbecility....'[70]

Among the Indian princes, the Nizam of Hyderabad was unique. His state had originated as the southern dominions of the much-mourned Mughal Empire in the early eighteenth century and considered itself an heir of that vanished realm. After the death of the founding nizam in 1749, his dynasty showed a great want of military, political, and administrative skills. The survival of the state depended on the support of outside allies and powerful internal factions, and so Hyderabad had to endure a continual tangle of court intrigues, family feuds, and the schemes of greedy and ambitious men, both Indian and British. Robert Knight, too, would become enmeshed in this murky web.

In 1798 and 1800, the nizam, menaced by Marathas, was persuaded by the British to sign treaties which replaced his French mercenary officers with a British protective force. These ruinous treaties also gave control of Hyderabad's external affairs to the East India Company and authorized the 'advice' of the British resident on administration.[71] They also required the nizam to provide a matching force of 15,000, which he could not afford. Its troopers went unpaid and mutinied in 1812. The British resident then took over the brigade, paid the salary arrears, and staffed it with company officers as the 'Hyderabad Contingent'.

By 1853 extravagance and mismanagement had run Hyderabad so deeply into debt that Dalhousie settled accounts by occupying some of its richest districts and applying their annual revenue to its debts. The nizam was furious but helpless; the only two reliable armed forces in Hyderabad were both British-run. He dared not make a major appointment without the approval of the British resident. Therefore, the contending factions—the Persian-descent Shi'ite family which ran the *dewani* (administration), the Arab-descent Sunni family which controlled the household troops, and the occasional shrewd and talented Hindu—sought the favours of the resident and his ever-expanding staff.

But in 1853 a genuinely capable and conscientious young man—Mir Turab Ali, known as Salar Jung—succeeded to the dewani. Sir Richard Temple, British resident in 1867, called Salar Jung 'qualified in an unprecedented degree for his public and official duties'.[72] As he worked to reform the administration, the Rebellion erupted. Salar Jung was credited with persuading the nizam not to join the uprising, thus preventing its spread to south India. Later, the British professed gratitude and offered a reward. Salar Jung (on orders from the nizam) pleaded for restoration of the territories seized in 1853, especially the four north-western Berar districts. This the British rejected harshly, and two years of angry bickering followed. It resulted in the British grasping the Berars adamantly and thereafter turning a suspicious eye on that 'cheeky' dewan. An intended goodwill offer thus had exactly the opposite effect.[73]

To Knight, defender of princes and champion of justice, this was a case of a hapless prince pushed into a hopeless debt, a state stripped of its richest districts, and a deserving dewan in danger of being unjustly broken and ruined. He would review and expose the entire Hyderabad mess twenty years later (see pp. 151–4).

CHAMPION OF PEASANTS AND RURAL DEVELOPMENT[74]

Most of the people of India were poor, unable to hire agents or reward helpful journalists. Nevertheless, Robert Knight remained a passionate defender of the peasants—handicapped by traditional social oppression, a strained economy, a heavy-handed government, and haughty British settlers who were starting to move into the mufassil. His basic solution, like that of most Victorians, was economic development, preferably by private enterprise.

One preliminary problem was ignorance of what existed beyond the immediate horizon. India had always been a land of legends and fanciful tales, with a paucity of mundane facts and figures, and so it was in 1847, when Knight arrived. W.W. Hunter later recalled:

No authoritative work existed, to which the public or the administrative body could refer, for the essential data concerning the princes or people of India. Districts now [i.e., 1895] within half a day's railway journey of the capital were [called] 'unexplored'....Famines, agrarian agitation, tribal or sectarian movements, in short all the less common but inevitable incidents of Indian rule, were wont to take the Government not less than the public by surprise. The actual revenues and administration of even a British District were official secrets into which no outsider could penetrate.[75]

Hunter was lauding Dalhousie, who as governor general reduced rural remoteness and isolation by launching a national postal service, telegraph lines, and the beginnings of the railroads (see pp. 22–3). Knight, too, wanted to open the interior; he demanded firm facts and figures from the mufassil on trade, crop yields, tax returns, etc. He sought public records and accountability from officials trained in the closed-door system of the East India Company. These were needed for government help to the peasantry, especially in time of famine (see pp. 108–9).

The Rebellion still smouldered when Knight set out his programme for rural India:

We must give them not merely an equitable and benevolent government, but...the means of making the most of the fertility of the land. We must not merely construct roads and canals; the country must be thrown open to English capital and English energy; lands must be let on long leases, and each and every encouragement given to intelligent settlers.[76]

He lyrically portrayed the benefits of attracting foreign capital and industry:

If a Chinese thinks he can cultivate tea, or produce silk, let him have land on a long lease to try the experiment. If an American has a notion that he can raise tobacco or cotton, let him try. If a coffee planter wants forest land now lying waste, let him have it at an almost nominal rental.... the face of India would be changed in twenty years, from the most poverty-stricken country in the world, to a land teeming with industry and wealth; towns would spring up in the interior, exhibiting all the marks of civilization and progress....the missionary, the schoolmaster, and the English language would do the rest.[77]

Nothing did more to stimulate rural development in India than the railway system. Wherever the rails went, forced isolation ended. They provided an easy and reliable means of movement of persons, goods, and ideas between city and countryside. A station every few miles meant, for instance, a stationmaster and ticket sellers, and jobs for guards, maintenance workers, sweepers, all stirring alien influences. In larger stations it meant vendors, canteens, and soon bookstalls, where bundles of newspapers from nearby cities were dropped off for sale. Trains also brought in the mail, including newspapers for subscribers. Thus the words of Knight and every other newspaper editor reached the mufassil.

The rapid construction of the main lines in India was truly astounding. Awesome tunnels, trestles, and bridges were built with mid-Victorian tools and engineering. Overcoming obstructions of jungles and mountains, monsoon rains and floods, intense heat and tropical diseases, wild animals and hostile tribes, the railway companies completed the main lines— more than five thousand miles of trackage criss-crossing the subcontinent—within twenty years of that first groundbreaking. Knight was especially impressed by the 93-span bridge which carried the Bombay, Baroda, and Central India Railroad from Bombay to nearby Bassein:

It has often been asserted that if the English were swept away suddenly from India there would be no great works to bear witness to the greatness of their power. Every day that assertion is being falsified. To the grand trunk road of Bengal, the Ganges canal, and other triumphs of engineering skill, we hope soon to be able to add the Bhore Ghaut incline [leading to Pune] and the Bassein railway bridge.[78]

By 1871 the major cities of India were linked to each other and to much of the interior.[79] In 1851 it normally took two weeks to get from Calcutta to Delhi; in 1871, it took two days. The British pushed the railroads to tighten their grip on India by providing troop and supply mobility;[80] actually, it led to the eventual demise of the empire by giving Indians a national scope and connection.

Knight enthusiastically supported railroad construction, not only for military efficiency, but because it would help powerfully to overcome 'thirty centuries of stagnation' and redeem India from its poverty. For instance, he reported that a cartload of Nagpur cotton, marketed via local roads and the Godavari River to the port of Coconada, underwent seven stops for road cesses (surcharges) and tolls, adding 25 per cent to its cost.[81]

However, he also saw that even economic progress did not justify the 'lamentable denudation' of India's forests. He wanted 'to enclose and preserve, properly and strictly, under the care of an efficient forester,…all the best forest tracts.'[82]

Knight urged the government to assist the settling of British planters and businessmen in the mufassil through such measures as the near-giveaway of 'wastelands' (apparently unoccupied lands). Plantations would stimulate the productive general development of rural India and 'the moral and material improvement' of the peasantry.[83] However, British settlers proved to be a disturbing and often an upsetting addition to rural society, and in one instance—that of the indigo planters of Bengal—their activities provoked a series of riots.

Indigo planters had settled in Bengal during the first half of the nineteenth century, bought the zamindari rights over much land, built their processing factories, and were able to coerce the ryots into growing this difficult crop against their wishes. Soon stories spread about brutal attacks on the peasants by strong-arm *goondas* hired by the planters, which the local magistrates and police seemed unable to stop. In 1859 the ryots organized boycotts against indigo-growing in several localities. They armed themselves with crude weapons, and bloody clashes were reported. The planters charged the peasants with violations of contract by refusing to grow indigo, for which most had taken advance payments. The planters demanded and obtained, in March 1860, a six-month law making breach of contract a criminal offence. Sir J.P. Grant, Lieutenant Governor of Bengal, tried to take a balanced role: he supported this contract law (Act XI of 1860), but he strengthened the magisterial and police forces in the indigo districts and appointed a committee of enquiry, which produced much evidence of planter abuse.[84]

The newspapers chose their sides. The leading Indian weekly, the *Hindoo Patriot*, supported the peasants and was filled with complaints against the planters.[85] The Anglo-Indian dailies, the *Englishman* and the *Bengal Hurkaru*, defended the indigo interests. Knight assailed the indigo planter across the subcontinent for 'the grossest abuses that man's selfishness can lead to' that were 'virtually above the law'. The ryot, a victim of cruel oppression, 'finds his own body at the mercy of the planter's foot and his heel, and his wife's at the mercy of his lusts,' he wrote.[86]

Reports of violence and threatened violence continued during the summer of 1860, but the reorganized police and additional magistrates in the indigo districts helped prevent the explosion which Knight and others had feared.[87] In August the enquiry committee brought in a report critical of the planters, and the Secretary of State, Charles Wood, vetoed attempts to renew the law making breach of contract a criminal offence.[88] Knight exulted that oppressive planters had been checked; 'that Lord Canning's administration should have been overawed by the bluster of these men and the attitude of their English allies...moved us to more indignation than we expressed.'[89] Instead of arrests and criminal charges, he said, mortgages on crops should simply be registered, and a procedure for summary enforcement of contracts developed. The dispute continued, but closer judicial and public scrutiny stopped (or at least reduced) the planters' bullying.[90]

These planters were not the stimulating entrepreneurs of Knight's vision. He said that they had virtually enslaved the ryot by purchasing zamindari rights and they refused to pay a fair price for their indigo.[91] He defended the Rev. James Long, a missionary convicted of criminal libel and jailed for distributing a Bengali play ridiculing the planters.[92] The planters deserved 'the contempt and abhorrence of all honest men', he raged; instead of honest capitalists, they were 'a race of needy adventurers' trying to make money by 'confiscating the ryots' toils'.[93]

Knight now opposed the virtual giveaway of wastelands to the planters, and he was no longer enthusiastic about how British settlers would benefit the local peoples. The planters, he wrote in 1863, pay trifles for land and eventually take their profits back to England. If only those aliens were enriched, what were the advantages to India of this cultivation and trade? He now rejected the idea that 'the mere presence of a body of Europeans' would help local prospects: 'what have the indigo planters done for Bengal during the half-century of their fortune-making therein? What could be more demoralizing to both races, than the nature of relations subsisting between them....?'[94]

To protect the peasantry, the Raj relied on the skills and opinions of the district officers and others in the Civil Service of India (CSI, usually called 'civilians'), which provided its administrative backbone. Young men now entered the service through competitive examination instead of the old patronage appointments of the East India Company, and Knight expected more broadly educated, more liberal and capable men to enter the service through this door.[95] He called for higher educational standards for the CSI appointments and instruction of the young men in Indian languages. 'An Indian language is just as good for intellectual training as a European one, and generally far more useful', he wrote. Without the language, judges were at the mercy of their *dubashes* (interpreters), 'often a venal crowd'.[96] Reform of the rural minor judiciary was similarly needed.

Britain, referred to as the foremost modern nation by Knight, was expected to provide India with, not just law and order, not just classic 'good government', but relief from the massive poverty, depravation, and hopelessness which it found there. He said that the Raj should stimulate public works, especially irrigation projects, which would greatly increase India's productivity and its import and export trade. Water is gold in India, Knight wrote, citing a report that revenues from the Tanjore district had more than doubled with completion of irrigation works. What might

India's foreign trade become 'if the vast plains of the Ganges were efficiently irrigated, and made to produce double and treble their present amounts?'[97]

But the crucial element of India's development was the peasant, whose enterprise would be stimulated by strengthening his individual ownership rights. Knight was still preaching classical liberal doctrine:

The joint tenancies of the North-West, whatever arrangements the villagers might make among themselves, are in this respect opposed to the principles of sound political economy. Joint liability is a species of communism, for which even the most advanced societies are as yet quite unprepared....[98]

India's traditional joint family system was also seen as economically counterproductive. If one man got a job, he would be expected to support a whole clan of kinfolk, said Knight, which not only discouraged the relatives' getting their own jobs but kept the worker from saving part of his pay and investing it productively. The grip of the *shroff*, the moneylender, had to be broken by the state's ousting him and even stepping into his place.[99] For some reason Knight's veneration of private enterprise did not extend to rural moneylenders, whom he sometimes called shroff, sometimes *sowkar* (moneylender), sometimes the more general *bania* (shopkeeper or other small businessman).

His classical liberalism was now tempered by a sympathetic defence of the peasantry. The peasantry was India's base, and an economic programme which ignored their welfare was built on sand.

RACISM AND REPRESENTATIVE GOVERNMENT

Knight, the dedicated liberal, denied that his was a 'pro-native' policy; it was, merely, a just and equitable approach:

Our political creed with reference to the country, is based on the deepest abhorrence of the doctrine, that India is to be governed for the English. We yield to no man in the conviction that it is only a trust in our hands, to be administered for the welfare of its people.[100]

He sought a representative assembly to share the governing responsibilities. India had had 'legislative councils' since the charter renewal of 1853, but representative they were not, consisting only of British officials appointed by the governor general.[101] The crown's assumption of the Government of India in 1858, said the editor, should bring in an elective and representative council.[102] He also urged Bombay business leaders to petition for a state legislature of non-officials, with the council meeting openly and its proceedings published.[103]

In a representative legislature, though, who would represent the Indian peoples? Presumably Indians themselves, chosen by some sort of elections. A binational assembly did not worry Knight, who believed all men were created (essentially) equal and should have equal status and rights. But among the British in 1860 India, such views were generally unpopular. Knight, calling for an understanding and a rapport across racial lines, found the tide running against him.

European evaluations of non-Europeans had dropped sharply in the century before 1860. This reappraisal was due largely to the widening gap in technology, wealth, and power, but also due to closer contacts with Africans, Asians, and Native Americans. The old image of the 'noble savage' had been replaced by one of backward, ignorant, and often barbaric peoples whose distance from Europeans appeared so great as to call into question their common humanity. Early naturalists such as Carolus Linnaeus and the Comte de Buffon tried to clarify the subject by dividing mankind into large classifications based essentially on physical features, and these they called races. In the early nineteenth century, 'race' was seen as a restrictive attribute which served to explain the 'natural superiority' of one people over others. Some (the polygenists) claimed that the differences were so great that non-whites must be separate orders of creation, that only whites were descendants of Adam and Eve. Race had thus moved from a descriptive to a determining characteristic. It also served to excuse the antipathy which many felt toward those who were 'different'.[104]

In India the optimistic liberalism of T.B. Macaulay, who believed that all Indians needed to do to enter the modern world was a European-type education and the English language, had already lost favour among Anglo-Indians before the Rebellion. The savage bloodletting (by both sides) in the Rebellion had left a legacy of fear and hatred.[105] The publication of Darwin's *Origin of the Species* in 1859 restored non-whites to the human race, but in the assumed role of a natural and permanent inferiority. Social Darwinians such as Herbert Spencer promptly embellished this into the brutally competitive notion of 'survival of the fittest', and they had no doubt who the fittest was. Charles W. Dilke, a Liberal Member of Parliament, toured the empire in 1866–7 and forecast the global triumph of 'Saxondom', that English settlers would displace the 'natives' in the temperate areas of South America, China, and the table lands of Africa, just as they had in North America, Australia, and New Zealand.[106] Race had become a banner to flaunt.

But not by Knight. One never sees in his newspapers this sort of racist braggadocio, nor demeaning nor insulting remarks about Indians as a people, or race, or nation. Instead, he deplored the worsening relations between the two communities:

It offends our selflove to be told, that the natives of India hate us at heart; and when slowly forced to recognize the fact, the same selflove whispers, that this hatred arises from no fault in us, but from the depravity of the people....a gulf now stands between the sympathies of the people and ourselves. It is not the people who have changed, but *we*, and it is unhappily the case, that the personal bearing of Englishmen toward natives, seems to have become marked by hauteur and violence....You can hardly introduce the subject in any society, but a chorus of voices lets you into the secret of the contempt and dislike, which are cherished for the people amongst whom we dwell.[107]

Knight, as an English editor engaged by Indian directors, was clearly vulnerable. This growing antagonism probably led the directors to sell the *Bombay Times* to Knight, to remove an impediment to 'the interests of truth'.[108] Nevertheless, the hostile *Bengal Hurkaru*, clearly referring to Knight, sneered: 'We think the most wretched of all sights is an Englishman, for the sake of lucre, uttering the ideas and fostering the prejudices of a native, his inferior in education, in religion, and—it ought to be so—in morality.'[109]

Knight, like Macaulay, felt Britain had an obligation to reform and modernize India, though he would have added economic development and Christianization to the latter's prescription of English education and law. But he felt that the 'thick cloud of prejudice' obscured the British view of the Indian people.[110]

The idea of interracial representative government, like that of economic assistance, was badly wounded by this growing racism. When it returned, it wore a different face: demands by angry Indians, wrung from a reluctant Raj.

IMPERIAL JUSTICE AND EXPLOITATION

Robert Knight, as a man concerned about morals, felt that the Raj needed moral justification. It was neither the booty of conquest nor the harvest of Darwinian natural selection but, as he put it, 'only a trust in our hands, to be administered for the welfare of its people.'[111] He appealed to his fellow-Anglos:

the substitution of European for native executive is the national calamity of India, to the mitigation of which, as far as possible, we are bound, by every consideration of humanity and justice. The time has come in our history, when we may bind this people to us forever, by a Christian and magnanimous policy, and if we allow the occasion to pass, it may never return.... To place it on a safe and enduring basis, it is but necessary that the people discern the purity and justice of our intentions.[112]

However, Knight knew that the reality of the Raj fell far short of 'purity and justice,' that British policy rested on 'an intensely selfish basis' and in adopting Machiavellian morals 'we have sown the wind, and in the rebellion [of 1857] have but reaped the first fruits of our harvest.'[113] The government's attempt to close its fiscal deficit through a new customs law showed 'the blundering Imperialism which flounders on from one difficulty to another'.[114]

Nothing, though, could ignite the editor's anti-imperial rage like a reminder of the Afghanistan invasion of 1838–42, such as the publication in 1859 of some Kabul dispatches. Knight (and others) saw the war as a disaster.[115] It was a diplomatic disaster because imprudent and headstrong British officials, responding to an imaginary Russian threat to India, showed the world how even the mighty British empire could blunder and fail. It was a military disaster because, through a chain of misjudgments, the political mission and then the entire British outpost at Kabul were massacred by gunslinging Afghans. It was a political disaster because the British, having ousted the amir of Kabul (Dost Muhammad) at great cost, had to restore him to the throne as the price of peace. Knight called it 'an insane adventure' in which the people of India had no voice and should not have been taxed to pay.[116]

Economic crimes required less fury, more careful explanations. From his start as editor Knight had assailed the Raj for its lack of an economic development programme and for keeping India poor by draining specie to Britain as profits and 'home charges'. From the 1853 report of the East India Company he discovered that during the previous twenty years it had collected £500 million in Indian revenues, of which it had spent only £5 million on public works, while the 'home charges' had reached £80 million. Even those five million were not spent on the development of India's resources, he said:

No such thing. They were expended on barracks, jails, churches, *cutcherries* [offices], military roads, harbours, lighthouses, postal communications, pilot establishments, and we know not what else. The outlay on roads, bridges, and other works for purely commercial purposes, and for the improvement of the country, was next to nothing. Can it be said, under these circumstances, that England has been faithful to the great trust committed to her in the dominion of the East? Surely not....[117]

(To be fair, during the 1850s the company constructed some large irrigation projects in north India and the huge railroad construction programme, both of which had significant impacts on India's economy.) The Raj, he said, should be compelled to guarantee a return on capital invested in the country, as an incentive; it had been 'unfaithful to its trust' and the British people shared the guilt by complacently looking on.[118]

Most maddening were the 'home charges'—bills incurred and paid in Britain but charged to the government (and taxpayers) of India. Knight considered this an unjust use of imperial power against a government too squeezed to nourish and develop India's economy. These 'home charges' included the pensions of retired military and civil officers, most of whom lived in Britain; sales of arms and most supplies to the British Indian Army, even though that army was used to pull imperial chestnuts out of firefights from Ethiopia to Hong Kong; salaries and costs of British troops training for future duty in India; the offices and expenses of the

India Council and the Secretary of State for India, even though they were a part of the British government; the payments to make up those five per cent railroad guarantees, and the interest payments on the massive debts accumulated by the late East India Company. The 'home charges' for 1858–9 were given officially as £6 million, nearly half of the Indian budget deficit of £13 ½ million.[119]

That company debt began when Parliament renewed the company's charter in 1813 but ordered it to end most commercial activities though continuing its payments of 10½ per cent annual dividends, or £632,000, to its shareholders. The debts were transferred in 1858 to the Government of India, whose annual deficits, plus the compound interest on those past debts, reached an alarming £69 million by 1874 (when the company and its obligations were officially dissolved).[120]

* * *

The outbreak of the American Civil War in 1861 shut off cotton supplies from the US and sent Manchester mill owners on a desperate search for raw cotton in India or anywhere. Knight, like a Biblical prophet, saw divine retribution for England's unjust squeezing of the Indian economy: 'God in History lights up before us as with a lightning flash, the hundred millions of capital wrongfully taken from the soil of India in the past, and still being taken while Manchester is in the very verge of perishing.'[121]

According to Knight, this unwise and unjust policy also contradicted his exalted view of the purpose of the Raj, which was '[t]he prosperity and wealth of India, and the contentment of her people.'[122] He recalled that when he had first landed on the Indian mainland in 1847, 'a fakeer' had heaped curses upon him and his party. 'The burden of the poor wretch's malediction was the complaint, that the white man had carried all the rupees out of the country.'[123] Indians, he said, generally believed there was a constant drain of silver, that a white man arrived with a box of clothes but went home with a box of silver.

In the years which followed, Knight continued his close and usually critical scrutiny of India's finances. He was always full of reform proposals, some of them wise: The government should try to promote Indian exports. British Burma and the Straits Settlements (Penang, Malacca, and Singapore) should be cut loose from India and its treasury and made separate crown territories within the empire. (This was done in 1935 and 1867, respectively.) India should shift from its silver rupee to a gold standard and a gold-based currency, as gold was more stable and reliable.[124] (Beginning in 1874, massive global mining and minting of silver nearly halved its value against gold, nearly doubling India's rupee payments on foreign debts within twenty years.)[125] But fiscal policies of the so-called 'Government of India', like its political and military policies, were shaped in Westminster by men answerable only to a British electorate.

Those years also saw the articulation of the 'drain theory', an elaboration of the complaint of Knight's 'fakeer', that India's poverty under the British was substantially due to the drainage of much of India's wealth overseas to pay for mass-produced manufactures dumped in India, repatriation of corporate profits and individual earnings, and of course those extorted 'home charges'. Therefore, a once-prosperous India had been reduced to penury and stripped of the capital needed for public works and normal commercial and industrial development.[126] (The British reply was, in effect, that India's poverty was due rather to rapid population growth, deteriorating natural resources, monsoon unreliability, and wasteful socio-economic-cultural patterns.) The drain theory became an essential argument of India's 'freedom movement' and it remains a topic for research and dispute. Its principal theorists were Dadabhai Naoroji and Romesh Chunder Dutt.[127] Although neither credited Knight (who never wholly embraced the theory), they developed and expanded upon facts, figures, and ideas which the editor had presented. Knight pointed the way.

THE ABHORRED INCOME TAX

The Government of India was clearly in financial trouble. Its debt was compounding each year. The crown takeover had led to an expansion of the costly administrative mechanism. The land revenue, the traditional source of royal revenue in India, was 'inelastic'; it had to be extracted from the few wealthy and powerful landholders and squeezed from masses of bare subsistence cultivators. The indirect taxes—various excises, duties, and fees—were limited in yields. Knight, as usual, viewed with alarm:

The financial embarrassment of the Government is most severe....it is rumored that a suspension of cash payments may be looked for, unless relief is obtained very speedily....we owe this state of matters to pure blundering....no one will embark money in an investment, that has been so cruelly mismanaged as the Indian funded debt.[128]

What the government needs, he wrote, is a competent finance minister. It was a wish he would quickly regret.

The first plan to meet this annual deficit of £10–12 million was a licensing tax, for which everyone in trade or following a profession would need an annual license at a cost of Rs 2 to Rs 2000, with ten levels of assessment. Knight said a better solution to the deficit than a licensing tax would be to cut the size of the army in half. 'Rule the people justly and in fear of God', he preached. 'Cease to covet their possessions, thus secure their confidence, and instead of an army of 350,000 men, you do very well with one of 200,000.'[129]

As the licensing tax debate ensued, Knight's opposition deepened. The confusing classifications and the proposed exemptions made a simple and straightforward income tax seem preferable, 'the wisest tax we can impose while the objections raised against it are either unreal or based on an exaggerated estimate of the difficulty attending its levy.'[130] Agitation against the licensing tax was spreading because of 'an almost universal conviction, that it is unjust in principle,...obnoxious, in the last degree in detail,' and would require 'a needlessly irritating and inquisitorial machinery.'[131]

The financial expert for whom Knight had wished arrived in late November of 1859. He was James Wilson, former paymaster general and vice president of the Board of Trade, whom the cabinet had appointed as the first finance member of the viceroy's executive council. Wilson presented his fiscal programme to the council on 18 February 1860. The highlights: an income tax of two per cent was to be levied on persons with an annual income of Rs 200 to 500, and four per cent on those of more than Rs 500; the licensing tax would be retained, but its rates would drop to insignificance; the tax on imported cotton yarn, twist, and thread would be doubled, to ten per cent; and a paper currency would be introduced.[132]

Knight at first was cautiously supportive of Wilson's programme. 'We are no great admirers of an Income Tax anywhere', he wrote, although in.principle it was perhaps the fairest of all taxes. He predicted 'no opposition anywhere' to that principle. Wilson deserved 'the thanks of all' for assuming such great responsibilities, 'while we may congratulate ourselves for having "the right man in the right place"'.[133]

It took the editor only five days to change his mind completely about Wilson and his programme. When he examined the proposals fully, he found some old skeletons: the assumptions that new taxes were needed to meet the expanding costs of governance, and that the Indian people were financially liable for the huge obligations and debts of the East India Company and the costs of suppressing the Rebellion, and the refusal of Britain to guarantee repayment of bank loans to the Government of India. Knight yearned for independent legislators who would question Wilson's assumptions and scrutinize his budget proposals. 'Divide the Indian debt fairly between India and England', he wrote; 'give us a non-official legislature, and an effective voice in the control of our own expenditure; remove the interdict which forces us to borrow at 6 per cent.' Wilson was now called a 'Financial Dictator', and Knight deplored 'the surrender of the whole power of the State into the hands of a gentleman utterly wanting in acquaintance with the real condition of the country....'[134]

Knight's anger seemed to feed upon itself. During late April 1860, he published three extensive articles on 'Indian Finance and Indian Debt' in which he expanded his arguments in fuller detail and harsher tone. Wilson's mistakes, he concluded, were to see himself as representing only British interests, with no responsibility for India's welfare. To dismiss India's pleas for help 'with twaddling platitudes upon the necessity of self-reliance to make us provident, when our fortunes lie wholly at the mercy of our advisors, is to mock our misfortunes.'[135]

Early May saw five long letters addressed to Wilson personally and signed by Knight. Then came a list of cost-cutting alternatives: the troop contingents assigned to princely states, the levying of such expenses as the home depots (that is, depots in Britain for the outfitting and maintaining of British Indian Army units), the Aden fortress on the Arabian coast, the Indian Navy, foreign wars such as those in Afghanistan, and 'the total cost of a rebellion begotten of misrule'. He reiterated that if Indian finances were equitably administered, there would be no deficit at all and no new taxes to so terribly burden the Indian people, for whom 'life is a struggle to make both ends meet'.[136]

This bombardment of Wilson's programme continued during the summer of 1860. The proposed paper currency would create inflation and hardship. The tax yield would be inadequate to fund development. The income tax would be inequitable as well as unjust: Would prostitutes be taxed, and how would their income be determined? What about priests? Those living on the charity of others? The military might be exempted because 'the Government dare not levy the obnoxious tax upon men with arms in their hands'.[137]

The unexpected death of James Wilson on 11 August brought no respite: 'were this melancholy event to result in the withdrawal of every financial measure introduced by the deceased gentleman', it would have been 'among the most fortunate interpositions of providence'.[138] Wilson, he explained later, opposed a tax system that relied on land and regarded the income tax as 'the perfection of fiscal science' whereas Knight saw it as 'a perfectly monstrous device'.[139] He broadcast shrill alarms: The income tax was likely 'to lead to a general rebellion from its obnoxious nature', and 'At the heels of every Income Tax Assessor you will have to send a score of European bayonets'.[140]

However, the government rejected Knight's warning and, despite Wilson's death, prepared to pass his tax programme (with a few modifications). A calmer Knight then issued some practical advice: Do not rely on the *mamlutdars* (a class of local officials) or other dubious authorities for collection. Keep the tax forms simple and in appropriate languages. Be cautious of the tricky bookkeeping and other subtle means of resistance by bazaar merchants. Do not enforce the collections harshly for the first year or two.[141] He also published an open secret of district administration under the Raj:

Our governmental system in India ever has been based upon the delusion that because each department had a European or two at its head, we had therefore taken sure precaution against corruption. And what is the result?....corruption and rascality have had an almost unchecked reign....[142]

A district, he explained, might be a hundred miles in diameter, including perhaps 5000 villages; what control could a lone European possibly maintain?

The income tax was enacted late in 1860, and complaints promptly began. Knight told of a Marwari (a member of an ethnic financial network) who had the temerity to appeal against a tax surcharge by a British assessor; the assessor had him arrested and jailed until a closed-door hearing at which he had neither a lawyer nor a subpoena right.[143] Samuel Laing, who succeeded Wilson as finance member, soon called the tax 'the most horrid hash conceivable. It is not possible, admitting the principle, to apply it worse....'[144] A year later the viceroy, Lord Elgin, thought it should be repealed; the cost of collection was great, it was attended by 'deceptions and extortions' and the yield was inconsiderable,[145] all of which Knight had warned. (But these admissions came only in private letters; there was no policy of public accountability.)

Knight remained devoted to the land revenue and its rigorous collection as India's fiscal salvation. 'The land is the one species of property which necessarily and perdurably increases in value by the mere growth of society,' he wrote, 'and which can therefore be charged with the support of the State.'[146] Not only could the income tax be repealed, but every custom house closed, and India would 'declare FREE TRADE at once and forever with the world.'[147]

The income tax had been enacted for five years, and it lapsed in 1865. However, it was later revived, and after independence it replaced the land revenue as the financial mainstay of the republic. It is generally considered the most socially equitable of major taxes. The 1860 levy had applied to those with an annual income of Rs 200 or more, which exempted all villagers and the urban poor. Knight's indignation was directed less against the tax itself than the circumstances of its enactment, such as the unjust assignment of imperial debt which necessitated a new revenue source, the authoritarian launch of a bold new tax in disdain of independent scrutiny or public reaction, and the lack of a collecting mechanism.

Perhaps this noisy dispute made the Raj more sensitive to public opinion. An 1861 law enabled the viceroy to appoint the first independent and non-official members to the legislative councils, even a few Indians, and a change in 1892 allowed those independent representatives to question and debate the annual budgets and tax proposals.[148] Knight's zigzag editorial policy may have puzzled, but it also prodded and challenged.

RELIGION, REFORM, AND THE RAJ

Knight's towering rages on issues such as the income tax and the Inam Commission might indicate a man so obsessed that he blotted out the rest of the world, but this was not so. His editorial page, like most, usually carried commentaries on several subjects, and on some other topics, he maintained a perpetual interest. One such was the question of religion and social reform in India and the appropriate policy of the government towards them.

Knight was (from all available evidence) always a believing and practising Christian. He shared the disdain of his countrymen for traditional Indian religious beliefs and practices, most of which they lumped together as 'Hinduism'. He also disliked the related social structure which foreigners called 'caste', in which persons were supposedly designated at birth for specified roles in life. Although caste rules were not followed as rigorously and rigidly as Hindu classics (such as the *Laws of Manu*) decreed, they were considered by Knight and others as a major deterrent to India's progress, as they supposedly confined and wasted much of its human resources.[149] Traditional religion, the traditional social order, and the traditional political order had supported and sanctified one another, and to attack one was to threaten all.[150]

The patronage of the monarch (or his local administrators) was necessary for the religious establishment, but also necessary for that monarch as a recognition of his (or her) political legitimacy. As the British took control of parts of India, their district officials were sometimes asked for the traditional support of the raja for local temples, usually at festival times, and they sometimes complied, in their quest for popular acceptance. In this way the East India Company and later the crown became the awkward patrons of what they called 'heathen idolatry'. The company, fearing strained business relation and perhaps popular disturbances, also barred Christian missionaries from its settlements (although it always provided chaplains to serve its employees). However, as the Evangelical movement spread, missionaries began moving to India, and the company was pressed to ease its restrictions. In 1813 it lost the power to bar missionaries and other undesirables (such as journalists) from its territories (see p. 20). Pro-Christian activities increased greatly, and their contributions to the outbreak of the Rebellion showed the wisdom of the company's earlier precautions.

Knight, then, had a dilemma: As a Christian and a humanitarian, he wanted to see the Gospel and related social reforms advance, but as a liberal he objected to interference with religion, to coercive or harassing tactics by the government or aggressive missionaries. His editorials show him wavering back and forth during his Bombay years. In 1858 he lashed out at 'the violent minority which is prepared to thrust a beef-steak...down the Brahmin's throat as the speediest method of converting the country.'[151] He also sought an end to government contributions and collection of Hindu temple revenues, but allowing the temples to keep properties which they already owned, and 'a total abandonment of our interference with their concerns.' For the Raj to reclaim endowments which earlier governments had granted was 'so monstrous a violation of morality that it hardly merits attention. We are not to present robbery to God as burnt offerings....'[152] The real issue was this:

Can we resume the endowments granted in perpetuity by our predecessors [because] they are dedicated to the support of idolatry? Is it consistent, either with justice or equity, to confiscate that which has been held as private property of the most inviolable kind, from time immemorial in the country, because it is devoted to the support of what we believe and know to be a false religion? We say that such a step would be indefensible, alike in morals and in policy....'[153]

But Knight also observed the growth of 'the moral influences of Christianity', a leaven whose 'mighty working is already felt by every educated native mind, in an awakening consciousness of the fact, that a higher morality exists than its fathers knew.'[154] He tied this to social progress, which he saw in the growing acceptance of the remarriage of Hindu widows. The old rule of enforced widow celibacy, he wrote, is held by many Hindus 'to be unreasonable and unnatural; and remarriages have been sufficiently numerous to show that the thin end of the wedge is fairly in.'[155]

During the indigo riots some missionaries defended the peasants, while others supported the European planters, who reciprocated. Knight applauded those who helped the ryots, but deplored those who took planter money to promote Christianity.[156] A frequent antagonist, the pro-planter *Hurkaru*, warned against those 'who, like the *Bombay Times*, will have everything for the native and nothing for the Englishman', while its only interest in India was that Englishmen were living and prospering there. So, replied Knight, this gentleman admits that except for making money out of India, he does not care what becomes of it. Such planter evangelism repelled his 'innermost nature'. The true supporter of missions, he concluded, should be a man of 'deep compassion for his native fellow-subjects' instead of 'these moneygetting, fierce Christianizers'.[157]

In sum, the planters wanted State coercion of the ryots, through assistance to missionaries preaching to them; Knight favoured missionary enterprise but opposed religious coercion, just as he had opposed legal coercion of the ryots.

A series of remarkable editorials followed during the next several weeks in Knight's *Bombay Times and Standard*, remarkable because calls for religious neutrality and a secular state would have shocked most of Europe in 1860. In an editorial, Knight advised the government not to support any religion because the government itself contained people of many religions. It hired on ability, not by religious tests:

We want a good financier to manage the public purse, and if the abilities of Mr. Rothschild who is a Jew, surpass those of Mr. Newdegate, who is a Christian, we unhesitatingly confer the trust on the former; on the same principle we take a Hindoo accountant into our office as a bookkeeper rather than an inefficient Englishman (30 August).

In an editorial on 5 September 1860, he sought 'fair play' for the Gospels but rejected a state role in the propagation of Christianity, which would require 'a mitred Bench and a whole Church system at its heels.' If the Raj had strayed from a neutral course, 'it has done so wrongly.'

In yet another article, on 7 September 1860, he denied that state neutrality meant 'upholding idolatry':

Neither the wrath of the Indian Press, nor any attitude the Indian Government may take up, will convert this country to the Gospel, and the missionary had better let both allies go without a regret. We live in times when God has so happily ordained matters that society demands the religious freedom of every man as his birthright. Let the missionary be content with this....

Knight specifically opposed the Christianizing programme of Sir Herbert Edwardes, a major general and high Punjab official noted for his religious zeal. Were Edwardes allowed to promote his views, 'you would find *his* conscience...set up as the only guide we need consult....The native populations would have rights neither civil nor religious; [India would be left] to the wildest excesses of fanaticism' (22 September 1860). He warned that hatred would spread to all of British India if matters came under the control of men who forget

that the native has feelings as sensitive and prejudices as strong as our own, and would force our higher morality and civilization upon them, by ceaseless invectives, legal disabilities, and if need be by European battalions. Let not these gentlemen imagine that the spirit of Christianity has anything in common with them (18 October 1860).

However, in 1862 Knight resumed his interventionist stance. He wrote that the government had a duty to 'civilize' India, where reform had to come from the outside. 'The government must directly or indirectly mould the popular intellect instead of conforming to them [sic], if we are to attract, or to compel Hindoos to any resemblance of our own type of civilization,' he said.[158]

An episode then occurred which reinforced this mood. Karsondas Mulji, a young Gujarati educator, journalist, and reformer, was sued for libel by the Vaishnavite Hindu sect of the Vallabhacharyas. Mulji had exposed and denounced the leaders of this community, called maharajas, who claimed they were mystical incarnations of Krishna and tried to copy his fabled sexual exploits with their devotees.[159]

Their lawsuit against Mulji outraged Knight. He saw the Vallabhacharyas as tools of Satan who were holding millions 'in the bonds of a superstition so degrading, that the page blushes to record its filthiness.' Instead of his previous tolerance he called the fables of the Vaishnavite incarnations 'a filthy and malignant parody upon the doctrines of the Gospel.'[160] When the court rejected the maharajas' libel suit, Knight called it the start of a reconciliation between God and man in India.[161] Mulji continued his reform efforts, and Knight continued to defend him. The leaders of his caste community of banias opposed and ostracized him, forcing him and his family to flee Bombay, to Knight's disgust.[162]

After this experience Knight came to believe that Christian conversion was necessary for social reform and the welfare of the Indian masses. For instance, any successful prison rehabilitation programme needed religious conversion: 'the idea of any moral teaching apart from Christianity, effecting a radical change in the character of the convicts, cannot surely be held by any reasonable person,' he wrote. 'Has the rising generation of Hindoos and Parsees thrown off the vices as well as the prejudices which enslaved their fathers?'[163]

However, Knight also spoke up for free scientific inquiry; the inquirer does not become an 'infidel', said Knight, just by propounding views not generally held by Christians. To a public just discovering Darwinian evolution, he urged support for the study of nature 'untrammeled by fear of misrepresentation, or of a narrow intolerance....'[164]

Education was another vehicle to liberate the Indian mind. But it had to be education in Indian culture and classical literature, said Knight. These were being obscured by layers of tradition and ignorance because the British-built school system ignored them and gave Indian youth a western-type education, in English. It had been created by reformers such as Macaulay, who were 'utterly ignorant of native thought, habits, languages, and literature.'[165]

Knight (perhaps with scholarly help) pointed out that a critical study of ancient texts in Europe had led to its Renaissance and

Reformation, and that India had a great history of the study of philology, grammar, and linguistics:

A powerful effect will be produced in India when the contents of all the Vedas and the Shastras are laid open to the eyes of the people, and the veil which has hitherto covered these revered records....shall have been lifted. Translation of all these books into the Indian vernaculars, and a critical and sound explanation of them, will render far greater service to the cause of reformation, than the mere teaching of natural sciences and mathematics by the medium of English, and the reading of English books.[166]

English classics cannot make natives into Englishmen, he continued. 'They can make them only mock Englishmen, to be laughed at and ridiculed. They make them strangers to their own country and home, despised and hated by their own people whose traditions they have forgotten....'

This extraordinary editorial of 14 March 1863 shows a rare insight and appreciation of Indian culture, either written or sanctioned by Knight. However, in his more familiar topic of economic improvements, he still worshipped at the feet of *his* traditional deities—private enterprise, foreign investment, and individual ownership of land. He promoted his views with vigour, insight, and compassion. But he remained a foreigner, prescribing foreign solutions for the ills of India.

THE GROWTH AND DRIVE OF BOMBAY

The years under discussion, 1857–64, were the years in which Bombay grew into a world-class city and seaport. The heart of the modern city arose, built by a tidal wave of investment and construction, public and private projects, by British and Indian entrepreneurs. Robert Knight, editor-proprietor of the city's leading paper, shared the pride and enthusiasm and would become involved personally, not just journalistically, in the resulting political and financial tumult.

The first steps in Bombay's amazing growth have already been described—the switch to the Egypt–Arabian Sea route from Europe, the start of steamship runs between Bombay and Suez, the first segments of the railway system (see pp. 17–18 and 22–3). However, a proposal for a subsidized steamer route to

Baghdad and intermediate ports, urged by Bombay officials and businessmen, was vetoed by Secretary of State Charles Wood. Knight was livid, and live steam rose from his *Bombay Times and Standard* office: 'It is very difficult to maintain moderation in speaking of such folly. What wonder if we are heartily sick of being told to rely upon ourselves, when the dictates of common sense are violated....'[167] Regular steamship runs would greatly promote Bombay trade, he continued, since that is where the merchants of Baghdad, Muscat, and the Persian coast look for European goods: 'they come down annually in large numbers in great unwieldly craft, bringing with them the produce of their countries for exchange against the piecegoods of Manchester and English iron, and large quantities of treasure as well.'[168]

Knight's answer, and not for the first time, was home rule:

There will never be good government in this country until we devolve the management of its own affairs upon each presidency, and place at the head of each a representative government of some kind or other. Bombay is as well able to furnish a representative assembly as New Zealand at all events, and while its community is treated as a pack of children, who do not understand what their real wants are, the progress of the presidency will be arrested by the incapacity of its guardians.[169]

His civic pride climbed to new heights on 18 May 1861, when he changed the name and scope of the *Bombay Times and Standard* and created the *Times of India*:

The *Bombay Times* this day loses its modest title to become the Imperial *Times of India*....Bombay is already the capital city of India, although not yet the seat of the Supreme Government. It is to the Bombay Press that the home public must look for intelligence from all parts of India, and upon it must the Indian public wait at no distant period for news of the world. The point of arrival and departure of all the mails; the centre of the great interest that binds the two countries together; imperial in its resources whether for commerce or for war, and the natural emporium and capital of Asia—there is a future before Bombay that the most sanguine of us cannot adequately forecast....[170]

His prophecy was fulfilled, as Bombay (later Mumbai) rapidly rose to become a world seaport and a commercial, industrial, and cultural centre; his *Times of India* has remained the predominant newspaper of Bombay and western India ever since.

The development of Bombay had been a steady but slow affair. The largest single step, as stated (see, p. 16), was construction of the Hornby Vellard in the 1770s, linking Bombay island with Worli, the ridge on its north-west, and Mazagaon, north of the Fort. Causeways in the early nineteenth century joined it to Mahim, to the north of Worli, and Colaba, at the southern tip. Shipping grew rapidly during the middle decades of the century, and construction of piers, shipyards, and other facilities began stretching north from the Fort, along the eastern side of the island. The largest project was the drainage and reclamation of Mody Bay, just north of the Fort, during the 1860s for the site of the terminal of the Great Indian Peninsula Railroad.[171] Completed in 1888, it is Bombay's largest station, that loaf of Indo-Victorian Gothic gingerbread named (until recently) Victoria Terminus.

Bombay's population, estimated at 236,000 in 1838, had jumped to 812,562 by its first official census in 1864. The rapid unplanned growth created predictable urban problems such as the water supply. Local wells were inadequate on those swampy seabound islands, and a monsoon failure in 1855 dried up some wells and led to emergency decrees. Cartmen and even the new railroad brought loads of water from nearby areas. The city then pressed ahead with a long-delayed project, tapping Vihar Lake, on Salsette Island to the north, and piping it fourteen miles into Bombay beginning in 1858.[172]

A costlier problem was waste disposal—sewage and market and slaughter-house wastes. The British Fort area had a drainage system, but the Indian neighbourhoods and close suburbs relied on ditches along a few main streets, feeding into a 'main town drain' which emptied into the Arabian Sea near Worli.[173] Sweepers also gathered wastes into their baskets, which they dumped on the beaches for the high tides to carry away. The odour can be imagined, but let Knight describe it:

The accumulation of filth and ordure which now lie festering along the Mazagon shore, and in every lane and gully of the Native Town, are almost incredible; and the marvel is, not that Bombay is never wholly free from cholera, but...that the place is not speedily converted into one great charnel house. Upon coming into Bombay by the early morning train, you have no sooner passed the Mazagon bridge, than you find yourself in an atmosphere of stench so dense and suffocating that it seems to leave a taste....[174]

Knight proposed running a large pipe far out to sea and pumping the wastes through it, but a litany of successive studies, delays, disputes, and fund shortages restricted the city to patchwork improvements in his day. Consequently, Bombay was ill-equipped for its massive immigration of the late nineteenth century.[175]

However, wild prosperity suddenly hit Bombay. The outbreak of the American Civil War in 1861 led to the effective blockade of the US southern ports and the cutoff of cotton supplies for the factories of Britain. Millowners sought new sources, and the demand for Indian raw cotton shot up. The amount of cotton exported through Bombay doubled during the first year of the war, the *Times of India* estimated, and at twice the price,[176] igniting massive inflation, booming land values, and many speculative business and banking ventures.

At first, the cotton was taken to Bombay by small boats along the coast and bullock caravans on land, either with backpacks or crude carts. But as the railroads stretched their steely tentacles through the hills, passes, and valleys of western India, the eased access to markets and rising prices spurred cotton cultivation, and the region's economy was forever altered. The Bombay, Baroda, and Central India Railroad began construction along the Arabian Sea coast to the north of Bombay, mastering the formidable problems of streams, ravines, and tidal inlets. The first section of the line opened in 1860, and in 1864 Bombay was linked with Ahmedabad, in Gujarat. The first city terminal was at midtown Grant Road, but the line was soon extended south, to Colaba.[177]

Meanwhile, the rival GIP Railway Company had been opening sections of track since 1853. To pierce the rugged range of the Western Ghats, where not even a cart path had been cut until 1830, different engineering wonders were needed—hairpin mountain turns, high viaducts, and many tunnels. The steep Bhor Ghat section, leading to Poona and the Deccan, was opened with much fanfare in April 1863, while the Thal Ghat, further north was surmounted to link Bombay with Nagpur in central India in 1865.[178]

Bombay now had a geographic and economic hinterland, and the British thought the city would dominate the peoples of the interior. Ironically, the reverse eventually happened. With easy access to the coast, masses of Maharashtrian people moved into the city for jobs and other urban benefits. After independence they took control of Bombay through elections.

The man who contributed most to the modern expansion and growth of Bombay was Sir H. Bartle E. Frere, who became governor on 22 April 1862. Frere was a senior official who had served mostly within the Bombay Presidency.[179] Knight applauded the appointment because of Frere's familiarity with Bombay's problems and his reputation as a vigorous administrator, and he hoped for a bolder policy on the appointment of Indians to the Bombay Legislative Council.[180]

Frere's first project was his most dramatic: demolition of the walls of the old Fort, whose protective purpose had long since lapsed, and which now blocked urban development and traffic. Knight approved the demolition, but not the accompanying plan to sell off the Esplanade, the park and recreation area outside the walls, for building lots. He wrote:

We have most of us seen the grassy slopes from the ramparts to Back Bay on a moonlight night in the hot weather dotted with groups of people of almost all creeds and ages, availing themselves of the only locality within reach, from which they can obtain a breath of cool and pure air....[181]

The Apollo, Bazaar, and Church gates (leading from the Fort to the south, north, and west, respectively) were pulled down in January 1863. By the end of that year the semicircular walls which had connected them had been demolished, and the outer moats and ditches filled in.[182] In their place was built the broad boulevard which serves as the main street for downtown Bombay (called Hornby Road initially, later Mahatma Gandhi and Dr Dadabhai Naoroji roads). Some of the Esplanade was used for restricted construction, but most remained (and remains) open green space.

The state next constructed some public buildings as stolid and imposing as the Raj itself (and, ultimately, more durable)—the Bombay Government Secretariat and the High Court building on the west side of Hornby Road and the General Post Office on the north, next to the planned Victoria Terminus. A softer touch was added by the Victoria Gardens in Byculla and Elphinstone Circle in the heart of the renovated Fort. Private benefactors (some of them newly-rich cotton brokers and financiers) generously endowed new cultural institutions, including the University of Bombay, whose signature structure was (and is) the graceful Rajabhai Tower, the university's library.[183]

Important new roads criss-crossed midtown and uptown Bombay. These eased the development of new neighbourhoods, as thousands of workers moved in from the interior. Sometimes they clustered around major sources of employment, such as Tardeo, in the west-central city, for the early cotton mills; Parel, in central Bombay, for the railroad workshops, and several locations along the eastern side of the island for shipping and dockyard work. Europeans and wealthy Indians built homes on Malabar Hill and the Breach Candy area, along the western shore.[184]

Conspicuously undeveloped was Back Bay, a shallow inlet south-west of the old Fort, and here too a company of investors, with state support, wanted to drain and fill the bay to create new building sites. Knight, the enthusiastic town booster, urged action and forecast: 'Ten years hence the reclamation will be the grandest moments of Sir Bartle Frere's reign, and should it be a work of great remuneration to its public-spirited projectors, all Bombay will rejoice.'[185]

Institutions of municipal government in Bombay were anaemic and slower to develop, as the real power was maintained by the governor. To hold any position of authority one needed an appointment as justice of the peace, and these were dispensed by the governor. However, a pluralistic commercial elite (sometimes called the *shetias*)[186]—British, Hindu, Jain, Parsi, Muslim—usually provided the impetus for economic progress as well as socio-cultural leadership. Different forms of city government were tried, such as a Board of Municipal Conservancy, created in 1845. This was replaced in 1858 by a board of three municipal commissioners, intended to give more attention and leadership to civic matters.[187] This commission would guide Bombay's boom of 1862 and 1863 before being superseded by a new civic structure in 1865.

During those prosperous years the Bombay municipality was severely handicapped by restricted finances and disputes within the elite on further taxation. An annual house tax of five per cent was the fiscal mainstay, aided by various minor taxes such as a 'wheel tax' on carriages and a shop and stall tax, until this last was adjudged illegal in 1854.[188] Then those of the elite who were principally men of property, fearing an increase in the house rate, urged the enactment of a system of octroi or town duties. This was opposed by those who were principally men of commerce. (In Bombay men of property were usually men of commerce as well, so there were some awkward divisions.) The octroi was approved in 1858, but the quarrel continued.[189] Knight's enthusiasm for civic improvements did not extend to the requisite taxation. He complained in 1862 that an octroi system, 'universally repudiated in England', was strangely accepted in Bombay, 'where nature herself makes provisions, firewood, and building materials comparatively scarce and dear, and nothing can be more unwise than to enhance their price by legislation....'[190]

By 1864 cotton imported into Great Britain from India had nearly tripled its pre-war yield of 560 four-hundred-pound bales to 1400. Demand and inflation had raised their value from £3.9 million to £38 million.[191] Gold and silver poured into Bombay. It was later estimated that a war on the opposite side of the globe had pumped £81 million into Bombay.[192] The speculative bubble of cotton futures also inflated dramatically during 1863 and into 1864. According to one account, a banker was lending at eighteen per cent interest, and local entrepreneurs scrambled to borrow at that rate to buy cotton in remote districts, yet still realized profits of thirty or forty per cent in six months.[193]

Perhaps as a warning, Knight's *Times of India* published an 'extra' edition on 10 August 1863, informing about the Union's capture of Vicksburg and victory at Gettysburg (which had actually occurred nearly six weeks earlier). It opined the next day that the Confederate Army would soon be hemmed in and forced to surrender, and said that cotton prices were dropping already. It also warned against 'time bargains'—investments in cotton futures—as not legitimate trade but gambling, betting whether prices would rise, and perhaps even trying to arrange it.[194] There were other warnings as well, but the frenzy continued through 1864. Dinshaw Wacha (who was there) later wrote: 'In the Bombay of 1864–5 every tenth man was either a promoter, embryo promoter, or director. And as to the number of bankers and managers, it was legion....'[195] So the businessmen of Bombay spurned all warnings, grabbed for instant fortunes—and grappled with each other to avoid petty local taxes.

THE EDITOR AND THE MAN

Knight's grand and gleaming vision of 1861, of Bombay as the commercial and communications centre, not just of India but of all Asia, was built upon two separate but related developments: the telegraphic cable and the news agency. The electric telegraph had spread through Europe in the 1840s, displacing earlier news transmitters such as carrier pigeons and relays of semaphore flagmen. But the telegraph only became intercontinental with the development of an insulated submarine cable. Such a cable was completed under the English Channel in 1851, and the technology prepared for further advances.[196]

The news agency grew out of the quest for rapid and reliable information, especially market prices and other commercial news, and whoever could provide it held a key to wealth and power. The first to do so commercially was a Frenchman, Charles-Louis Havas; from 1831 his Agence Havas sent copies of articles to all subscribing newspapers, banks, brokers, etc. One of his staff, Paul Julius Reuter, moved to London and set up a rival agency in 1851. In 1858 Reuter expanded the news coverage he offered British papers, sending out his own reporters and engaging 'stringer' (space-rate) correspondents in Europe and beyond.[197]

No one appreciated the submarine cable and Reuter's agency more than the British government. For centuries it had tried to run its far-flung empire from a distance, adroitly juggling resources and alliances, struggling to control wilful colonial governors and other ambitious men-on-the-spot. Reuters received official encouragement, concessions, and other favours.[198] By 1860 contacts between Britain and India no longer depended on the winds or took months, but they were still slow enough to upset officials and editors alike. Parliamentary coverage by 'Our

London correspondent' dated 4 February 1861, appeared in the
Bombay Times and Standard of 1 March, and a piece by 'Our Paris
Correspondent' also dated 4 February, was published on 2 March.
The sudden death of Prince Albert (husband of Queen Victoria)
was announced in London on 14 December 1861, but was not
known in Bombay until 7 January 1862, twenty-four days later.
As noted, news of the Battle of Gettysburg reached Bombay six
weeks later. It even took almost three weeks for a newsletter
from nearby Bushire, on the Persian Gulf, to reach Bombay by
steam frigate.[199]

Both Reuters and the Indo-European cable were advancing
toward Bombay to fill that need, but an 1859 attempt to lay a
cable through the Red and Arabian seas broke down. Knight
didn't wait. In 1860 he wrote: 'We have the pleasure to intimate
Mr Reuter has made us the offer of his sole agency, not in the
Western presidency only, but in all of India....'[200] A year later,
as shown, he changed his newspaper to the *Times of India.* He
then formed a Times of India Telegraphic Agency to sell news
dispatches, including those received from Reuters, to other
newspapers around India, and, he said, 'all the leading Anglo-
Indian newspapers' subscribed at Rs 500 a month.[201] Clearly Knight
intended to be the provider of international and, apparently,
intercity news to the journals of India. There was even a separate
commercial service for the mercantile community. However,
Reuter, whatever he had offered Knight, had grand ideas of his
own: he wanted an exclusive news agency for the entire British
Empire. Knight later explained: 'When Reuter came into the
field with a capital of £100,000, we saw at once that it would be
hopeless for us to compete with his Company, and so we sold
our services to him....'[202] Neither Reuters nor the *Times of India*
has retained any explicit record of this sale, although Reuters has
an unexplained entry of a draft for £30 to 'R. Knight' in 1862.[203]
(Knight gave the date of the sale as 1864, but this could have
been a fuzzy recollection a quarter-century later.)

The cable marched forward, and messages from it first
reached Bombay in 1865. The line ran through the Austrian and
Turkish empires to Baghdad, then by land and sea to Karachi,
in north-west India (now Pakistan), where it connected to the
Indian network. Its use, however, became a nightmare of delays,

breakdowns, and garbled transmissions. A reliable line was opened in 1870, through Russia and Persia to Karachi. But the British were not satisfied until they had a line to India under their own control, and this they obtained later in 1870 with the successful completion of a cable from Gibraltar, through the Mediterranean and Arabian Seas by three British companies (which merged in 1872).[204]

Meanwhile, Reuters sent Henry M. Collins to Bombay in 1866 to set up a centre for operations. After a few stumbles, he succeeded in opening offices and signing up subscribers, including the Government of India. As the cable moved beyond India, so did Collins, to Singapore, East Asia, and Australia.[205] Knight's vision of Bombay as communications entrepôt for Asia was thus fulfilled, but only after Knight himself had been pushed aside.

Knight's accession as editor and then proprietor of the *Bombay Times* has already been explained. The newspaper apparently expanded and thrived under Knight. This is difficult to verify, since profit statements and circulation figures were a secret. However, the *Times* played a larger and more prominent role in the city's life and politics while its competitors faded. George Buist, ousted as editor of the *Bombay Times* in the passions of the Rebellion, returned as editor of the *Bombay Standard*, founded by his friends on 4 January 1858. Knight felt no animus toward Buist and said that the earlier ill will had died.[206] However, the *Standard* never caught on, and it merged into the *Bombay Times and Standard* on 1 January 1860. Knight remained editor and took as a proprietary partner Mathias Mull, a typographer and businessman who had been business manager of the *Standard*.[207] The *Telegraph and Courier*, itself the result of an 1847 merger, was merged into the *Times of India* on 18 November 1861, which is thus the descendant of four separate papers.[208]

During the late 1850s a sharp and at times abusive relationship had developed among Knight, George Craig of the *Telegraph and Courier*, and John Connon of the *Bombay Gazette*. With the absorption of the *Telegraph and Courier*, the *Bombay Gazette* became Knight's remaining rival, first under Connon and, from 1859, under James Mackenzie Maclean, newly arrived from Britain.[209] Maclean in his memoirs disparaged Bombay journalism as 'forlorn' with disorganized news offices and scarce resources.[210]

He resigned after a few years, but admirers kept him in the city, and he founded a *Saturday Review.* Knight claimed that this new weekly was intended to counter the influence of his the *Times of India,* which favoured 'the people of the country' as against 'the Colonist party'.[211] In 1864 Maclean and a friend bought control of the *Bombay Gazette,* and he returned to it as editor until 1880, despite his earlier misgivings.[212]

One sign of the *Times of India*'s robust health was its added enterprises, such as the weekly overseas edition and the telegraphic service. Another was its successive moves into more prominent quarters. The *Bombay Times* was first published from 'Petit's Building' off Colaba Causeway. Then it moved to Rutterfield Street, Military Square; then into a house in the Fort, off Medows Street. After the merger it moved to no. 2 Churchgate Street (the main east-west avenue in the downtown), where it remained for a quarter-century.[213] It had become a sturdy institution.

Knight's vision, though, outreached the construction of a single newspaper, or even of a free and independent press. He still saw the British Raj as the vehicle for the liberation and uplift of the Indian people, not their exploitation or enslavement. They were citizens of Victoria's India and entitled to the same rights as citizens of Victoria's England—due process of law; freedom of speech, press, and religion; open, honest, and efficient government. He often attacked the practice of conducting public business in private; under the queen's administration, he wrote, it could not last.[214]

He disagreed sharply with those who held that a free press was incompatible with an authoritarian government. Without a representative legislature for India, the role of the press was all the more vital, since it alone could publicly scrutinize and criticize the operations of government—what a later generation would call 'adversary journalism'. It is the mission of the press, he wrote, 'freely to submit all acts of the administration, whether local or imperial, to vigorous and wholesale criticism.'[215] An example was the income tax budget which James Wilson had presented in 1860; the Legislative Council had applied no critical judgment, said Knight, so the press had to supply it.[216]

He offered a 'brotherly hand' to Indian newspapers, which were growing in number and influence. As long as they showed 'a loyal, cordial adhesion to British rule', the *Bombay Times and Standard* would 'readily unite with the ranks of our native friends' and resist

those creeds and arbitrary measures which an uncontrolled government, be it Anglo-Saxon, is too ready to adopt. We are also prepared to [resist] the doctrine too prevalent in many circles, and especially in Calcutta, that the Anglo-Saxon ought to be recognized in India as the dominant race. We hold, on the other hand, the rights of our Hindoo fellow subjects as regards liberty and religion, as equal with our own....[217]

Bold words for the India of 1860!

With Knight and his paper showing the way, independent public opinion began to emerge in Bombay. Governor Frere was struck by the new interest in public questions among 'the more intelligent classes' of Indians, in place of the previous indifference. But he found the English press 'often hostile' to the government, and its Indian readership 'rapidly increasing',[218] but even more rapid was the increase of those influenced indirectly, that is, through opinion leaders in towns, villages, and neighbourhoods, as well as the practice by vernacular (that is, Indian language) newspapers of lifting, translating, and commenting upon articles from the major papers. Two years earlier, the Inam Commission's Cowper had similarly complained that the spread of such articles written by Knight was teaching 'discontent and sedition' to Indians. The *Times'* influence far surpassed its paid circulation.

While Knight's newspaper grew rapidly, so did his family. As mentioned, a daughter, Alice, was born to Robert and Catherine in 1856. A second daughter, Edith (called 'Blossie' by the family), was born in 1857; then a son, Paul, in 1858; then a second son, Robert (known later as 'Young Rob') in 1860; then a third son, William Hugh, in 1861; then a third daughter, Violet, in 1863.[219] The birth notices show the family living in Sewri, a midtown waterfront area, in 1857; Bandra, a suburb across Mahim Bay, in 1858 and 1860; and Chinchpokli, north of midtown Byculla, in 1861—all remote from the downtown and none a prestigious neighbourhood.[220] Knight was later described by a daughter as having had a graceful form and handsome features, with brown hair and bright grey eyes.[221]

Knight played an active role in Bombay commercial and civic affairs during those years. He claimed credit for preventing a split in the Bombay Chamber of Commerce in 1861. He founded a 'Strangers' Home' for destitute Europeans and organized and served as first secretary of a Strangers' Friend Society, 'to extinguish loaferism in Bombay altogether'.[222] The editor recruited the approval and support of a half-dozen leading European merchants, and he obtained an endowment for the home. He explained this prime example of mid-Victorian 'tough love' in a memoir fragment:

When we started the Strangers' Home in Bombay in 1861 or 1862, we kept the management in our own hands for a while. We received every vagrant into the Home, whatever his character, and the moment we ascertained that there was no hope of his doing any good in India, we deported him, clearing the Home every few weeks by sending the men away in batches of 15 to 20 at a time. The poor fellows were only too glad to go. If a man is a drunkard, he is the very first man to send away....[223]

In 1863 he contributed £100 for the relief of unemployed and destitute workmen in Lancashire.[224]

One day Knight disclosed that he had bought an interest in a coffee plantation in the Wynaad, a plateau east of the Western Ghats, in south India. 'There is no denying, then, that the *Times of India* is, after all, a planter's journal,' he exulted. 'It is literally true that the responsible editorial "we" of the journal is a coffee planter....'[225] The bank clerk's son had risen in the world.

Few accounts of Knight as a personality have survived from those Bombay years, but there is one which speaks volumes. Many years later, in 1914, S.K. Ratcliffe, a retired editor of the *Statesman*, was speaking to the East India Association of London on 'The Press in India', during which he called Knight 'the ablest Englishman who has so far devoted himself to the career of journalism in India.' In the audience that day was 82-year-old Dr George Birdwood, who had been a physician, science professor, and civic leader in Bombay in the 1860s. In the discussion following Ratcliffe's talk, Birdwood recalled how he had filled in as *Bombay Times* editor for three weeks while Knight was ill with fever. But he mischievously changed the paper's policy with an editorial favouring the politics of Pope Pius IX, where Knight had supported Garibaldi and the Italian nationalists. His editorship ended abruptly when, on the paper being read to Knight, he at once sprang out of his bed in Colaba, and sending for a buggy while he dressed, galloped off in it to the Fort, and presently had literally emptied me out of the editorial chair, and all but literally kicked me downstairs—a very steep, dark flight—into Medows Street.[226]

Knight relinquished editorial control of the *Times of India* on 1 March 1864, in anticipation of an extended 'home leave' (that is, in England) for both business and family reasons. During his seven years as editor he had built a vigorous, thoughtful, and conscientious newspaper which had stimulated and stirred Bombay and its governing authorities. He had helped churn Bombay's wave of prosperity, which would soon crest. A delegation of grateful Indian businessmen met the editor ten days later and presented a cheque for Rs 1500. Knight replied to the leader, Kursendas Madhudas, 'Your munificence really distresses me. I do not know what I have done to deserve such returns. I have simply striven to be *just*, and you pay me for it thus.'[227]

A rising generation of educated Indians, including students of Bombay's new colleges and university, were aroused by Knight and his reform causes. One such was Dinshaw E. Wacha, later a businessman and founder of the Indian National Congress. Wacha wrote a generous appreciation of Knight, stating that he

had earned the sobriquet of 'Bayard of Indian Journalism' for his sterling integrity, righteousness of purpose, manly independence, and unique grasp of all the burning political and economic problems of India....from the day that he unmasked the Inam Commission of odious memory to the heyday of Bombay's financial prosperity, during the American Civil War, Mr. Knight was a power and influence in Bombay. The highest officials sought his advice....At times he may have been wrong in his opinion or fact, but...there was such an unsophisticated frankness about him, such love of justice, such burning love of truth, that those who came into contact with him could not but be impressed by his singular personality.[228]

Further accolades came at a testimonial meeting for Knight on 10 May 1864, at Mazagon Castle. Dozens of Bombay's eminent citizens—British, Parsi, Hindu, and Muslim—participated. Presiding over the meeting was Sir Jamsetji Jijibhai (or 'Jejeebhoy'), Bart., who expressed appreciation for Knight's conduct as a public journalist and especially his unique work 'to promote cordiality and good feeling between Natives and Europeans.'[229] A dozen speakers heaped praise on Knight, not just for the newspaper he had built, but for his work in promoting intercommunal cooperation and understanding. Sir Alexander Grant, Bart., vice chancellor of the University of Bombay, said he had enlisted men 'of standing and capacity' as contributors to 'the first daily journal in the British Empire'. Mangaldas Nathubhoy, civic leader and philanthropist, declared: 'We are all, high and low, rich and poor, men of all races and languages and religions of the Native community of Bombay, moved by one common sentiment of gratitude and admiration towards him....' A public purse for Knight was opened, which soon reached more than £8000.

Two days later, editors of Gujarati and Marathi-language papers waited upon Knight and praised his efforts 'to redress the grievances and raise the status of natives of India,' citing the Rebellion, the Inam Commission, etc. In reply, Knight told the editors of their growing importance:

You have an immense advantage over your English contemporaries in your exact acquaintance with native society, native thought, and native opinion. I believe the native Press of India will play an important and prominent part in the history of the next thirty years. The Universities will be pouring a steady stream of highly educated men into every channel of employment, and one cannot reasonably expect that the English Press of the country should maintain its present great ascendancy....[230]

These must have been proud and exhilarating moments for Knight. Seventeen years earlier he had landed in Bombay as a young shop manager, a nobody. By 1864 he had become a man of importance and influence, editor and co-owner of the city's outstanding newspaper. He had married and was siring an expanding family. He remained confident that the British Empire, despite its defects, held the best prospects for the well-being of the Indian people. He could also look forward confidently toward his future, personally and politically. He could not have foreseen the storm of misfortunes that awaited him. In some ways Knight never stood higher than at that farewell of 1864.

NOTES

1. *Bombay Times* (hereafter *BT*), 1 January 1857.
2. Ibid., 14 March 1857.
3. Ibid., 12 March 1857.
4. Ibid., 10 April 1857.
5. Ibid., 10 August 1857.
6. *Overseas Bombay Times* (weekly edition sent to Europe), 2 April 1857.
7. *BT*, 14 April 1857.
8. Ibid., 10 July 1857. His pronoun is significant. Knight sometimes identified with 'the people of India' or 'the taxpayers of India' or 'the Indian subjects of Her Majesty' but never with 'the ruling class' or 'the conquering race'. The *anna* was a small coin, like a penny.
9. Ibid., 21 March 1857.
10. Ibid., 6 February 1858 (weekly edn).
11. Ibid., 12 January 1858.
12. Many sepoy battalions were recruited from particular social communities. Many in the Bengal Army came from Brahman and Rajput castes of Bihar and Oudh. Lt Col Sir Wolseley Haig, 'The Armies of the East India Company', in H.H. Dodwell (ed.), *The Cambridge History of India*, vol. 6 (Delhi: S. Chand, 1958 [1932], p. 159; Seema Alavi, *The Sepoys and the Company, Tradition and Transition in Northern India, 1770–1830* (New Delhi: Oxford University Press, 1995), pp. 50 and 75.
13. Ibid., 11 May 1857.
14. The insurrection of 1857 began as an army mutiny, but it became much more, and it has been called 'Great Revolt', 'First War of Indian Independence', etc. 'Rebellion' is a general and neutral identification, and it will be used herein as a shorthand or code name, despite its inadequacies.
15. *BT*, 12 and 15 May 1857 (as reprinted in *Bombay Times Overland Summary* of 27 May).
16. Ibid.
17. Ibid., 10 July 1857.
18. . *BT*, 10 August 1857.
19. *Times of India* (Bombay), 9 October 1861. One Bombay journalist said Knight was 'reviled by his contemporaries, and his writings were misrepresented....With nearly the whole of the Press of India arrayed against him...he wrote as his conscience dictated to him.' Sanial, 'History of the Press in India—IX', *Calcutta Review* (hereafter *CR*), vol. 130, April 1910, p. 269n.

20. *BT*, 17 and 19 October and 26 November 1857. This was apparently a sharp break with Buist's previous attitudes. See Aroon Tikekar, 'Dr. George Buist of the Bombay Times: A Study of Self-Proclaimed Messianism of an Anglo-Indian Editor, 1840–57', in N. K. Wagle (ed.), *Writers, Editors and Reformers, Social and Political Transformation of Maharashtra, 1830–1930* (New Delhi: Manohar, 1990), p. 106.

21. The account of the meeting was given in a special supplement in the *BT* of 6 November 1858.

22. Ibid., 4 January 1858; Sanial, 'The Father of Indian Journalism—I', *CR*, vol. 19 of 3rd series, May–June 1926, pp. 304–5.

23. *BT*, 4 January 1858.

24. Ibid., 1 January and 7 December 1859.

25. Ibid., 14 January and 8 January 1858.

26. Ibid., 13 December 1859.

27. Ibid., 15 January 1858.

28. Ibid., 1 January 1859.

29. Ibid., 7 September 1859. For another such expression, see ibid., 1 May 1858.

30. See for instances 15 and 17 November 1858, and 19 January 1859.

31. H. Fukazawa, 'Western India', in Dharma Kumar (ed.), *Cambridge Economic History of India*, vol. 2 (Hyderabad: Orient Longman, 1984), pp. 179–82.

32. An *imam* or gift commonly referred to a grant of revenue-free land by a ruler; British officials called it 'alienated land'. B.H. Baden-Powell, *The Land Systems of British* India (Oxford: Clarendon Press, 1892), vol. 3, p. 299. The Inam Commission estimated the overall revenue loss at 16 per cent of the potential total. Fukazawa, p. 181n. See also Eric Stokes, *The Peasant and the Raj* (Cambridge: Cambridge University Press, 1978), pp. 51–2.

33. Baden-Powell, *The Land Systems*, vol. 3, p. 300.

34. India, *Act XI of 1852*, secs 5 and 7, and Schedule A, sec. 2; Thomas Etheridge, *Narrative of the Bombay Inam Commission*, n.s. 132, *Selections from the Records of the Bombay Government* (Poona: Deccan Herald Press, 1873), pp. 22–5.

35. John William Kaye, *History of the Sepoy War in India* (London: W. H. Allen, 1889), vol. 1, p. 175. Kaye claimed that more than half of the titles examined from 1852 through 1857 were confiscated. Etheridge, a member of the commission's staff, claimed in response (pp. 3 and 54) that no one had been evicted, no inam lands seized, and most titles confirmed, at least through the lifetime of the holder. However, the Maharashtra State Archives (successor to the Bombay Records office) holds a packet of letters

addressed to Captain Cowper appealing decisions from the field, pleading for instance that 'our Enam be restored' (Bombay, Revenue Dept, vol. 71 of 1860, n.p.). No records of hearings or judgments have survived. Baden-Powell, a land-tenure expert of the next generation, wrote that the records showed that most of the commission's cases involved occupancy, not just revenue rights (vol. 3, p. 300). Penderel Moon wrote that more than 20,000 estates were confiscated (*The British Conquest and Dominion of India* [London: Duckworth, 1989], pp. 667–8, his source not given). How, then, could Etheridge have claimed no lands were seized and no one expelled? Perhaps his Pune office was not informed of everything done in that loose-knit, stretched-thin operation. Perhaps the British took title to lands of which they dared not take possession, at least during the lifetime of the inamdar.

36. *BT*, 6 January 1859.
37. Ibid., 10 November 1858.
38. Ibid.
39. *BT*, 6 January 1858.
40. Ibid., 11 November 1858.
41. Ibid., 25 August 1858, 31 August 1858, 17 November 1858, 19 January 1859, and 9 April 1859.
42. Cowper to H.L. Anderson, secretary of the Bombay government, 5 January 1859, and Minute of Elphinstone, 8 January 1859, both in India, Home, Public Consultations, vol. 58, 25 March 1859, entry nos 64 and 65.
43. *The Inam Commission Unmasked* (London: Effingham Wilson, 1859), p. 74.
44. Ibid., pp. 75–7. This is one of Knight's few critiques of the socio-economic consequences of Inam Commission operations. He usually attacked its judicial and administrative misdeeds, areas in which the British were supposedly serving as role models for the Indians.
45. Great Britain, *Hansard's Parliamentary Debates*, 3rd series (London: Cornelius Buck, 1859), vol. 152, p. 375.
46. *BT*, 14 March 1859.
47. Ibid.
48. *Bombay Times and Standard* (hereafter *BT & S*), 8 March and 5 December 1860. For a contrary view, see Neil Charlesworth, *Peasants and Imperial Rule, Agriculture and Agrarian Society in the Bombay Presidency, 1850–1935* (Cambridge: University Press, 1985), pp. 53–5. Citing government reports and letters of officials, Charlesworth depicts.

49. Ibid., 17 January 1861; Etheridge, pp. 36, 37, and 90. This may be why Etheridge could write that no one had been actually expelled from his lands (see n. 35).

50. Treaties with major princes read like alliances between two independent and sovereign powers. See for instance the 1804 treaty between the company and Daulat Rao Sindia in India, Foreign and Political Dept, *A Collection of Treaties, Engagements, and Sunnuds Relating to India and Neighboring Countries*, compiled by Charles U. Aitchison, vol. 4 (Calcutta: Supt of Government Printing, 1893), p. 51. However, later treaties with lesser princes, such as the 1818 pact with the Nawab of Bhopal, include a pledge to act 'in subordinate co-operation with the British Government and acknowledge its supremacy....' ibid., p. 261.

51. William Lee-Warner, *The Native States of India* (New York: AMS Press, 1971 [1910]), pp. 281–7. Ian Copland has described British efforts to give a legal basis, or at least an appearance of legality, to what was essentially a power relationship, in *The British and the Indian Princes, Paramountcy in Western India, 1857–1930* (Bombay: Orient Longman, 1982), esp. pp. 211–21. Put simply, might made right.

52. Great Britain, India Office Records, L/MIL/9, 199, pp. 332–5; Bell Papers, National Army Museum, London, entry nos 5806–45.

53. William Wilson Hunter, *The Marquess of Dalhousie and the Final Development of the Company Rule*, in the Rulers of India series (Delhi: S. Chand, 1961 [1895]), pp. 85–90.

54. R.C. Majumdar, 'The Annexations of Dalhousie', in R.C. Majumdar (gen. ed.), *British Paramountcy and Indian Renaissance*, pt I (*The History and Culture of the Indian People* (Bombay: Bharatiya Vidya Bhavan, 1970), vol. 9, pp. 70–1; Sorabji Jehangir [or Jahangir], *Representative Men of India* (London: W.H. Allen, n.d., ap. 1889), p.139. For a strong defence of Dalhousie and his annexation policy, see Hunter, *The Marquess of Dalhousie*, pp. 104–6.

55. Jehangir, *Representative Men of India*, p. 140; Buckland, *Dictionary of Indian Biography* (hereafter *DIB*), pp. 33–4.

56. (London: Trubner, 1865). See also C.S. Srinavasachari, 'Introduction', in Evans Bell, *The Empire in India, Letters From Madras and Other Places* (Madras: G.A. Natesan, 1935 [1864]), pp. 72–5; also the *Times of India* (hereafter *TOI*) (Bombay), 1 October 1868. For Bell's fullest critique of both the 'annexation' and 'residency' policies of the Raj, see his *Retrospects and Prospects of Indian Policy* (London: Trubner, 1868).

57. Sanial, 'Father of Indian Journalism', *CR*, p. 288.

58. F.H. Skrine, *An Indian Journalist: Being the Life, Letters, and Correspondence of Dr. Sambhu C. Mookerjee* (Calcutta: Thacker, Spink, 1895), p. 157. The letter was sent by Bell to Mookerjee.

59. *BT*, 13 December 1859.

60. Ibid., 11 November 1858.

61. Ibid., 31 March 1859.

62. Great Britain, *Royal and Other Proclamations...to the Princes and People of India, 1858-1919*, #1.

63. *BT*, 10 November 1858.

64. 11 February 1859, *Hansard*, vol. 152, p. 275; *BT*, 14 March 1859.

65. Ibid., 2 April 1859.

66. Ibid., 11 April 1859.

67. Ibid., 22 June 1859.

68. Ibid., 4 October 1859.

69. *T & S*, 12 October 1860. See also *T & S*, 23 February 1860.

70. Ibid., 6 March and 14 March 1860. See also *T & S*, 2 August 18[ʃ ʋ.

71. A meticulous study of these matters is Nani Gopal Chaudhuri, *British Relations with Hyderabad (1798-1843)* (Calcutta: University of Calcutta, 1964), pp. 51-149.

72. Sir Richard Temple, *Men and Events of my Time in India* (London: John Murray, 1882), p. 288.

73. This account is drawn from those of Henry George Briggs, *The Nizam: His History and Relations With the British Government* (Delhi: Manas, 1985 [1861]; Bharati Ray, *Hyderabad and British Paramountcy, 1858-1883* (New Delhi: Oxford University Press, 1988), and Michael H. Fisher, *Indirect Rule in India, Residents and the Residency System, 1764-1858* (New Delhi: Oxford University Press, 1991).

74. The term 'peasant' is used here in its general sense of a rural dweller, usually a cultivator, rather than a specifically defined social or economic role. Its Indian equivalent is ryot, sometimes transliterated as raiyat, raiat, etc.

75. Hunter, *The Marquess of Dalhousie*, pp. 107-8.

76. *BT*, 6 November 1858.

77. Ibid.

78. *TOI*, Bombay, 8 October 1861.

79. India, *History of Indian Railways....*(Simla: Govt of India Press, 1924); Edward Davidson, *The Railways of India, With an Account of Their Rise, Progress, and Construction, Written With the Aid of the Records of the India Office* (London: E. and F.N. Spon, 1868), pp. 368-9. Davidson gives copious detail on the early construction.

80. R.C. Majumdar and K.K. Datta, 'Administrative System', in *History and Culture of the Indian People*, vol. 9, pp. 384-5.

81. *BT*, 24 March 1859; *TOI*, 23 May 1861. However, the financial drain of the 5 per cent guarantee also loomed in Knight's mind as he criticized officials for extending money-losing lines ever-further. *BT & S*, 1 March 1860. (See Chapter 2, for the succession of these Knight newspapers.)
82. *TOI*, 1 March 1864.
83. Ibid., 3 November 1861.
84. C.E. Buckland, *Bengal Under the Lieutenant-Governors* (Calcutta: Kedernath Bose, 1902), vol. 1, pp. 183–96 and 238–71. One thorough and thoughtful account is Blair B. Kling, *The Blue Mutiny: The Indigo Disturbances in Bengal, 1859–1862* (Philadelphia: University of Pennsylvania Press, 1956).
85. Kling, *The Blue Mutiny*, pp. 118–21; R.C. Majumdar, *History of Modern Bengal* (Calcutta: G. Baradwaj, 1978), p. 69.
86. *BT & S*, 26 March 1860.
87. Ibid., 4 and 6 April 1860.
88. Ibid., 26 September 1860; Kling, *The Blue Mutiny*, pp.139–46.
89. *TOI*, 22 May 1861.
90. Kling, *The Blue Mutiny*, pp. 193–4.
91. *TOI*, 15 July 1861.
92. Ibid., 12 August 1861.
93. Ibid., 3 April 1862.
94. Ibid., 11 May and 7 August, 1863. Cf. n. 78.
95. *BT & S*, 6 September 1860.
96. *TOI*, 20 May 1863; 2 and 4 February 1864.
97. Ibid., 27 May 1863. See also *TOI*, 6 February 1864.
98. Ibid., 10 February 1864. Were the ryots more enterprising in Bombay and Madras presidencies, where individual ownership was recognized, than in the north and north-west, with their systems of village controls? No one has ever claimed so.
99. *BT*, 24 February 1858.
100. Ibid., 25 March 1858.
101. Great Britain, 16 and 17 Vic., c. 95.
102. *BT*, 25 April 1859.
103. Ibid., 20 and 30 April 1859.
104. Recent studies of the development of modern European racism include Peter Gay, *The Cultivation of Hatred, The Bourgeois Experience, Victoria to Freud* (New York: W.W. Norton, 1993), vol. 3, esp. pp. 35–95 and Ivan Hannaford, *Race, The History of an Idea in the West* (Washington: Woodrow Wilson Center Press, 1996), esp. pp. 187–276.
105. For a recent study of racism in British India, see Thomas R. Metcalf, *The New Cambridge History of India*, 3.4, *Ideologies of the*

Raj (Cambridge: Cambridge University Press, 1995), esp. pp. 80–6 and 160–7.

106. Charles Wentworth Dilke, *Greater Britain: A Record of Travel in English-Speaking Countries During 1866 and 1867* (London: Macmillan, 1869), pp. 572–3.

107. *BT*, 2 July 1859.

108. Ibid., 7 December 1859.

109. *BT & S*, 16 January 1861.

110. *TOI*, 4 October 1861. See also ibid., 20 May 1861.

111. *BT*, 1 January 1859.

112. Ibid., 22 June 1859.

113. Ibid., 11 April 1859.

114. Ibid., 24 March 1859.

115. The classic account of this First Afghan War is John W. Kaye, *A History of the War in Afghanistan* (London: Richard Bentley, 1851). A more recent study is John H. Waller, *Beyond the Khyber Pass: The Road to British Disaster in the First Afghan War* (New York: Random House, 1990).

116. *BT*, 1 September 1859.

117. Ibid., 11 July 1859, as reprinted in *Bombay Times Overland Summary* of 14 July 1859.

118. Ibid., 13 July 1859, as reprinted in *Bombay Times Overland Summary* of 14 July 1859.

119. Great Britain, *Parliamentary Papers*, vol. 49 (1860), col. 305, pp. 82–3. If a British royal troop was assigned to India, its pay for the six months before departure was charged to the Government of India. *TOI*, 4 October 1861.

120. Great Britain, *55 Geo. III*, chapter 155, 2nd and 6th resolutions; Majumdar, *British Paramountcy and Indian Renaissance*, vol. 9, pt 1, of *History and Culture of the Indian People*, p. 1153.

121. *TOI*, 7 November 1861.

122. *BT & S*, 28 January 1861.

123. *TOI*, 28 November 1863.

124. Ibid., 3, 7, and 5 December 1863.

125. A.G. Chandavarkar, 'Money and Credit, 1858–1947', in *Cambridge Economic History of India*, vol. 2, p. 770.

126. Robert Knight, *A Letter to His Grace the Duke of Argyle, K.C., Upon the Annual Claim Made by the Proprietors of East India Stock Upon the Revenues of India* (Bombay: Oriental Press, 1870), pp. 11 and 18.

127. See Dadabhai Naoroji, *The Poverty of India* (London: Brooks, Day and Son, 1878), and *The Condition of India* (Bombay: Ranina, 1881); and R.C. Dutt, *The Economic History of India in the Victorian Age From the Accession of Queen Victoria to the Commencement*

of the Twentieth Century, 2nd edn (London: Kegan Paul, Trench Trubner, 1906).

128. *BT*, 14 March 1859.
129. Ibid., 27 August 1859.
130. Ibid., 10 September 1859.
131. Ibid., 28 December 1859.
132. *BT & S*, 21 and 27 February 1860.
133. Ibid., 21, 27, and 28 February 1860, respectively.
134. Ibid., 3 and 5 March 1860.
135. Ibid., 23 April 1860.
136. Ibid., 8 May 1860, as reprinted in Overland Edition of 10 May 1860.
137. Ibid., 10 July and 6 August 1860.
138. Ibid., 14 August 1860. Buckland presents a much more positive estimate of Wilson and his achievements. *DIB*, p. 456.
139. *BT & S*, 20 September 1860.
140. Ibid., 17 and 30 August 1860. Note the dates: August in Bombay probably meant monsoons, wet discomfort, and short tempers.
141. Ibid., 7 September, 11 October, 13 and 8 November, and 25 August 1860, respectively.
142. Ibid., 7 September 1860.
143. Ibid., 17 January 1861.
144. Laing to Sir Charles Wood, Secretary State for India, 21 March 1861, Wood Papers, Box 3D, as quoted in S. Gopal, *British Policy in India, 1858–1905* (Cambridge: University Press, 1965), p. 51.
145. Elgin to Wood, 9 April 1862, Wood Papers, MSS Eur. F78, 56 (1).
146. *TOI*, 10 November 1862.
147. Ibid., 15 November 1862.
148. Great Britain, *Indian Councils Acts* (24 and 25 Vic., c. 67, and 55 and 56 Vic., c. 14).
149. The most famous and controversial such critic was sociologist Max Weber, whose *The Religion of India* has gone through many editions. One, translated by Hans H. Gerth and Don Martindale, was published by the Free Press (Glencoe, Ill., 1958).
150. This pattern, usually associated with Asian societies, was actually far more common. The British, in Knight's day and since, have had an official national church as an arm of the state, whose officials sanctify and crown the monarch and depend on his or her patronage.
151. *BT*, 5 March 1858.
152. Ibid., 20 February (biweekly edn) and 1 November 1858.
153. Ibid., 3 January 1859.
154. Ibid., 16 November 1858 and *T & S*, 9 September 1859.
155. Ibid., 19 March 1860. He tells about one widow who was remarried

to a Brahman. But the Brahman already had another wife, so this was not such a good example.

156. Ibid., 29 March 1860.

157. Ibid., 8 August 1860.

158. Ibid., 8 January 1862.

159. B.N. Motiwala, *Karsondas Mulji: A Biographical Study* (Bombay: Karsondas Mulji Centenary Celebration Committee, 1936), pp. 80 and 120–2.

160. *TOI*, 20 February 1862.

161. Ibid., 22 July 1862.

162. Ibid., 2 December 1863 and 9 March 1864; S. Natarajan, *A Century of Social Reform in India* (Bombay: Asian Publishing House, 1959), p. 58.

163. *TOI*, 5 January 1863.

164. Ibid., 12 July 1862.

165. Ibid., 14 March 1863.

166. Ibid. Contrast this with n. 163. Knight himself lacked scholarly credentials, but his writings show a general familiarity with the peoples and cultures of India.

167. *BT & S*, 24 April 1860.

168. Ibid.

169. Ibid. A report that the government was considering moving the provincial capital from Bombay to Poona, the old Maratha capital, provoked another sputtering outrage—ibid., 16 October 1860.

170. He even called Bombay 'the centre of the world'. James Douglas, *Bombay and Western India* (London: Sampson, Low, Marston, 1893), vol. 1, p. 253.

171. Mariam Dossal, *Imperial Designs and Indian Realities: The Planning of Bombay City* (Bombay: Oxford University Press, 1991), pp. 184–5. Knight blamed official mismanagement and delays for the lack of a proper terminus in 1863; *TOI*, 13 August 1863.

172. Dossal, *Imperial Designs*, pp. 104–16.

173. Ibid., pp. 130–4. See also D(inshaw) E. Wacha, *The Rise and Growth of Bombay Municipal Government* (Madras: G.A. Natesan , n.d., ap. 1913), pp. 41–5.

174. *BT*, 12 January 1858.

175. Ira Klein, 'Urban Development and Death: Bombay City, 1870–1914', *Modern Asian Studies*, vol. 20 (October 1986), p. 754.

176. *TOI*, 24 March 1862.

177. India, *The History of Indian Railways, Constructed and in Progress, Corrected up to 31st March, 1923* (Simla: Govt of India Press, 1924), n.p.; Edward Davidson, *The Railways of India, Written With an Account of Their Rise, Progress, and Construction* (London: E. & F. N.

90　✸　ROBERT KNIGHT

Spon, 1868), pp. 290–302. For a recent study see Ian J. Kerr, *Building the Railways of the Raj* (New Delhi: Oxford University Press, 1995).

178. *The History of Indian Railways...*, Davidson, *The Railways of India*, pp. 273–9; Dossal, *Imperial Designs*, pp. 180–3. One hairpin curve on the Bhor Ghat could only be managed by construction of a huge switchback, which allowed a train to reverse directions and run down an adjoining track. For further data on construction of the railroads and their impact, see Chapter 1 of this volume.
179. The standard biography is John Martineau, *The Life and Correspondence of the Rt. Hon. Sir Bartle Frere* (London: John Murray, 1892).
180. *TOI*, 2 April 1862.
181. Ibid., 13 June 1862.
182. 'There was a great shout, as when a whole people are the subjects of a mighty deliverance, for the ditch had been a harbour of every unclean thing, and the walls a harbour for all the badmashes of the town.' Douglas, *Bombay and Western India*, vol. 1, p. 225. See also Dossal, *Imperial Designs*, pp.192–3. The picturesque and mostly antique area formerly enclosed by the walls is still commonly called 'The Fort'.
183. Dossal, *Imperial Designs*, pp. 194–5 and 201; Teresa Albuquerque, *Urbs Prima in Indis, An Epoch in the History of Bombay, 1840–1865* (New Delhi: Promilla and Co., 1985), pp. 157–9 and 179–80.
184. S(tephen) M. Edwardes, *The Rise of Bombay, A Retrospect* (Bombay: The Times of India, 1902), pp. 267–8 and 295–303.
185. *TOI*, 8 February 1864.
186. The term is used prominently by J.C. Masselos, *Towards Nationalism, Group Affiliations and the Politics of Public Associations in Nineteenth Century Western India* (Bombay: Popular Prakashan, 1974), esp. pp. 15–19.
187. Wacha, *The Rise and Growth*, pp. 9–15. Wacha feels the board's inaction on health and sanitation problems led to its replacement.
188. Ibid., p. 77; Dossal, *Imperial Designs*, p .71.
189. Dossal, *Imperial Designs*, pp. 71–7; Masselos, *Towards Nationalism*, pp. 136–41.
190. *TOI*, 20 January 1862.
191. Isaac Watts, *The Cotton Supply Association, Its Origin and Progress* (Manchester: Tubbs and Brook, 1871), p. 138.
192. Edwardes, *The Rise of Bombay*, p. 273.
193. Martineau, *Sir Bartle Frere*, vol. 2, p. 2.
194. *TOI*, 11 and 15 August 1863.
195. p. 21. For a fuller description see Edwardes, *The Rise of Bombay*, pp. 274–6.
196. Robert W. Desmond, *The Information Process, World News Reporting*

to the *Twentieth Century* (Iowa City: University of Iowa Press, 1978), pp. 110-11.

197. Ibid., pp. 134-6 and 146-9; Graham Storey, *Reuters' Century, 1851-1951* (London: Max Parrish, 1951), pp. 13-17.

198. Storey, *Reuters' Century*, pp. 45-7 and 62-5.

199. *TOI*, 7 January 1862 and 10 August 1863, and *BT*, 10 March 1857, respectively.

200. *BT & S*, 12 April 1860.

201. Sanial, 'Father of Indian Journalism—I', p. 322; *Statesman and Friend of India* (Calcutta), 26 January 1889.

202. Ibid., 3 December 1883.

203. John G. Entwisle, manager, Reuter Archive, to the author, 10 October 1995. Entwisle calculated that £30 of 1862 was the equivalent of £1072 in 1995, 'quite a considerable sum'. It could not have been merely for purchase of a few dispatches.

204. India, *Report on the Indo-European Telegraph Dept., 1863 to 1888* (n.p., n.d.; found in National Archives of India, New Delhi), pp. 3-9; Daniel R. Headrick, *The Tentacles of Progress, Technology Transfer in an Age of Imperialism, 1850-1940* (New York: Oxford University Press, 1988), pp. 100-1; Desmond, pp. 115 and 119.

205. Donald Read, *The Power of News, The History of Reuters, 1849-1989* (Oxford: Oxford University Press, 1992), pp. 59-60; Storey, *Reuters' Century*, pp. 68-71. For Collins' own account, see his *From Pigeon Post to Wireless* (London: Hodder and Stoughton, 1925).

206. *BT*, 15 June 1859.

207. Buckland, *DIB*, p. 306; 'Sixty Years of the Times of India: A Chapter in the History of the Anglo-Indian Press', *CR*, 108 (215), April 1899, pp. 64-9.

208. The *Times of India* management considers their paper the direct descendant of the *Bombay Times* only and dates all anniversaries from 1838. The view here is that it had two or three or even four parents, and that it was born on the day the masthead first proclaimed the *Times of India*: 18 May 1861.

209. Sanial, 'History of the Press in India—II', *CR*, vol. 130, part 2, April 1910, p. 116; S(waminath) Natarajan, *A History of the Press in India* (Bombay: Asia Publishing House, 1962), pp. 82-3 and 119.

210. J.M. Maclean, *Recollections of Westminster and India* (Manchester: Sherratt and Hughes, n.d. [ap. 1900]), pp. 16-17.

211. *TOI*, 6 January 1863.

212. Maclean, *Recollections*, pp. 17ff.

213. S(tephen) M. Edwardes, *Gazetteer of Bombay City and Island* (Bombay: Times Press, 1909), vol. 3, p. 148; 'Sixty Years of the Times of India', p. 104.

214. *BT*, 24 January 1859 (and reiterated frequently during the next thirty years).
215. *BT & S*, 24 October 1860.
216. Ibid., 10 March 1860.
217. *BT & S*, 24 October 1860. See also *TOI*, 15 July 1861.
218. Minute of Sir H.B.E. Frere, 16 March 1860, in India, Home Dept, Public Proceedings, 31 January 1861, entry nos 76–80.
219. India, *Bombay Register of Baptisms, Marriages, and Burials*, vol. 30, p. 399; vol. 31, p. 451; vol. 33, p. 370; vol. 35, p. 197, and vol. 37, p. 190.
220. Bombay Calendar and Almanac for 1858 (Bombay: Times Press, 1858), p. 1827; *Bombay Almanac and Directory for 1858*, (Bombay: Gazette Press, 1858), p. 890; ibid....*for 1861*, p. 825.
221. Interview with Hilda (Knight) Kidd, 21 August 1968.
222. Sanial, 'The Father of Indian Journalism—III', *CR*, vol. 20 of 3rd series, pt 2, p. 342.
223. *Friend of India* (Calcutta), 2 September 1876, p. 795. (Knight had bought that venerable weekly in 1875.)
224. *Times* (London), 24 March 1863, p. 12.
225. *TOI*, 27 November 1862.
226. *Asiatic Review*, New Series, vol. 5 (July 1914), pp. 199–215.
227. Sanial, 'History of the Press in India—X', *CR*, 131 (1), July, 1910, p. 361.
228. Wacha, *The Rise and Growth*, p. 153. See also *Famous Parsis* (Madras: G.A. Natesan, 1930), pp. 293–4.
229. This and other remarks at the testimonial meeting come from a printed transcript of that meeting, a photocopy of which was sent to the author by Hilda Kidd. Excerpts may also be found in Sanial, 'History of the Press in India—X', *CR*, p. 362n.
230. *TOI*, 13 May 1864. Others had noted the potential power of the Indian press despite its youth. Mountstuart Elphinstone, former Governor of Bombay, said even that small quantity of printing could set off 'a great quantity of manuscript, as well as declamation, conversation, dissemination of rumours and alarms.' John Wilson, 'A Short Memorial to the Honourable Mountstuart Elphinstone, and of his Contributions to Oriental Geography and History', *Journal of the Bombay Branch of the Royal Asiatic Society*, vol. 6, 1861, p. 105n., as quoted in David Finkelstein and Douglas M. Peers, 'A Great System of Circulation: Introducing India into the Nineteenth-Century Media', in David Finkelstein and Douglas M. Peers, *Negotiating India in the Nineteenth Century Media* (Basingstoke: Macmillan, 2000), pp. 1–2.

3

The Making of a Dissident, 1864–72

ENGLISH INTERLUDE

Before Robert Knight reached England in 1864, he was preceded by a letter from Sir Bartle Frere, Governor of Bombay, to Sir Charles Wood, Secretary of State for India, in which he called Knight one of the few successful and able editors in India. Frere continued:

I know nothing of him personally, except through his writings in the Bombay Times....But it was as a very voluminous and careful writer on Land Tax and Political Economy, currency, prices and statistics, that he struck me even when I did not agree with his views as more able and trustworthy than any of our periodical writers, here or at home. I know nothing whatever of his objects or intentions in visiting England and very little of his pre-editorial history, but as a very able and accurate writer on a very important class of subjects it struck me that you might like to know he was in England.[1]

It was a thoughtful and gracious compliment, and yet it shows a distance. The governor of the province did not know the editor and proprietor of its leading newspaper, and very little of his background. He had not attended the testimonial to Knight, nor had any of his councillors. Knight was active in civic affairs, and his friends seem to have been business and professional men, but he himself was not a part of the imperial establishment, which might explain his underlying hostility towards it. Anglo-India had its factions and class structure.[2] Most literature, whether fiction or memoir, concerns the small-town or mufassil stereotype of a small group of Europeans clinging to each other for mutual protection (Forster's *A Passage to India* being among the best known). But in a large city such as Bombay, the Europeans were many and varied, and confined to no set role, socially or culturally, just as Indians were not.

Knight was certainly singular, but in lifestyle and family matters he seems to have lived the standard middle-class Anglo-Indian life. This meant his sons had to be sent 'home' to England for their education—an education in India, even by missionaries, was not yet considered *pukka* (proper).[3] Daughters, on the other hand, might be taught at home by private tutors. So it was with the Knights. Of the five daughters who grew to maturity, none pursued a formal education nor a career or profession (according to family tradition); all were married in due course to appropriate young Englishmen. For the sons, however, schooling had to be arranged on this 1864 trip to England, when Paul was six and Rob was four. The school selected for them was St Paul's, in Stony Stratford, Buckinghamshire. It advertised its awareness of the difficulties of parents of modest means, 'such as the majority of Anglo-Indian officials may be taken to be.'[4]

Knight's family affairs included arrangements for his widowed mother, his father having died in 1855 (see p. 22). In addition, his oldest sister, Anna Maria, remained unmarried and had to be maintained. Robert also had three married sisters in 1864, Sarah Riddle, Emma Burnside, and (after a brief widowhood and remarriage) Esther Zorn. There were also two younger brothers, Henry and Edward;[5] whether they shared these family responsibilities is not known.

Catherine and their six children had preceded Robert to England; he did not arrive until September of 1864.[6] Meanwhile, baby Violet died in England on 10 July.[7] A fourth son, Raymont (*sic*), was born there in December.

One matter which detained Knight in India was his coffee plantation. Some of his Bombay gift money was invested in the plantation, run by his partner and friend, H.E. James, and Knight lingered to help.[8] The Wynaad was the centre of a promising coffee industry, with about 50,000 acres under cultivation. He had visited it about a year earlier, and his thorough description faulted only the quality of the sherry at the planters' club at Manantoddy.[9] Estates were cleared, coolie labour was hired, and roads were built to market the crop through Tellicherry and Kozhikode (Calicut) on the Arabian Sea.

However, the presence of the white borer or coffee fly was noticed in 1865. In 1867 it caused 'great havoc', an ecological disaster blamed on the stripping of shady jungles.[10] During the 1870s and 1880s, borers and leaf-blight (and Brazilian competition) led to the abandonment of hundreds of plantations.[11] What came of Knight's particular plantation is not recorded, but it was never mentioned after 1868.

The Britain to which Knight returned in 1864 had changed since his departure in 1847. The old liberal ideals, funnelled through the Chartist movement, had faded, and British politics, like that of most major powers, now fed on a headier diet of nationalism and imperialism. Viscount Palmerston, who had guided this assertive foreign policy for a generation, had already ridden the popular fears of Russia into the bloody blind alley of the Crimean War; now, as prime minister, he watched helplessly as *that* canal was being dug at Suez—by the French! European statesmen of 1860, much like those of 1760, treated the globe as a huge chessboard on which to work their amoral strategies of position and power, manoeuvre and manipulation.

This amorality of imperialism received a further rationalization from the 1859 publication of *The Origin of the Species*. Killing and robbing were no longer seen by Social Darwinians as sinful, perhaps not even criminal, when they were moves on that global chessboard; they were simply the result of instinctive masculinity, or the natural ordering of life, or 'manifest destiny'.

Knight had no use for this line of thought. He clung to his old ideals of the British Empire as a vehicle for the enlightenment and well-being of all of its peoples, of *all* races. He deplored British Indian Army invasions into far corners of Asia or beyond, especially since the taxpayers of India were paying the bill. To present the viewpoint from India to those who decided its fate (the British electorate), he planned a pro-Indian newspaper for London.[12] He had an interview with Sir Charles Wood, who found him 'most intelligent'.[13] Through reformer John Bright (who had in 1858 advocated appointing Indians to legislative councils), he met several prominent politicians, including Henry Fawcett, a member of Parliament who became known as a spokesman for Indian causes.[14] Knight was elected a Fellow of the Royal Statistical Society in 1865. He retained that membership until 1874, though the society has no record of his active participation in its programmes.[15]

In 1865 Knight, like much of Europe, was watching the conclusion of the American Civil War and trying to assess its significance. However, his immediate concern was an old ogre which had again emerged: the 'permanent settlement' (or 'perpetual settlement') of Indian land revenues (see pp. 14–15). The zamindari settlement in Bengal, he complained, had stripped the peasants of their land rights, crippled the state by pledging never to increase its revenue demand, and donated a percentage of its yield to the zamindars as collectors. In 1862 Knight published a table showing that Bengal Presidency, though more than twice as large as Madras Presidency, was yielding less than half its revenue; that settlement was 'a fraud upon the rest of India,' which carried 'burdens that should be borne by Bengal'.[16]

Knight was upset when, six months later, Sir Charles Wood announced that he wanted to extend a permanent settlement to other parts of India.[17] Local conditions would determine the pace of change, but Wood had as his immediate target the populous North-Western Provinces (today's Uttar Pradesh). He blamed the special poverty of Madras on taxes so high as to discourage 'the improving element'; besides, like Cornwallis before him, Wood sought the political support of 'the natural chiefs and leaders of the people'.[18] On the opposing side, people such as Knight felt that the answer to Indian poverty was public improvements such as roads and irrigation projects to increase productivity and market access. This required financial resources for the government, which (without that dreadful income tax) meant an elastic land revenue. As objections, doubts, and requests for local exceptions arrived from India, Wood began losing his confidence and delayed extension of the permanent settlement. Surely Knight presented opposing views at their 1865 meeting.

The editor also used as a platform a special conference arranged by the Manchester Chamber of Commerce on 24 January 1866. He asserted that extending the permanent settlement to the

North-West would be impolitic, unjust, and foolish; reduced taxes might benefit landlords and European planters, but there was no assurance that the reduction would reach the cultivators. Moreover, they would be required to pay cash instead of the traditional share of the harvest, which had protected them against fluctuating market prices. After chiding the Chamber of Commerce for its opposition to all forms of taxation, he introduced a new concern:

The time is coming, gentlemen, when interpellations upon this subject will reach you from the native mind of India itself. It is not for nothing that the young men of India are pressing through the Universities that you have established in its chief cities. Their voices are mute now, for they know not political warfare; but the time is coming when you will have to give an account to the sons of India of the trust so long confided to your hands, and, as I in my conscience believe, so inequitably used....[19]

This may have been the first time a British audience heard a warning of impending Indian national anti-imperialism.

A few weeks later Wood resigned as Secretary of State. His successor, Lord de Grey (later Ripon) did not support permanent settlements. When the Conservatives took office later in 1866, Viscount Cranborne (later Salisbury) became India Secretary, and he told Knight in an interview that the 1862 dispatch had been a mistake.[20] The permanent settlement scheme had lost, and Knight had won.

Knight gave a different sort of talk to a different sort of audience on 25 May 1866. This was the newly-formed London Indian Society, composed of Indians residing in Britain, mostly students but initiated by businessman Dadabhai Naoroji.[21] Knight began by denouncing 'personal discourtesies which men of vulgar nature—albeit Englishmen—sometimes show to natives of the country.' He rejected the pseudo-Darwinian imperial view that might makes right: 'conquest, in the history of the world, has been a crime ninety-nine times out of a hundred, and can convey no rights whatever.' Robbing a subject people shows the morals of a highwayman. But, he concluded, England had made them free and educated men, that they might 'force us to be just towards you'.[22]

A flame which lit a torch? The audience probably included Dadabhai, the society's president, and W.C. Bonnerjee, its secretary and later the first president of the Indian National Congress.[23] Dadabhai, in his later writings on economics, found the journals published by Knight the only ones which supplied him with necessary data.[24] The London Indian Society made Knight an honorary member,[25] and when the Congress later organized strength, its approach was to 'force us to be just'.

FINANCIAL DISASTERS

At the time of these English speeches, Knight's concerns were already shifting from the ideological to the mundane, as he and his city faced financial disasters. When he left Bombay in 1864, a rising tide of cotton profits was lifting all ships (see pp. 72–3). Massive construction projects were transforming the shape and appearance of the island-city, and get-rich-quick speculation was inflating dozens of banks and developers. Presiding over these developments was Sir Bartle Frere, the builder-governor.

Two developments were integral and necessary parts of Bombay's future as a metropolis and world port. The 'Mody Bay Scheme' for developing the harbour along the east side of the island was contracted by the Bombay Presidency to the Elphinstone Land and Press Company in 1861. Also called the 'Elphinstone Land Company' or just the 'Elphinstone Company', its project was to reclaim the land, develop harbour facilities, and erect and maintain warehouses and factories, including machinery to press raw cotton into bales.[26] A comparable company on the west side of the island, the Back Bay Reclamation Company, became the centre of the wildest speculative bubble. Back Bay, south of Malabar Hill, was too shallow for harbour facilities, but developers envisioned land reclamation, building lots, and a new city centre, including a railway station; speculators deliberately pumped up this bubble for rapid profits.[27] In 1864 Frere's government was forced by the viceroy to auction off its 400 Back Bay Company shares; each, with a face value of £500, brought an average price of £2650.[28]

In 1863 Knight had warned of irresponsible speculation. In 1864 the Bombay Chamber of Commerce had warned about it. In 1865 Sir Charles Wood warned about the same.[29] Nevertheless, shares were selling for four to eight times their face value in

April, 1865, when the US Civil War ended, and American cotton began returning to the British market.[30] Cotton prices in Bombay dropped sharply, and a wave of bankruptcies flowed. Desperate juggling kept commerce afloat until August of 1866, when the leading juggler, Premchund Roychund, went bankrupt. This broke his leading vehicle, the Asiatic Bank, which was also financing the Back Bay Reclamation Company, which then shut down. This also collapsed the respected Bank of Bombay, since the Asiatic Bank owed it Rs 1.9 million. A later commission of inquiry showed that Roychund had hoodwinked the Bank of Bombay manager, who had authorized large loans on unsecured promissory notes.[31]

In England, Knight watched helplessly. He lost Rs 50,000 when the Bank of Bombay crashed, and another large sum in the 'Black Friday' panic in England in 1866. These, along with the loss of his coffee plantation, wiped him out, even the gifts of the earlier few years, and left him insolvent.[32] His project for a journal in England had to be abandoned (though not forever).

Innocents hurt in the crash included the shareholders of the Elphinstone Company. That company was solid, but its shareholders had to sell at a loss for cash needed to cover their debts elsewhere; shares which had once brought Rs 3000 were now selling for Rs 400.[33] Knight took up their cause. In an interview with Lord Cranborne, he argued that the company had begun work necessary for Bombay, and therefore the State should relieve its burden.[34] This issue was clouded by the growing strain between Frere and the viceroy, Sir John Lawrence, who disliked the governor's reckless and extravagant ways.[35] Therefore, Cranborne, while sympathizing with the Elphinstone shareholders, deferred matters until the imminent succession of Frere by Sir Seymour Fitzgerald.[36]

Knight then journeyed to Bombay at the end of 1866, resumed control of the *Times of India*, and publicized the matter. He arrived in time to send Frere off with a sharply critical editorial, charging the retiring governor with irresponsible neglect of the fiscal danger. Frere, he said, had encouraged the 'mad excitement' and then shelved plans for 'the restrictive and bracing regimen needed'.[37] The editor broadcast his case for government relief of the Elphinstone shareholders by repurchase of the foreshore lands.[38] He returned to England in May 1867, and through a letter and interview with the next India secretary, Sir Stafford Northcote, again urged the repurchase.[39]

Again back in Bombay, Knight examined the events which had so shattered the city's economy. He called Roychund 'the grey eminence behind the bank crash', but he also blamed the managers and directors of the several banks who were his 'secret partners'.[40] There was an official inquiry, but no criminal charges emerged in those days of very free enterprise. Even the critical Knight said that there was no rascality involved, just venality on the part of the 'good-natured idiot' who opened the vaults (Bank of Bombay manager James Blair) and the directors who gave him full authority and never inquired.[41] Apparently it was considered bad manners to ask a friend to provide security for a bank loan.

Knight went further. This episode, he held, showed the need for decentralization of the imperial structure, with local fiscal autonomy and the governor general as merely the head of a loose confederation of local governments. Clashing personalities had compounded the problem:

Sir John Lawrence in Calcutta and Sir Bartle Frere in Bombay got into such ill relations with each other, through the narrow provincialism of one and the ambitious folly of the other....Both men are profound blunderers in finance, and both were accomplished in the folly that brought about the mania of 1864 in this place; and when the crisis came, neither of them having the least idea of the way in which its evils might be mitigated, they took to quarreling with each other over the pettiest details....[42]

Not until 1869 did the government agree to buy out the Elphinstone shareholders, easing the city's financial squeeze.[43] In 1873 the Bombay Port Trust was created, the construction of harbour facilities and the rail terminus resumed, and Bombay again marched toward its prosperous destiny. Even the Back Bay reclamation resumed, although its completion took more than a century. (Today the reclaimed land is the site of high-rise office and apartment towers.)

But Knight never truly recovered. Although he soon satisfied his creditors, he never again seemed secure, and economic considerations swayed his future actions. At his death in 1890, according to his daughter, he left only his life insurance and Rs 100 cash in the cupboard.[44]

LOSS OF THE *TIMES OF INDIA*

Robert Knight and his family returned to Bombay in May 1868, and he resumed the editorship of the *Times of India*. Robert and Catherine's family continued to grow; their fifth son, Phillip, was born on 27 October 1868.[45]

Knight's editorials then show a harsher, sharper criticism of British rule. He issued an 'unqualified condemnation' of the Lawrence viceroyalty, then in its last year. The phrase 'masterly inactivity', already coined to describe Sir John's patient foreign policy, was attached by Knight to his entire administration, and internally it meant 'simply stagnation and disaster'. With 'masterly inactivity' Lawrence looked on while a million people perished of famine 'at the gates of Calcutta'.[46] (This referred to the Orissa famine of 1866, to be discussed in the next section.)

However, Knight approved that inactivity's halting a march of British troops through the Khyber Pass. Alarms in Britain had been touched off by the Russian seizure of Bokhara in Central Asia and their proposal for a railroad into the region. Do not, he said, send troops to 'help' the amir of Kabul unless he requests it; '[E]verybody knows the patience and forbearance of the Afghan race, how gladly they hail the interference of strangers in their domestic concerns....'[47]

Knight also continued his sniping at Bengal and its permanent revenue settlement. Bombay Presidency was contributing three times as much revenue as Bengal, he claimed, so there should be a special compensatory tax of 25 per cent in Bengal. But it would never happen, because of the strong Bengal influences on the Government of India; half the European business houses of Calcutta 'are mixed up with the zamindari interests'.[48]

Jabbing the powers-that-be in distant Calcutta or London was brave; intervening in a local catfight over municipal taxes was merely foolhardy. While Knight had been in England, Bombay Presidency had responded to the city's growth by founding a municipal corporation through Act II of 1865. It created a Bench of

Justices to serve as the corporate body, consisting of more than a hundred men (the majority European), appointed justices of the peace by the governor. He named prominent men from business, professional, and official ranks (Knight included), but it was not meant to be representative and certainly not democratic.[49]

Another provision of Act II repealed the octroi or town duties, which, some merchants feared, had hurt Bombay's commercial development. However, this thrust most of the cost of the city's expanding services onto the small number of property owners who paid the town rates. Those rates were initially set at five per cent of the estimated rent, then raised to six, then seven per cent. The unhappy ratepayers organized and agitated, demanding a return of the town duties.[50]

Knight waded into the fight on the side of the ratepayers. Transit duties, he wrote, were justified levies for services rendered, often to people who did not live in the city or own property there. Shunning his usual devotion to classical economic doctrine, he said its 'copybook maxims' against direct taxation were ridiculous when they meant trifling and bothersome levies.[51]

Not content with his editorial columns, Knight made a provocative and belligerent speech to the Bench of Justices on 5 November 1868, which he then published. In it he assailed Indian businessmen as narrow and selfish for trying to foist all local tax burdens onto the ratepayers, so that trade could be 'cheap and convenient'. The European Justices of the Peace really represented 'forty or fifty European firms and banks', and some did not even live in Bombay. He found it 'impossible to treat with respect the diarrhea of stuff they put forth as a flood upon us....'[52] Showing scars of earlier combat, Knight recalled a time (presumably during the Rebellion)

when for weeks together I could not open an Indian newspaper without finding myself the object of attacks so violent, so fierce, and sometimes so slanderous, that nothing could have sustained me under them but the consciousness that they were undeserved.[53]

He closed with cryptic remarks about leaving India and hoping this would be his last fight here. He already knew, and perhaps his listeners knew, that he was about to lose control of his newspaper. The Bench of Justices restored the town duties in

1869. Whether Knight's extraordinary speech had any impact, positive or negative, is not known.

Knight's departure from the *Times of India* followed 'many years of painful differences' (unspecified) with his partner, Mathias Mull.[54] Mull, who handled the business side, had become partner in 1860 by merging his *Standard* with Knight's the *Times of India* (see p. 75). The partnership had become intolerable, and Knight offered to buy out Mull's share, according to his account; instead Mull persuaded him to sell out to himself (because Knight lacked the capital?). Mull and his unnamed friends had been 'very greatly offended' by some of Knight's writings, and the money to purchase Knight's share was being furnished by unnamed parties 'desirous of changing the editorship of the journal permanently'.[55] Negotiations led to an agreement on 11 July 1868, in which Knight sold his share of the *Times of India* for Rs 100,000, of which Rs 40,000 was to be paid immediately. Knight was to remain editor until the following 1 July and was not to edit or be connected with any other newspaper or periodical in Bombay Presidency.[56] Knight's shares were eventually bought by General William Nassau Lees, principal of the Calcutta Madrassah, and William Martin Wood, who was to succeed Knight as editor.

During the interim, however, the quarrel between Knight and Mull exploded. Mull, by letter of 23 January 1869, accused Knight of showing telegrams of the *Times of India* to William Sim, editor of Calcutta's *Hurkaru*, in 1862, for a payment of Rs 4000, a sum not entered on the company's books and therefore a 'private Transaction' which benefited only Knight. Knight replied that the 'insolent and calumnious charge' was false, and Mull knew it to be false. Mull retorted that he had Sim's confirmation of his charge, and for Knight to deny it 'reveals a depth of degradation not altogether unknown to me, but only now visible in its broadest and darkest colours.' And therefore: 'I deem you unfit to conduct for one hour longer the editorial duties of the *Times of India* and besides I also deem you a dangerous man to be on the premises. I, therefore, prohibit your entering this office as editor any longer....'[57]

The furious exchange continued: Knight claimed he had found the relevant correspondence with Sim on the 1862 transaction. Mull challenged him to produce it. Instead, Knight went to the Bombay High Court, where his lawyers cited the contract confirming Knight's editorship until 30 June. The court therefore ordered Knight's interim restoration as editor on 2 February.[58] The next day Knight told his side in the newspaper. He said that he had agreed to retire from the paper, 'as it was more important for Mr. Mull to remain by the property than for Mr. Knight to do so' (with no explanation). But Mull, he continued, had systematically violated the proviso that Knight should remain the sole editor until 30 June:

For many months Mr. Knight has never known when leaving office in the evening what would appear in the paper next morning. Living upon the premises, Mr. Mull has claimed and exercised the right of putting whatever he pleased in the paper, and on several occasions has published in its columns communications expressly intended...as reflections upon Mr. Knight. At midnight, in one instance, long after Mr. Knight had left the office, Mr. Mull compelled the printers to append a footnote to a leading article of Mr. Knight's, reflecting grossly upon Mr. Knight's article....a letter headed 'Beware' was published in its correspondence columns, warning the public not to trust the editorial columns of the journal....[59]

Knight concluded his article with a promise that when his injunction came up for a hearing, 'all correspondence connected with the case will be laid before the Court.' But no open hearing was ever held, and no evidence was ever produced for the public by either Knight or Mull. Instead, the High Court appointed two arbitrators, who decided that if Mull could pay Knight's salary for the remainder of the contractual year, Knight should cease his work as editor. This was done on 1 April 1869.

With this puzzling decision the bitter episode ended, and Robert Knight was ousted from the newspaper which he had founded and built into a power in India's public life.[60] Under Nassau Lees, Martin Wood, and their successors, the *Times of India* became a sturdy pillar of the Anglo-Indian establishment and soon forgot its founder (See Epilogue for comments on Knight's death).

THE *INDIAN ECONOMIST* AND THE FAMINE MENACE

If Knight had expected to leave India (as his 1868 speech indicated) and had fought his last battle there, he was wrong. If the Bombay establishment thought it had got rid of the cantankerous editor, it was also mistaken.

Later in 1869 Knight launched a monthly journal, the *Indian Economist and Statistical Reporter* (henceforth *Indian Economist*), in which he could concentrate on this area of special interest. In those pre-census years, local reports on crop yields, prices, and agrarian problems and developments were generally fragmented and haphazard; Knight would study official and private reports and statistics and write coherent summaries and commentaries on them.[61]

Before starting his new venture, he approached the Government of India and sought its support by, first, asking its officers to supply him with 'reasonable information' from their districts and, second, subscribing to at least one hundred copies at Rs 24 a year each.[62] The collection of the land revenue had grown lax, the government thought, and detailed reports, thoughtful opinions, and vigorous discussion of economic and fiscal matters would stimulate interest in it. As Allan Octavian Hume, soon to become Revenue, Agriculture, and Commerce secretary, explained, when Knight proposed to start a paper to discuss economic subjects,

a paper open to all well-considered views, — a paper which should tempt working revenue officers to record their views and experiences, and, with a freedom impossible in official correspondence, to discuss and dispute over and so exhaust all moot points connected...the Government of India most readily accepted the proposal, and agreed cordially to support the undertaking.[63]

The first issue, dated 10 August 1869, was laden with statistics but included a variety of relevant dispatches. One was a Parliamentary report on the financing of Indian railways; another told how the extension of railways was equalizing grain prices, as surpluses from the Central Provinces were being shipped into Bombay Presidency and lowering market prices there. There were price quotations on securities, directors' reports, and an analysis of the English Bank Act. There was also a trenchant, Knight-style feature on how the retirement of those East India Company bonds (see pp. 54–5) was costing Indian taxpayers £630,000 a year.[64] Its 36 pages had few advertisements, clearly relying on subscriptions to meet expenses.

Knight's contract with Mull forbade his connection with any Bombay Presidency journal for three years, but the *Indian*

Economist stated that it was published by Wyman and Company, Calcutta, although it was printed in Bombay by William Boyd, Oriental Press, and communications to the editor were to be addressed to Mr Knight, Bombay. Mull complained bitterly to the viceroy, Lord Mayo, that Knight was taking a state subsidy under false pretence. 'It has been my painful experience,' he raged, 'to know much of Mr. Knight's capacity for prevarication and for mystification not consistent with a love of truth; but that he dared to violate a compact the terms of which are so patent, exceeds the bounds of all I could conceive....'[65]

Otherwise, the *Indian Economist* was apparently well received. It claimed after six months: 'No journal perhaps ever before published in India achieved so complete a success in so short a time.'[66]

Knight's editorial views ranged freely through India's economy and society as he sought answers to its persisting poverty. He saw free enterprise capitalism as the cure, though he found more and more exceptions. He also kept his unwavering faith in land revenue as the principal, and if possible the only, state-funding source. Echoing Malthusian-Ricardian rent theory, he maintained that the proper 'rent' which the state should charge the cultivator was whatever income exceeded the costs of production (see pp. 14–15).[67] The state's share of the harvest (called *khiraj* under Muslim rule) had traditionally been a third, a half, or even more of the yield, Knight said.[68] Consequently, the 1869 reassessment of Soopa taluk in Surat district 'reduces us almost to despair', because the Raj, instead of claiming sixty per cent of the harvest, was settling for a mere six.[69]

If the state were to spend 'ten or twelve millions a year', he told a Bombay audience, 'upon railways, canals, roads, tanks, and wells, increasing the value of the land', that land must carry that burden.[70] An income tax, on the contrary, would be practically restricted to the towns and cities with their cash economies, and indirect taxes such as sales taxes, customs, and excise would draw too little, because Indians consumed little; most had simple wants, while the rich hoarded their wealth in silver. If the state used that silver, for instance, to build a canal or tramway linking Raipur, a rice-surplus district, with Nagpur, the Central Provinces capital, it would 'double the value of the harvests at once'.[71]

Without state aid, he wrote two months later, the cultivator would remain in hopeless debt to the local moneylender; 'by lowering the assessment we simply enrich the *sowcar*; for what we abandon as rent he takes as interest.'[72] There was another slap at the Bengal zamindars, who were fighting against a local levy for roads and education. The zamindars, Knight said, claimed that Cornwallis' permanent settlement made them 'absolute owners of the land' with 'an absolute immunity from direct taxation for all time.'[73]

The moneylender and the landlord had become Knight's spotlit oppressors, against whom the Raj should be protecting the peasantry. Instead, he charged, it was creating a new class of parasitic landlords in the Central Provinces under the chief commissioner, Sir Richard Temple—middlemen who would 'rack-rent the actual cultivator':

Whether it is the Irish landlord, the Bengal zemindar, the English nobleman, the Welsh commoner, or the Oudh talookdar,...the judgment is still the same. Landlords as a class do nothing to improve the land.

The world has never yet seen a race of landlords that was not marked by the vices which idleness begets in the human character, and the attempt deliberately to create such a class would be a treason to the society in which it is made, were it not an act of simple folly.[74]

Knight made occasional disparaging remarks about the 'infantile' Indian peasant, but in a more thoughtful mood he remarked:

We do not believe the ryot to be the thriftless, improvident creature, he is commonly declared to be....in the main the cultivator is frugal as well as industrious. It is a terrible reproach to our rule that the class should be so miserably oppressed under us, and we refuse to believe that their redemption is hopeless....[75]

He said if he could run a district for six years, bind the hands of the moneylender, make crop advances to the cultivators, and collect the land revenue in kind instead of cash, he would then show 'a district full of prosperous yeomen'.

Shouldn't the state step aside and let nature take its course? 'In the name of God, no! If the British Government cannot alter it, it is no Government at all.'[76] But wouldn't such an activist government violate all the cherished principles of political economy? No, because political economy 'assumes a certain condition of things' and when conditions change, new principles must be adopted. India is not England, and 'Adam Smith's philosophy may be utterly inapplicable to a native community.'[77] Economic heresy, perhaps, but so he said.

Knight's prime example of economic laws misapplied during those years was the famine policy. Nothing ignited his indignation as much as the perceived indifference and/or ineptness of the British in handling famine.

The threat of famine had been a constant of Indian history. Classical literature contained many references to frequent famines.[78] However, the threat had enlarged in recent centuries by rapid population growth, combined with diminished rainfall, reduced forest cover, and depleted soil productivity. As early as 1861 Knight had urged a programme of canal and road construction to reduce the 'frightful evils' of famine,[79] and in 1863 he called for prompt reports by field officers of crop failures or rising grain prices, and the shipment of grain from surplus areas for market distribution. He shunned the concept of non-interference with the markets 'though the people starve before our eyes'.[80] (The classical free-market view was that a food shortage would raise market prices, attracting imports from nearby unaffected areas, thus meeting the needs.)

The free-market solution failed badly in the Orissa famine of 1866, the first great disaster after the crown's takeover of British India. The all-important summer monsoon rains were skimpy and untimely in 1865 in coastal Orissa, then a part of Bengal Presidency. Local appeals for rice for the temple town of Puri were rejected by the Bengal Board of Revenue, which decreed: 'If the market favours importers rice will find its way to Puri without Government interference, which can only do harm.'[81] By May 1866, officials could find no grain in the markets for army messes, jails, and other establishments. Urgent appeals were then sent to Calcutta, but before relief could be organized, heavy monsoon rains hit and isolated Orissa. Swollen rivers washed out roads and bridges, while storms prevented shipments by sea. Before the famine eased, an estimated one million people, a third or fourth of the affected population, had died of starvation or related diseases.

These dread particulars were set forth by the Orissa Famine Commission in its prompt and severe report. There was no attempt to hide the disastrous consequences. The British Raj considered itself an exemplary effective and humane government, and such losses were intolerable and unforgivable. Robert Knight had spent 1866 in England and so missed the famine itself, but he returned in time to see the repercussions and recriminations, to which he contributed. He blamed T.E. Ravenshaw, commissioner for Orissa, for ignoring the warnings of local officials, and the Board of Revenue for blindly selling Orissa rice for export, confident that other grain would somehow appear in markets.[82]

When famine was next reported, in 1870 in Rajputana, in the north-west, Knight demanded an inquest and full inquiry as to whether those deaths were inevitable. 'We are entitled and we are bound by our own trust', he argued, 'to demand proof that these poor wretches could not have been saved alive.'[83] The British, he wrote, should emulate the Biblical Joseph and store up grain against the seven lean years; once supplies were depleted, it was too late to ship from other regions.[84] Reserve stocks of grain could be stored in rural towns as a buffer against famine, more readily if the land revenue were taken in kind instead of demanding cash. In 1872 Knight applauded those local officials who had apprehended drought and warned promptly, but scolded the Raj:

The notion must finally be got rid of, that when these calamities occur, it is but natural that multitudes should perish of hunger. It is most *unnatural*, and inexcusable. Instead of warning our district officers at such periods against doing too much, the stereotyped way of consigning people to death by tens of thousands, and reducing the fragment of survivors to an emaciated host made ready for plague, [we should intimate] that all mistakes will be overlooked and forgiven, but the mistake of letting people die....[85]

The *Indian Economist* also took an occasional swat at 'the idol temples of India, with their nameless abominations and demoralizing influences.' Knight called the temples, their priesthoods, dancing girls, and devotees 'the mainstay of that deadly system of so-called religion, the overthrow of which is the very first condition of the regeneration of the people.'[86] Dreadful Hindu practices also prevented social reforms:

The elevation of native women, widow re-marriage, the suppression of infanticide, the abolition of caste are utterly inconsistent with the maintenance of temples, the strongholds of superstition, which hangs like a funeral pall over the country, and has filled it with pollution and with blood.[87]

On this topic, Knight remained adamant.

NEW QUARRELS AND A NEW PAPER

By 1870 Bombay had recovered from its financial disaster and was once again expanding its capacities and moving towards the global prominence which Knight had foreseen. The Suez Canal opened in 1869 and proved a major factor in integrating India into the world trade pattern, mostly through Bombay.

The editor, in an 1871 speech, urged a farsighted restructure of the empire. Building on a proposal by the viceroy, Lord Mayo, for provincial authority and stronger municipal institutions, he called for provincial legislative assemblies which included the heads of all important associations and ethnic groups; a federal structure, with provinces having their own taxing, budgeting, and borrowing powers; and the renewal of the old imperial capital of Delhi as the seat of the Raj.[88] His first idea was partially adopted in 1892, his second in 1935, and his third in 1912.

Knight was not proposing modern democratic elections; his idea of assemblies was a thoughtful blend of old and new concepts· 'Thus I would see the Governor of Bombay assemble a Mahratta Council every year in Poona during the rains, and a Guzeratee assembly...in Bombay in the winter months. We want to bring the people into a habit of intelligent cooperation with us, and the practice of intelligent criticism upon its acts....'[89]

However, Knight was again drawn into the vortex of Bombay's angry factionalism, and again he emerged badly bruised. The city's first attempt at municipal self-government (see p. 71) had produced a loose-knit Bench of Justices, but placed executive authority in the hands of a town commissioner. Arthur T. Crawford, an able and personable civil servant, had been engaged as the first town commissioner, in 1865. At first Crawford and his programme of municipal improvements were generally popular, but then complaints of extravagance and corrupt favouritism were heard. It was also reported that the municipality was deeply in debt and heading for bankruptcy. Since the landowners provided most of the revenue through the property rates, they organized a Ratepayers' Association, headed by J.A. Forbes, one of the foremost businessmen. They not only wanted Crawford dismissed, but the town government revised, with a new town council elected by the ratepayers sharing power with the commissioner. They were joined by the Bombay Association, originally a group of educated Indians, now led by Mangaldas Nathubai, the largest landowner on the island. Together they called themselves 'the reform movement'.[90]

Knight had championed reform and elected government before, but his immediate priority was to defend Crawford and his programme of farsighted town improvements. He denied charges of waste, or that local taxes were too high, though he still favoured a broader distribution of the tax load. He also openly berated his fellow justices for talking 'twaddle'.[91]

Tempers rose on 30 June 1871, when, after a buildup of public rallies and demonstrations, Forbes presented his reform plan to the Bench of Justices. In the ensuing debate Knight spoke in opposition. He had prepared a speech laden with economic arguments and fiscal principles, but he was not allowed to deliver it; members objected that set speeches violated the rules. He was required to speak extemporaneously (which Wacha says he did very well), but this led to *ad libs*, interruptions, and retorts by justices (in what was probably a steamy midsummer evening). Knight heatedly denied that Commissioner Crawford was out of control: 'I have full power to rule him under the Act. It is your twaddlers, Sir, who cannot rule him, for he is a man whom twaddlers cannot rule.' This drew a warning from the chair that Mr. Knight should avoid personalities, but, as Wacha put it, 'Mr Knight was oftener than not an earnest but misguided enthusiast and carried away by his own hobbies. He was not to be moved on that day from his purpose....'[92]

To rub it in, he then published his original talk as 'The Speech Which Mr. Knight Was Not Permitted to Deliver at the Bench Meeting, Dedicated Without Permission to "The Twaddlers"'. [93] And he inserted a preface:

as one man finds his dissipation in billiards, and another at the theatre, so there are men in Bombay, it seems, who take it out in the mild way of twaddling at the Bench upon every subject....its members are bored to death by men who will talk, and enquire, and object, and talk again and again....These talking apparatuses are simply my horror. They are wind-bags every one, and have about as much real insight into out Municipal difficulties as the peons who stand gaping at them from the doors....[94]

For further insult Knight then published an essay on municipal finance, with a postscript abusing the justices as 'capricious and as unintelligent as they well could be'. He compared them to parish vestries in England that 'look upon all expenditures as a swindle upon the parishioners, and who, if left to themselves, would leave the towns undrained, the streets unlit, the roads unwatered, the water unfiltered, and the whole country unclean.'[95]

All of Knight's passion, however, could not save Arthur Crawford, for whom he had been 'a most fearless and gallant advocate'.[96] A committee inquiring into allegations of corruption, extortion, and leading a dissolute personal life presented a severely critical report in October 1871. With a majority of the justices now hostile, Crawford resigned as commissioner and fled to escape criminal proceedings. Though never indicted, he was dismissed from the CSI.[97] Meanwhile, the charter reform proposal was wrangled over and amended, then sent to the Bombay Legislative Council, where it was further wrangled over and amended. Finally passed as Act III of 1872, it replaced the Bench of Justices with a town council, of which some of the members would be elected by some of the ratepayers.[98]

The bitterness of this angry battle lingered. It had pitted Knight against old friends such as the two leaders of the Bombay Association, Mangaldas Nathubhai, who had feted the editor at that 1864 party, and Furdoonji Naoroji, his friend and ally from the *Bombay Times* back in 1857. He later wrote: 'I stood by Mr. Nowrojee Furdoonji when he was intensely unpopular in Bombay, because I knew him to be what he still is, an honest and good man, and I opposed his pursuit of Mr. Crawford because it was blind and unjust.'[99] Even after Crawford's departure, Knight supported a faction of the association which broke away and formed a rival Western India Association in 1873.[100]

Meanwhile, a new daily paper had appeared in Bombay, the *Star of India*, with no acknowledged editor. In its first issue, 1 July 1870, it announced: 'When a star first rises above the horizon, it is difficult, especially in such an atmosphere as prevails in Bombay at present, to determine what its magnitude may be, and what it portends....'

It was asked whether Robert Knight was behind this new venture, especially as the *Star* contained a long extract from the *Indian Economist*. Knight's contract with Mull had barred his participation with any other Bombay publication for three years— until July 1871. The anonymous editor denied a connection, but said Knight would be welcome to contribute to the *Star*'s columns.[101] Letters signed by Knight, usually on economic matters, did appear at times.[102]

After almost one-and-a-half years of the *Star of India*, a notice stated that it would be incorporated on 1 January 1872, into a new daily, the *Gazette of Asia*, 'under the direction of the well-known editor, Mr. Robert Knight.'[103] The *Star of India*'s last issue announced that Knight had bought it and would incorporate it into his new daily. This was followed by a strange warning:

Of his [Knight's] liveliness, energy, and cleverness it would be difficult to speak too highly and we heartily wish him success...[but] of late, he has displayed signs either of great unscrupulousness or of great recklessness and a desperate self-assertion—characteristics which, it may be hoped, will disappear as he feels himself once again at home in Bombay and no longer subjected to unworthy treatment....[104]

However, this seems to have been a charade and self-admonition, because the mysterious editor was apparently Knight himself! Knight's great admirer, Dinshaw Wacha, wrote of 'the *Star of India*, edited by Mr. Knight' as an accepted fact.[105]

The *Gazette of Asia* title drew objections from the rival *Bombay Gazette*, which claimed it would create confusion. Therefore, a new title was lifted from a defunct Madras paper, and the new daily became the *Indian Statesman and Gazette of Asia*.[106] Into this venture, Knight later wrote, he sank the remains of his fortune, about Rs 40,000.[107]

By 1872 Knight had endured much and fallen far from his peak of public acclaim of 1864, but he was still full of fight. Episodes such as the Bombay financial crash, the Orissa famine, and the unjust imperial drain of Indian wealth showed how much the Raj needed an outspoken critic.

THE MOVE TO CALCUTTA

The nameplate—*Indian Statesman*—was new to the people of Bombay in 1872, but the rhetoric and arguments were familiar Robert Knight. First, he still argued for town duties rather than let the municipal tax burden fall entirely on 'an impoverished and wretched class of nominal house-owners...while the well-to-do masses of the industrial population, our domestic servants, the boat and harbour men, the artisans, and the workmen pay nothing whatsoever.'[108]

Second, the 'reformers' had disposed of Arthur Crawford and revised the municipal structure, but Knight said that it met none of Bombay's real needs:

With our cities undrained and their streets half-lit, their water unfiltered and impure and insufficient in quantity, and wide districts crowded with miserable dwellings into which neither God's sunlight nor air can get entrance, who can listen with patience to the men who drivel like parish vestrymen about economy?[109]

He claimed that in four years 20,000–25,000 Bombayites had died from such sins of omission.

Third, he continued sniping at the Bengal zamindars and the settlement which relinquished state lands to them. If India ever should ever elect a parliament through manhood suffrage, he prophesied (correctly), the zamindars would have to repay dearly to retain that settlement. To call the state the universal landlord, he said, meant no landholder had rights independent of 'the laws and social arrangements' of the nation, and so the surplus produce beyond the costs of labour and return of capital should be taken by the state in the public interest, which gave a quasi-socialist turn to the Ricardo-Malthus rent theory.[110]

Fourth, he still promoted Christianity: 'Our own conviction is profound that India will never possess Home rule, until she has cast away and abjured the false systems of religion that have been the cause of her degradation, and become Christian.' However, he still opposed 'proselytism', which he called 'utterly foreign to the Christian system....no power but that of the Almighty Himself can make India Christian.'[111]

Finally, Knight continued his active involvement in Bombay politics, supporting those Indian leaders who had formed the

Western India Association in April 1873. He suggested a municipal income tax to ease the revenue burden on the property owners.[112]

It must have come as a surprise, then, when Knight and his family abruptly left Bombay, wholly and permanently, in mid-1873 for a position in Calcutta. A year earlier he had written to Sir John Strachey, a member of the viceregal council, offering his services to the state. He explained, 'I have for a good many years wished to be in some position under Government in which the special aptitudes I am conscious of possessing for economic and fiscal matters might be directly at the service of the Government.'[113]

Sir George Campbell, whose forthright report on the Orissa famine has been cited, became Lieutenant Governor of Bengal in March 1871. Little had been compiled about the Bengal mufassil and its products, and so he began ordering district reports on weather, crop prospects, yields, etc. He wanted a statistical branch of the province secretariat to supervise the surveys.[114] Strachey passed Knight's letter to him, and on 12 November 1872, Campbell wrote to Knight:

We are plunging into Statistical inquiries in Bengal,...a vast and unknown sea. For that and our Provincial Finance, we wish to establish a Financial-Statistical Department of the Office, and have already got sanction to some additional establishment. I believe it would be a great advantage if we could make it worth your while to undertake the Superintendence of these duties....[115]

He offered Knight a position as assistant secretary, at a salary of Rs 1000 a month.

Knight replied that he wished to place his aptitude at the service of the government, but not at that salary. He candidly explained his problem:

the salary you name, while high as an entrance salary for a young man without encumbrances, is small for one who has had twenty-five years' experience in Indian life, and no longer stands alone, but has many to provide for. I have two daughters whose education is just finished, and who are now with me here; four little ones under eight years of age, and three boys at school in England; while I have two life insurance policies to keep up, and a mother and two sisters in England dependent upon me....Live economically as I might in Calcutta, I could not, I fear, with my family, count upon my expenses being less than Rs. 800 or 900 a month, while my home encumbrances and life policies between them come to Rs. 300 or 400 more....[116]

Campbell wrote in response that there were no salary emoluments for an assistant secretary and he could not promise any promotion, though appointments for European gentlemen opened from time to time. 'The only additional inducement I could think of as possible would be that, if the Viceroy did not think it unconstitutional, you might bring the *Indian Economist* here and continue it as a sort of semi-official Statistical Journal.'[117] One month later he made a firm offer of an assistant secretaryship,

with liberty and encouragement to keep and bring over the *Economist*. Lord Northbrook [the viceroy] says that it would not do that it should be considered in any degree official, and that you would have to avoid controversial sentiments....Our object would be to give you a special department, and not fritter away your time opening letters, & c....[118]

Knight considered for several days, then took the fateful plunge. He wrote that although the appointment offered him no pecuniary gain, 'I have determined to accept it, as it will release me from the strain of daily journalism, while it opens to me a field which I have long desired to enter. It is the tone of your letters perhaps, as much as anything else, that decides me to go....'[119]

Departing from Bombay must have been difficult for Catherine (who had lived practically her entire life there) and the children. The four 'little ones' to whom Knight had referred were a sixth son, Duncan, born in 1871, and a third surviving daughter, Emily Mabel (generally called 'Bonnie' by the family), born in 1872, in addition to the aforementioned Raymont and Phillip.[120]

The Knights' parenting concluded with the birth of two more daughters, Imogen, in 1874, and Hilda, in 1875, while Robert worked in Calcutta.[121] However, the registry lists Hilda's birthplace as Agra. Many years later she wrote that she had lived in Agra at 'Jacob's Castle' (otherwise unidentified) until the age of four.[122] This was confirmed by Hilda's nephew, George Knight, who wrote that his mother, Emily, had told him that she grew up in Agra.[123]

Presumably Knight's family lived in Agra while he worked in Calcutta because of the cost of raising a large family in Calcutta, which had worried him. By 1873 the East Indian Railway had been completed between Agra and Calcutta's Howrah Station, but even in the twenty-first century that trip of 1426 kilometres takes more than twenty-four hours. If Knight had worked regular office hours in the secretariat, he could not have seen his family often. Since Knight was, from all indications, a devoted family man, this separation must have been difficult for him. Perhaps it contributed to the discontent with his new position, which developed rapidly.

POLITICAL AND CULTURAL FERMENT IN CALCUTTA

The city to which Robert Knight relocated had, like Bombay, begun life as a trading post of the East India Company, but the similarity ended there. Bombay had been a group of offshore islands, separated from significant hinterland by sea and mountains. Calcutta began as a temple and three villages set on a low-lying open plain beside the Hughli River. The river brought oceangoing ships into Calcutta and provided a broad highway into north India through the connecting Ganges.

Where Bombay was a city made for commerce, Calcutta was a city made for politics. Clive's victory at the Battle of Plassey in 1757 made the East India Company the effective ruler of Bengal, with Calcutta as its capital. This was India's wealthiest province at the time and included the present-day states of West Bengal, Bihar, and Orissa, and the nation of Bangladesh. The 'permanent settlement' of 1793 created a rich and influential landed elite. The zamindars sold, leased, or simply milked their estates, and many moved into Calcutta, where they built handsome, even palatial, town houses. Since the governor general had the entire Indian empire to supervise, a separate provincial government for Bengal, headed by a lieutenant governor, was created in 1854.[124] Calcutta's good fortune, then, was to serve as a subcontinental capital, the centre of a rich agricultural region and the focal point for a vast trade and, later, an investment network.

Accounts and pictures of the Calcutta of Knight's day show a sturdy and prosperous city, called 'the Second City of the Empire'. There was no suggestion of the bloated, grossly overcrowded metropolis which it became in the twentieth century. Its most distinctive feature was the *maidan*, a park which ran along two miles of riverfront and about a mile inland. The maidan was created when Clive built a new Fort William, a stolid, defensible bastion, and cleared the adjacent wooded area. As Calcutta grew around it, the city needed this open green space, and it has been maintained intact, except for a few encroaching monuments, roads, and vendors' stalls.

The imposing Government House was built at the north end of the maidan by Governor General Lord Wellesley in 1804. A quarter-mile further north was Dalhousie Square (since renamed BBD Bagh), centre of the banking and big business activities. As people flocked into Calcutta, the city grew mostly to the north and east; in 1875 the first tram line opened, along Bow Bazar Street west to Dalhousie Square. But Calcutta's 'main street' was Chowringhee (since renamed Jawaharlal Nehru Road), running the length of the maidan, along its eastern side. It was lined with well-to-do houses, offices, and fashionable shops.[125] On Chowringhee Knight would plant his the *Statesman*.

Power and prestige in Calcutta resided with two elites, the British and the Bengali, who sometimes cooperated, sometimes contended. As the nineteenth century proceeded, the contentions grew more conspicuous. On the one side developed a heightened racial pride and exclusiveness, on the other, a renewed awareness of its religious and cultural heritage. Many Bengalis took an increasing interest in political matters and resented the constrictions of the imperial order. Bombay also had its racial and communal identities, but the edges seemed less sharp, the gaps not so wide. Bombay commerce exhibited more of the pattern of a plural society, of the interaction of many groups with specialized roles.[126]

The British elite were divided into official (military and civilian) and non-official. The administrative mechanism expanded after the crown takeover, but the ranks of private persons grew even faster, due to more career opportunities and easier travel. The local census of 1876 showed 9003 Europeans in Calcutta alone (along with 278,224 Hindus and 123,556 'Mahomedans'). The city was also a 'home base' for Europeans who had infiltrated the mufassil, especially in eastern India, as planters, railroaders, churchmen, etc. Most of the plantations and other large mufassil enterprises were supervised or at least represented by Calcutta's huge managing agencies on behalf of their distant British owners.[127] Altogether, they made a powerful and influential community.

The Bengali elite, often called the *bhadralok* (respectable people), consisted largely of high-caste Hindus—Brahmans, Kayasths, and Vaidyas. These were wealthy and cultured gentlemen, some with zamindari estates, who set the pattern and tone for Bengali society.[128] While they lacked formal political power, these bhadralok had substantial influence. To articulate it, they formed the British Indian Association in 1851. They had accepted British rule and would try to use it for their advantage.

However, the bhadralok had factions and rivalries among themselves. A significant rift had opened between those who sought modernizing reforms in their Hindu practices and lifestyle, and those who defended the traditional ways and even worked for their revival. Most conspicuous on the reform side was the Brahmo Samaj, which since 1843 had worked toward a reformed and iconoclastic type of Hinduism. On the revivalist side, many Indians (and even a few Europeans) were attracted to the mystical saint-philosopher known as Shri Ramakrishna, who lived, taught, and meditated in a Calcutta suburban temple.

All of these groups had their journalistic advocates. Most prominent was the *Englishman*, voice of the Anglo-Indian Establishment in Calcutta. The middle-class British had the *Indian Daily News*, which had replaced the aforementioned *Bengal Hurkaru* in 1864. Speaking for the Bengalis, there was the English-language *Hindoo Patriot* of the British Indian Association, the *Indian Mirror* of the Brahmo Samaj, the sassy bilingual *Amrita Bazar Patrika*, and plenty of Indian-language papers, mostly in Bengali.[129]

Many of the bhadralok sent their sons to the new University of Calcutta or its affiliated colleges to learn the language, culture, and manners of the British and thereby qualify for government positions or business contacts with European firms. Many received clerkships, secretaryships, etc., around British India, but some soon resented the racial limitations and arrogant attitudes of the British. In 1873-4, their martyr-hero was Surendranath Banerjea, a young Bengali Brahman. He was one of the first Indians to travel to Britain and earn a coveted place in the covenanted civil service, but was soon expelled for a trivial error. The British resented Bengali pushiness and derided their obsequious manner and fumbling English. 'Babu', a term of respect in Bengali, became a stereotype and a sneer on British tongues.

Such was the Calcutta which Robert Knight entered in 1873. It was not a congenial setting for a liberal.

THE MYSTERIOUS BIRTH OF CALCUTTA'S THE *STATESMAN*

The *Indian Economist* of 21 June 1873 announced the move to Calcutta, due to Knight's appointment as 'Head of the Statistical Bureau of the Lower Provinces'. The monthly lauded the enthusiasm of Sir George Campbell, but promised not to become his organ nor that of the Bengal government: 'We have had but one conception of a journalist's duties from the day we first entered upon their discharge. We look upon the office simply as a trust, and have ever done so....'[130]

The issue of 30 August announced that offices had been set up in Calcutta by 'Robert Knight, Proprietor' and the usual forthright and feisty spirit of the *Indian Economist* (and all Knight journals) arose. There was strong criticism of the oppression of the ryots by petty landholders, a demand for a protective tariff against a flood of cotton textiles from Britain (see Chapter 4), and a call for imperial guarantees of the Government of India's debt.[131]

All discretion vanished when there appeared to be a danger of another massive famine. The vital monsoon rains fell normally in northern Bengal and adjacent Bihar during July and August of 1873, but then shut down prematurely, killing the *rabi* (winter) crops of rice and coarse grains in northern Bengal and Bihar. Unlike Orissa in 1866, supplies of grain had been stored away, but with no work available, rural labourers could not afford them, and millions faced starvation.[132] The region needed public works projects as well as imports of rice to keep market prices stable. But September and October passed without either. Again, Knight was infuriated by official inaction when famine threatened. His late October editorial was almost revolutionary: 'A people starving in the actual presence of food,' he wrote, was 'one of those horrible anomalies which a weak, hide-bound government may tolerate, but no other.' He continued:

If food is in the country, and the people are allowed to die of starvation in its presence, the entire executive administration that suffers them so to die deserves impeachment. Does not everyone see that in the presence of such a calamity, all so-called 'rights of property' are...in abeyance, and that the State is bound to *take* from the well-to-do whatever may be necessary to save the people alive?[133]

Lieutenant Governor Campbell, his investigation of the Orissa famine fresh in his memory, needed little persuasion. He applied to the Government of India for funds to launch public works and to purchase and import rice, and he received them. But his other proposal, prohibiting the export of surplus rice from southern Bengal so it would be shipped to markets in the drought area, was rejected by the viceroy, Lord Northbrook. Campbell later wrote in his memoirs that the viceroy would not hear of such a sharp departure from the free market gospel; he 'looked on my proposal as a sort of abominable heresy.'[134] This rare rift in the ruling ranks soon became known and was reported by Knight.[135]

Despite the extra costs and delays, the Indian and Bengal governments succeeded in shipping and distributing relief rice in time to avert starvations. For once Knight could rejoice to see 'that the almost superhuman exertions of the Government...will be crowned with success; and that, for the first time in modern history, we shall have seen a terrible famine fairly surmounted by the humanity and resolution of the Government....'[136]

However, his earlier attacks on viceregal policies had stirred enmity within official circles. Robert Chapman, a financial secretary, objected to the growing cost and irregular procedure of *Indian Economist* subscriptions, but he also admitted his distaste for Knight's 'extreme views' on revenue matters.[137] Knight was also said to have used his insider role to obtain and publish confidential figures on grain purchases.[138]

Demand for the monthly had grown. By 1874 officials were receiving 339 subscriptions (mostly on the provincial and local levels) at Rs 30 each annually, a total of Rs 10,170, and more were requested.[139]

The subscription arrangement was defended by Allan Octavian Hume, Secretary of Revenue, Agriculture, and Commerce (and later instrumental in founding the Indian National Congress).

Hume, in a memo, appreciated such a stimulating and outspoken journal as the *Indian Economist* and said that one need not agree with Knight's editorial views to value the ideas and information which he was marshalling and presenting.[140]

Two months after his rift with Northbrook was disclosed, Sir George Campbell suddenly resigned and left India in April 1874—for reasons of health, it was announced.[141] This was disastrous for Knight, who had been his protégé and was now left unprotected. The very next month, the viceregal council halved the allotment for the *Indian Economist* subscriptions, forbade the provincial governments' subscribing directly, and rejected any commitment to subscribe at all after one year.[142] A dissenting councillor, Barrow H. Ellis, said that the only argument for this action had been a dislike of the journal's editorial views.[143]

This further irked Knight, who was already greatly disappointed with his situation. He complained to the new lieutenant governor, Sir Richard Temple, an energetic and assertive man (whose correspondence with Knight always sounded remote and chilly).[144] Knight explained:

I looked upon it as a new and special office, and never dreamed that it meant a routine Assistant Secretaryship with the charge of accounts and the Printing Press, the correction of proofs, and the numerous purely clerkly duties of which the work so largely consists....When I found that I had to devote nearly all my time to work which in my own office I had employed assistants and clerks to do, my disappointment was, I confess, very great....with more exact knowledge of matters I can see how ill-advised and impossible the proposal really was.[145]

But he could not return to Bombay, where he had cut his ties and engaged another editor for his *Indian Statesman.*

Temple spurned his request for an interview and professed his inability to relieve Knight's difficulties. Instead, he asked for a resume of his achievements in sixteen months' employment or what he hoped to achieve. Knight responded with an extensive memo proposing a fuller and better-integrated handling of agricultural and other data and statistics.[146]

Three months after this rebuff, on 1 January 1875, a prospectus for a third Anglo-Indian daily paper in Calcutta was distributed. The would-be editor, a Mr Dawson, had not arrived from England, but the proprietors and managers felt that enough support had been built from subscribers and advertisers to launch their venture, and so Calcutta first saw the *Indian Statesman* on 15 January. The proprietors (never identified) decided to undercut the established four-*anna* (like a penny) papers by hawking theirs for one anna 'at all the Ghats and Railway Stations, and at every great centre of transit in the city.'[147]

The appearance of this new paper drew the attention of the Bengal government, which asked Knight to explain his connection with it. Knight responded with a sad story: He had sunk the remains of his fortune into the *Indian Statesman* in Bombay; he had tried to sell it before moving to Calcutta but had been unable to do so; the people in whose hands he had left the paper had made some unwise changes and managed matters so badly that he was threatened with the loss, not only of income which he had counted on, but his entire investment. 'I then heard casually that there was a project on foot to start a third daily paper in Calcutta, and I proposed to the projectors that they should buy the *Indian Statesman* from me and bring it here.'[148] But this arrangement broke down over 'insuperable difficulties' involved in the transfer:

It was then suggested that the new Calcutta paper should take the same name as mine, and adopt the same rates, and co-operate with it closely, the two being worked by one literary staff for the sake of economy to both. I of course gladly made this arrangement, as it promised to redeem the position of the Bombay paper, and I was to receive a few paid-up shares in the Calcutta one for the use of our name and for the desired co-operation.

Beyond this, there is no connection whatever between the two papers, the only shareholder common to both being myself, who am in the embarrassing position of having a white elephant on my hands....[149]

Knight minimized his influence on his anonymous partners: 'I have no power whatever to make the proprietors of the Calcutta paper (who are 25 or 26 in number in addition to myself) change its name....They are all strangers to me with one or two exceptions....'[150] The informal *Brief History of the Statesman* refers to the founders only as 'twenty-four merchants'.[151] Managers of the *Statesman* have said their archives were long ago cleared of such unnecessary records.

The early editorship of the paper is also murky. Knight admitted involvement: 'The failure of Mr. Dawson to reach Calcutta, although he arrived in Bombay a week ago, has embarrassed the paper here very much,' he wrote on 24 January 'and I and others have been writing editorials perforce pending his arrival, to keep it going.'[152]

Further embarrassment ensued a week later when Dawson telegraphed the proprietors that he had never left Britain. He had been stopped by news of the serious illness of his sister, and he was needed in Ireland on business, a later letter explained. His name remained on the manifest of passengers arriving in Bombay, and so it was assumed that he had arrived. One J.W.O. Sullivan (or J.W. O'Sullivan) was filling in as interim editor.[153] *Brief History* assures that whoever was the nominal editor, Knight's was the dominant voice,[154] and the editorial tone supports that.

Despite these difficulties, the *Statesman* (it dropped *Indian* from its title the following September) seems to have been an instant success. It claimed that within its first month it had built a circulation second-highest in eastern India.[155] In May 1875 the directors declared that the paper had

in the teeth of unlooked-for difficulties, achieved a large and steadily increasing circulation. The accounts to 30th April last show that the Company is already working at a profit, and that with arrangements for securing a larger literary staff and early telegraphic intelligence, the journal will take a high position and return handsome dividends....[156]

Plans were announced for a sale of shares to raise capital and expand facilities.

However, as the *Statesman* was taking root, its principal founder was suffering his own crisis.

THE RUDE END OF AN OFFICIAL CAREER

Historically, monolithic regimes have used various techniques to handle unwelcome internal critics and dissidents. Imprisonment and assassination have been frequent. In Mughal times, men in power sometimes terminated the lives of bitter enemies and probably some in the Raj wished they could do the same for Knight. But dealing with Victorian Englishmen required something subtler. An economic squeeze could prove effective, especially when the culprit had ten or eleven dependent children. Were Lord Northbrook and Sir Richard Temple being clever and crafty—the viceroy would soon resurrect a perceived slight—or simply aloof and oblivious?

The lieutenant governor asked Knight (by formal letter through a secretary, as always) whether the *Indian Statesman* was a daily paper and still sold in Calcutta,[157] although it was being hawked on the city streets, right under his eyes. He apparently considered it improper, perhaps even an affront, that it should be a product of one of his secretariat. He told Knight that it was incompatible with official service; had he been asked, he never would have given his consent. He demanded Knight's immediate severance from the Calcutta *Statesman* and from the Bombay paper within a year. Until that was done, he could not guarantee that the government's subscriptions to the *Indian Economist*, already due to be halved, would be continued at all.[158] That would have strangled the monthly.

Knight was appalled. This edict, he replied, contained views 'that really change the whole conditions of my service.' The government had not objected to its servants editing or writing for the press during the past forty years, and even encouraged it as a means of helping the public understand state policies; some eminent officials had done so. In his own case, he had been engaged by Sir George Campbell *because* of his work with the press, and his *Indian Economist* had been approved as a supplement to his slender salary. However, Knight was willing to part with the *Statesman*, 'for it is a fact that I am tired of journalism, and would gladly escape from its troubled waters altogether into purely official life.'[159]

As for his *Economist*, Knight had a proposal: let the government take it over and convert it into a non-controversial agricultural gazette; let it engage him as editor at Rs 1000 a month, to compensate for his loss of income from the paper. He was already doing two jobs; why should not he draw two salaries? The lieutenant governor accepted this idea but said the government could only give him Rs 500 as editor. Northbrook agreed, adding 'Mr. Knight not to have permission to edit any other paper or journal'.[160] Knight asked for Rs 38,000 for the purchase of his journal; Temple refused to pay more than Rs 20,000. The protracted correspondence, despite formal courtesies, grew sharp and confrontational. Knight complained bitterly that the government had broken its promises to him and was making it impossible for him to meet his obligations.[161]

However, the viceroy recalled that a year earlier, in the dispute over famine relief measures, the *Indian Economist* had published (and criticized) reports of the government's purchase and export of grain, which 'might have been detrimental to the public interests'.[162] He said no officer was permitted to edit a newspaper in India 'without the express sanction of the Government' (by order of the Secretary of State, no. 12, 6 November 1864). Knight had received that sanction 'upon the condition that those journals would be confined to statistical and economic questions, and avoid any controversial subjects.' But recent articles had questioned the loyalty of the native press and commented on the ongoing Baroda trial, and he demanded: 'What does the Lieutenant-Governor propose to do about this?'[163]

The Baroda trial, then in progress, was probably the most sensational criminal trial of all nineteenth-century India, and there must have been few newspapers or journals which did not report or comment on it. Baroda, on India's west coast, was one of the largest and most prominent of the princely states. Mulhar Rao Gaekwar, who had ascended the throne in 1870, was criticized by the British for severe misgovernment and such alleged crimes as poisoning his enemies. The resident, Colonel Robert Phayre, was an assertive man whose scoldings had angered Mulhar Rao. On 9 November 1874, Phayre found arsenic in his fruit sherbet, and he immediately accused the Gaekwar of trying to murder him.[164]

This presented an awkward problem for Northbrook. The Raj could not ignore a threat to its representative, but the Gaekwar was a sovereign ruler (theoretically) and thus immune from criminal law. Moreover, whatever the man's defects, he was seen as a part of Indian culture and tradition, and as word spread of his danger from the *angrezi* (English) conquerors, many thousands of Indians rallied to show their sympathy and support for him and against the feared annexation of Baroda by the empire. The viceroy appointed a special commission of inquiry, consisting of three British officers and three prominent Indians, to conduct open hearings into the charges against Mulhar Rao. The trial which followed was a tangled web of accusations of deceit, perjury, and altered evidence, all spread to a waiting world by an eager press.

Knight had defended the Indian princes whom he saw as cheated or bullied by the Raj, but for Mulhar Rao he had no kind or supportive word. He called him 'one of the meanest, cruelest, most effeminate of mankind. Revenge, avarice, and sensuality are his ruling passions.'[165] He objected only that 'we are going to try Mulharrao for attempting to murder our Resident: but we care nothing that he is charged by his own people with a succession of crimes....'[166] To ask this outspoken editor not to comment was to ask the unnatural.

However, this was just what the Government of India demanded. Nothing 'political' or 'controversial' was to be included in the *Indian Economist*, and to enforce this Knight was required to submit the journal's proofs in advance for approval. This was done for the February 1875 issue, and about half the articles were rejected, including all references to the Baroda trial. Knight said it was impossible to run an independent paper under such restrictions, that replacing the banned articles would cause the paper to miss its production schedule. Besides, the whole idea of censorship was 'something of a degradation to an old publicist like myself'.[167]

Unable to move the government on either its demand for pre-censorship or the amount it would pay for the *Indian Economist*, Knight accepted its offer of Rs 20,000 on 13 March.[168] The lieutenant governor and his staff must have rejoiced that their Knight problem was apparently over. Their consternation, perhaps even fury, can only be imagined (since it did not stain their formal correspondence) when Knight used their Rs 20,000 to buy two weekly newspapers, the *Friend of India* and the *Indian Observer*, merged the second into the first, and proceeded to edit and publish it.[169]

The *Friend of India* had had a long and notable history. It was begun in 1818 by the Baptist missionaries in Serampore (actually, Srirampur), a Danish trading post upriver from Calcutta. It had provided thoughtful and independent commentaries on public affairs in an era when few dared to do so. The previous editor, George Smith, had retired to Britain, and the proprietors wanted to sell the *Friend of India* to someone who would conduct it 'in harmony with its antecedents'; they cheerily announced that 'a man who is possessed of great journalistic experience made an offer to the proprietors, and in his case no objection could possibly apply.'[170] The *Indian Observer* had been founded in 1871 by Major (later Lieutenant Colonel) Robert D. Osborn, who had been posted to Calcutta in the doldrums of a military career. He picked up extra rupees by tutoring and spent some on his weekly, in which he broadcast views largely critical of the Raj. After selling his *Observer* to Knight, he retired from the army and joined *The Statesman* staff as a colleague and friend of Knight.[171]

The Bengal government asked Knight to explain his actions. Knight again asked for a personal interview with Temple, which the lieutenant governor again refused. He then wrote of his grievances: Campbell had persuaded him to accept the Bengal office at a meager salary, with the understanding that he could supplement it through journalistic earnings; that if this was contrary to regulations, they had become obsolete and he had not been informed; that the government had forced him to sell his *Indian Economist*, while his Bombay paper, once a moneymaker, had become a dead loss. Therefore, he had bought the two weeklies for their income, to make up partially for losses from the forced sale of the *Indian Economist* and thus maintain the original terms of his engagement. Knight concluded boldly:

I have striven, throughout this letter to write respectfully, but I feel it is impossible to conceal my sense of the wrong I have suffered from the Government of India: and I have formally to request that permission may be obtained for me to memorialize the Home Government against the injustice of its course, as I am sure that Her Majesty's Secretary of State, who knows something of my services to the country, will not sustain what has been done.[172]

Temple was unmoved by this challenge. His secretary wrote that Knight's status as sole or principal proprietor of four newspapers was incompatible with his official position, and so 'the Lieutenant-Governor is obliged to inquire whether you propose to resign your appointment as Assistant Secretary to this Government.'[173] Knight had no wish to resign, and so he cited his family responsibilities. He threatened to appeal to the High Court, even if it meant a scandal 'such as has not happened before in my time; for I did not seek to come into Government service, but was seduced into it, and am now ruined by it.'[174] Again, the challenge seems to have stiffened Temple; he officially asked the Government of India whether, under the circumstances, Knight could be permitted to retain his appointment.[175]

Under the procedures of the day, this inquiry and its accompanying file were circulated among the viceroy's executive council for opinions. Northbrook himself took an uncompromising stand: Knight had been told to avoid any political or controversial matter, his continuing connections with the press were inconsistent with his secretarial position, and if he would not resign his position, he would have to be terminated.[176]

One councillor defended Knight: Allan Octavian Hume. 'His reputation is higher than that of any other Indian journalist since Marshman,' Hume wrote. 'He is considered flighty and at times intemperate' but still always honest and conscientious. Many others in government had owned or written for newspapers, he said, including Temple himself, though of course always pro-government. Rather than drive Knight out of the service, Hume suggested a 'golden bridge', a transfer to some other province or department where his talents would be better utilized.[177]

Arthur Hobhouse, the legal member of the council, carefully reviewed the arguments and accepted Knight's grievances. But his was a cold sort of support, with a gratuitous sneer:

I know next to nothing of Mr. Knight....I myself should think it the most probable result of putting into a Secretariat a man who for 20 years and upwards had been accustomed to the hasty, shifting loose mental habits of a daily newspaper writer. But for all that we did it, and did it with our eyes open. We took a man without official habits and at such a rate of pay as he could not live on....[178]

Hobhouse endorsed Hume's idea of a 'golden bridge' for Knight, as did another councillor, Lord Napier of Magdala, the army commander-in-chief.

Meanwhile, the hearing on the Gaekwar of Baroda moved to its conclusion, amid a rising tumult of public protests and threats of disorder. The verdict, announced on 19 April 1875, seems to have disappointed everyone. The three British members of the panel stated that the attempted murder case had been proved; the three Indian members insisted it had not. The deadlock ended the murder charge, but Northbrook then ousted Mulhar

Rao from his throne on grounds of misgovernment. Baroda would not be annexed, but a child of the royal family would reign nominally, with a British-appointed administrator.[179] Journalistic critics included Knight's *Friend of India*, which called the trial a 'blunder' by Northbrook. He should have deposed the Gaekwar without a trial on receiving the report from Colonel Phayre; to have the Secretary of State order it in spite of the verdict was 'an emphatic condemnation of Lord Northbrook's proceedings'.[180]

Perhaps this swayed Northbrook's decision on Knight or perhaps he had already set his mind. Certainly Hobhouse changed *his* mind about a 'golden bridge' for Knight because of it. 'There appeared in the *Friend of India*,' he wrote in a later addendum, 'some personal attacks on the Viceroy which were mendacious, scurrilous, and malignant....Mr. Knight cannot maintain the position of servant of the Government and also its hostile critic. I think he should be dismissed....' [181]

The official response to the Bengal government's query reflected only the harsh view of the viceroy. The Government of India, it stated, had 'no hesitation in stating that Mr. Knight cannot be permitted to retain his appointment.' A government servant who writes for a newspaper is expected to refrain from 'personal criticism of his official superiors' but the last two issues of the *Friend of India* had opposed the viceroy 'in intemperate and improper language' which amounted to 'a breach of the relations between that servant and his employers.'[182] Therefore, Knight had to resign or have his services terminated by the lieutenant governor.

Knight called this decree 'very cruel' and reiterated that the government had not kept its promise with him. He grasped at a suggestion that the viceroy might reconsider his case if he were to sever all press connections, and he preferred that to losing his appointment. He asked Temple for two months' leave to close out affairs in Bombay and remarked, 'I would rather face the loss of everything than go back into editorial work, which is nothing but a distress and a snare to me, and has ever been so from my peculiar temperament.'[183]

Northbrook and Temple agreed privately that in case of distress they would find some opening for 'the poor creature Knight'. But the lieutenant governor said that Knight's conduct had for some time been 'causing a certain sort of scandal, and everyone expects that he will be, as they know he ought to be, removed from his appointment.' A government which permitted an officer to do such things 'would lose all respect'.[184] So Knight was informed that 'the Lieutenant-Governor regrets that he cannot accede to this request.' Within a fortnight 'you will make over the charge of your office as Assistant Secretary to Mr. Easton, who has been appointed to relieve you.'[185] With this humiliating rebuff, Knight was thrust back to an editor's desk. He never again held a government appointment.

On examining this extensive file, one must conclude that Knight brought this debacle upon himself through his reckless acts and indiscreet words. But there were mitigating circumstances: his family had to be maintained. Sir George Campbell promised more than he could deliver and then apparently made no effort to repair the situation. Northbrook showed a spiteful and vindictive side. Temple could have unbent a little; a requested interview, which he twice rejected, could have led to an understanding and rapport. The official Establishment, which could have tried to ease or explain matters, apparently did not (except for Hume, himself a rebel). To them, Knight was an outsider, not part of that great fraternity of the covenanted service, a mere scribbler, of insignificant family and education, and a man of strange opinions. Woodruff compared the CSI to Platonic guardians, wise and selfless, and Kipling depicted them as self-sacrificing, burdened white men, but they could also be fractious, spiteful, resentful politicians.[186] A prime example was Charles E. Buckland (Eton, Oxford, a CSI son of a CSI father), who as private secretary to Temple wrote some of those rigid and frigid letters to Knight. His later books, *Bengal Under the Lieutenant-Governors* and *Dictionary of Indian Biography*, omitted any mention of Knight, though many lesser journalists were included in the latter. It appears to be a case of personal spite.

In 1875 Knight still considered the British Empire the likeliest vehicle for the reform, progress, and well-being of the Indian people. But he also felt that the empire, and India especially, had fallen into the hands of greedy and narrow-minded men who cared little about its people. However, Knight was mistaken when he said he was temperamentally unsuited for editorial work; cut loose from that hostile secretariat, he could soar.

NOTES

1. Frere to Wood, 14 April 1864, Wood Papers, Mss Eur. F78, 88/10.
2. See David Cannadine, *Ornamentalism, How the British Saw Their Empire* (Oxford: University Press, 2001) for a treatise on the importance to the British of hierarchical class order.
3. Anglo-Indian family life has been a popular subject for study and memoirs. One helpful history is Margaret MacMillan, *Women of the Raj* (New York: Thames and Hudson, 1988), esp. p. 139.
4. Advertisement, *Friend of India* (Calcutta), 3 July 1875, p. 613.
5. Constructed from family recollections in letters sent to the author, and held by him, from Hilda (Knight) Kidd, 26 August and 2 September 1968; George Knight, 12 December 1984, and Evelyn ('Eve') Knight, 15 December 1991; S.C. Sanial, 'The Father of Indian Journalism—III: Robert Knight, His Life and Work', *Calcutta Review* (hereafter *CR*), vol. 20 of 3rd series, pt 2 (August 1926), p. 305.
6. Ibid.
7. From an old family ledger kept by Catherine Knight, in possession of her daughter Hilda Kidd, in 1968.
8. Sanial, 'The Father of Indian Journalism—II', *CR*, vol. 20 of 3rd series, pt 1, (July 1926), p. 38.
9. The *Times of India* (Bombay) (hereafter *TOI*), 10 January 1863.
10. Lt Col C.P. Taylor, *A Short Campaign Against the White Borer in the Coffee Districts of Coorg, Munzerabad, and Nuggur* (Madras: William Thomas, 1868), pp. 3 and 24; E.C.P. Hull, *Coffee Planting in South India and Ceylon* (London: E. and F.N. Spon, 1877), pp. 24 and 268–70.
11. O.H.K. Spate and A.T.A. Learmonth, *India and Pakistan, A General and Regional Geography* (London: Methuen, 1967), 3rd edn, pp. 252–3.
12. Sanial, 'Father of Indian Journalism—III', *CR*, p. 305.
13. Addendum to Frere to Woods, 14 April 1864, Wood Papers.
14. Sanial, 'Father of Indian Journalism—III', *CR*, pp. 309–10; George Macaulay Trevelyan, *The Life of John Bright* (Boston: Houghton Mifflin, 1913), pp. 266–7. One writer cites Knight as a 'business associate' of Bright's but gives no particulars or sources: Marjorie Sykes, *Quakers in India: A Forgotten Century* (London: George Allen & Unwin, 1980), p. 32.
15. Letter to the author from the Royal Statistical Society, 14 December 1971.
16. *TOI*, 7 January 1862.
17. Great Britain, *Revenue Despatches to India*, 1862, 10(14), 9 July 1862. Wood's memo spoke only of creation and encouragement

of middle-class occupants, not of losses of tenure or rights by cultivators.

18. Wood's policy is explained carefully in R.J. Moore, *Sir Charles Wood's Indian Policy, 1853-66* (Manchester: University Press, 1966), pp. 180-202.

19. Knight's Manchester speech was published anonymously. A copy is held by the British Library, in which that final quotation is on p. 57. Sanial has a partial version, 'Father of Indian Journalism—III', pp. 317-20.

20. According to Knight. Sanial, 'Father of Indian Journalism—III', p. 312.

21. Anil Seal, *The Emergence of Indian Nationalism: Competition and Collaboration in the Later Nineteenth Century* (Cambridge: University Press, 1968), p. 246.

22. Robert Knight, *The Indian Empire and Our Financial Relations Therewith* (London: Trubner, 1866), pp. 6, 20, and 42.

23. Bimanbehari Majumdar, *Indian Political Associations and Reform of Legislature (1818-1917)* (Calcutta: Firma K.L. Mukhopadhyay, 1965), p. 97.

24. R.P. Masani, *Dadabhai Naoroji: The Grand Old Man of India* (London: George Allen and Unwin, 1939), p. 120.

25. Munni Rawal, *Dadabhai Naoroji: A Prophet of Indian Nationalism (1855-1900)* (New Delhi: Anmol Publications, 1989), p. 13.

26. Dinshaw E. Wacha, *A Financial Chapter in the History of Bombay City* (Bombay: Cambridge Press, 1910), p. 191.

27. Ibid., p. 197. Wacha so declared, and he was there.

28. John Martineau, *The Life and Correspondence of the Rt. Hon. Sir Bartle Frere* (London: John Murray, 1892), vol. 2, pp. 4-6.

29. Ibid., p. 19.

30. Wacha, *A Financial Chapter*, p. 97.

31. Ibid., pp. 88-93, 140, and 160; Martineau, *The Life and Correspondence*, vol. 2, pp. 20-6. For a recent retelling see Teresa Albuquerque, *Urbs Prima in Indis, An Epoch in the History of Bombay, 1840-1865* (New Delhi: Promilla, 1985), pp. 18-27, or Mariam Dossal, *Imperial Designs and Indian Realities: The Planning of Bombay City, 1845-1875* (Bombay: Oxford University Press, 1991), pp. 80-3.

32. Sanial, 'The Father of Indian Journalism—III', pp. 308-9.

33. Wacha, *A Financial Chapter*, p. 200.

34. Sanial, 'The Father of Indian Journalism—III', p. 328.

35. Lawrence to Cranborne, 18 October 1866, Lawrence Papers, MSS Eur. F90, 31; Wacha, *A Financial Chapter*, p. 101.

36. Sanial, 'The Father of Indian Journalism—III', p. 328.

37. *TOI*, 23 February 1867.

38. See for instance *TOI*, 5 April 1867.

39. It was published as 'Letter to the Right Hon. Sir Stafford Northcote Upon the Present Condition of Bombay, With Suggestions for its Relief' (London: Trubner, 1867). Did Knight, then ostensibly penniless, make this six-month trip to Bombay just for the Elphinstone shareholders? He said he himself had no personal interest in any company on the island. Neither Sanial nor anyone else has offered any explanation. Sanial's 1910 statement that Knight remained in England until March of 1867 ('History of the Press in India—X', *CR*, vol. 131 (July 1910), p. 363n) was inaccurate and superseded by his 1926 account ('The Father of Indian Journalism—III', vol. 20 of 3rd series, no. 2, pp. 328–9).

40. *TOI*, 16 July 1868.

41. Ibid., 7 and 8 July 1868. For details of the inquiry see Wacha, p. 93, or Martineau, vol. 2, pp. 26–7.

42. *TOI*, 17 July 1868.

43. Wacha, *A Financial Chapter*, pp. 70–1.

44. Letter of Hilda Kidd to the author, 26 August 1968. Her remark may have been hyperbolic; somehow the family was sustained.

45. *Times of India Calendar and Directory for 1869* (Bombay: Exchange Press, 1869), p. 353.

46. *TOI*, 29 July 1868. In a better mood, however, he foresaw a time when Britain would treat India with strict equity and take pride in it. Ibid., 9 January 1869.

47. Ibid., 6 July 1868 and 6 January 1869.

48. Ibid., 10 and 14 July 1868.

49. See Chapter 2; Wacha, *A Financial Chapter*, pp. 16–19; J.C. Masselos, *Towards Nationalism: Group Affiliations and the Politics of Public Associations in Nineteenth Century Western India* (Bombay: Popular Prakashan, 1974), pp. 132–4. Masselos, citing Bombay Council archives, says the JP's quickly broke into factions, and that by 1872 almost seven hundred had been appointed, but more than half were Europeans no longer resident in Bombay.

50. Wacha, *A Financial Chapter*, pp. 47–8; Masselos, *Towards Nationalism*, pp. 134–6. Masselos says Bombay had about 150 large property owners and about 15,000 owner–occupants of houses.

51. *TOI*, 2 October 1868.

52. *Speech on Local Taxation and the Constitution of the Bench, Delivered in Town Hall, Bombay, 5th of November, 1868* (Bombay: Times of India, 1868), pp. 5–7 and 21.

53. Ibid., p. 4.
54. *TOI*, 3 February 1869. The extensive and angry interchange between Knight and Mull was fully iterated in that issue and reiterated in Sanial, 'The Father of Indian Journalism—III', pp. 330–43.
55. Ibid.
56. Sanial, 'Father of Indian Journalism—III', p. 331. The signing of the agreement was delayed until 28 November.
57. Ibid., pp. 331–3.
58. Ibid., pp. 333–9.
59. *TOI*, 3 February 1869; Sanial, The rival *Bombay Gazette* also reprinted the angry correspondence (4 February 1869) and remarked: 'It's an ill bird that fouls its own nest.'
60. S. Natarajan, in his *A History of the Press in India*, observes (p. 83): 'There is some mystery about the event because Knight never fully explained his case.' Natarajan does not address the possibility that Knight might have been pressured or even cheated out of his paper by enemies. For Mull to dredge up a seven-year-old incident and use it to seize control of the paper smacks of a well-laid plot.
61. Some issues included *Agricultural Gazette* in the title, others *Statistical Reporter*, still others neither. Sometimes these were supplements distinct from the *Indian Economist* (hereafter *IE*) and at other times integrated.
62. Memo by 'J.B.R.,' 12 January 1874, in India, Revenue, Agriculture and Commerce, General Proceedings (June, 1874), progs 1–5, 7–10.
63. Memo of Hume, 3 February 1874, in India, Revenue, Agriculture and Commerce, General (RAC) Proceedings (June, 1874), pp. 10–12.
64. p. 3. For Knight's fullest expostulation on those oft-cited securities, see his 'A Letter to His Grace the Duke of Argyll, KG, Upon the Annual Claim Made by the Proprietors of East India Stock Upon the Revenues of India' (Bombay: Oriental Press, 1870).
65. *TOI*, 9 July 1869.
66. 10 February 1870, p. 201. (Pages were numbered consecutively for an entire one-year volume.)
67. *IE*, 15 April 1871, pp. 234–5. See also ibid., 29 November 1873, p. 37. Presumably this did not include the portion of the harvest which the ryot kept to feed his family.
68. *IE*, 10 December 1869, p.141. Accounts vary on the traditional percentage of the harvest taken by the state, which was often a compromise of the original demand. Half was the famous demand of Sultan Allauddin Khalji in the 14th century. But A.L. Basham

found a consensus of about a fourth of the harvest, with 'numerous exemptions and remissions', *The Wonder That Was India*, 3rd rev. edn (New York: Taplinger, 1967), p. 108. It was, in a word, flexible.

69. Knight, 'The Land Revenue of India, Is It Being Sacrificed or Not?' (Bombay: Thacker Vining, n.d.), pp. 4–6. This is a reprint of an undated *IE* article.

70. Lecture delivered in Bombay's Town Hall, 28 February 1870, published in *IE*, 10 March 1870 and reprinted separately as 'Fiscal Science in India, as Illustrated by the Income Tax' (Bombay: Oriental Press, 1870).

71. Ibid., p. 14.

72. *IE*, 10 May 1870, p. 285.

73. Ibid., 10 June 1870, p. 313.

74. Ibid., 11 July 1870, p. 350. This rebuke might explain Temple's harsh treatment of Knight in 1875. See pp. 122–31.

75. Ibid., 21 October 1871, p. 87.

76. Ibid., p. 58.

77. Ibid., 21 March 1872, p. 103.

78. Basham, p. 194. The most authoritative of these classical sources is Kautilya's *Arthashastra*, in which famine relief is discussed in book 4, chapter 3, verses 17–20, and book 8, chapter 4, verse 1. For a modern edition of Kautilya, see L.N. Rangarajan (ed.) (New Delhi: Penguin Books India, 1992).

79. *Bombay Times and Standard*, 1 March 1861. See also *TOI*, 20 May 1861.

80. Ibid., 4 May 1863.

81. India, *Report of the Famine Commission*, 1867, as quoted in C.E. Buckland, *Bengal Under the Lieutenant-Governors*, 2nd edn (Calcutta: Kedernath Bose, 1902), vol. 1, pp. 329–91, esp. pp. 340–1. See also Lawrence to Cranborne, 18 October 1866, Lawrence Papers, F90, vol. 31, entry no. 42.

82. *TOI*, 4 February 1867.

83. *IE*, 10 January 1870, p. 173.

84. Ibid., 21 September 1871, pp. 27–8.

85. Ibid., 21 October 1872, p. 65. Such a stockpiling policy was adopted successfully by the government of independent India about a century later.

86. Ibid., 10 January 1870, p. 173.

87. Ibid., 10 February 1870, p. 206.

88. Knight, 'Decentralization of the Finances of India', paper read before the Bengal Social Science Congress, 22 April 1871 (Bombay: Perseverance Press, 1871).

89. Ibid., p. 29.
90. Wacha, *A Financial Chapter*, pp. 93–126; Christine Dobbin, *Urban Leadership in Western India* (London: Oxford University Press, 1972), pp. 135–42; S.R. Mehrotra, *The Emergence of the Indian National Congress* (New York: Barnes and Noble, 1971), pp. 171–4.
91. Wacha, *A Financial Chapter*, p. 154.
92. Ibid., pp. 157–62.
93. Published in Bombay by Thacker, Vining, in 1871.
94. Ibid.
95. *IE*, 21 August 1871, pp. 2–8. Reprinted as 'Memorandum on the Municipal Finance of Bombay' (Bombay: Economist Press, 1871).
96. Wacha, *A Financial Chapter*, p. 211.
97. Ronald Smith, 'Indian Magistrates and the Secretary of State for India', *Westminster Review*, vol. 133, (January–June, 1890), pp. 669–72; David Gilmour, *The Ruling Caste, Imperial Lives in the Victorian Raj* (New York: Farrar, Strauss and Giroux, 2005), pp. 151–2.
98. Wacha, *A Financial Chapter*, pp. 206–9 and 242–61. See also Masselos, *Towards Nationalism*, pp. 144–6, and Dobbin, *Urban Leadership*, pp. 146–7.
99. Unpublished memoir, quoted in Sanial, 'Father of Indian Journalism—III', p. 347. Crawford's shady later career casts some doubt on Knight as a judge of character.
100. Mehrotra, *The Emergence of INC*, pp. 176–8.
101. *Star of India* (Bombay), 3 July 1870.
102. For instance 25 and 27 September 1871.
103. *Star of India*, 20 December 1871.
104. *Star of India*, 30 December 1871.
105. Wacha, *A Financial Chapter*, pp. 115 and 211. Wacha's account, though written thirty or forty years later, is precise, detailed, and apparently accurate.
106. *Indian Statesman and Gazette of Asia* (Bombay), 1 January 1872.
107. Knight to C.E. Buckland, private secretary to the Lt Governor of Bengal, 21 January 1875, included in India, General Department (hereafter Gen. Dept), Public Proceedings, entry no. 65 of June, 1875.
108. *Indian Statesman* (Bombay), 15 August and 3 September 1872.
109. Ibid., 4 January 1872.
110. Ibid., 3 January 1872.
111. Ibid., 13 December 1872.
112. Ibid., 7 January 1873.
113. Sir George Campbell, Lt Governor of Bengal, to Knight, 12 November 1872, and Knight to Campbell, n.d., both excerpted in

Knight to Sir Richard Temple (Campbell's successor as lieutenant governor.), 9 September 1875, included in India, Gen. Dept, Public Proceedings, June 1875, entry no. 66, pp. 787–8.

114. Buckland, pp. 518–22.

115. Also included in Knight to Temple, 9 September 1875, India, Gen. Dept, Public Proceedings, entry no. 66.

116. Knight to Campbell, n.d., ibid.

117. Campbell to Knight, 3 December 1872, ibid.

118. Ibid., 2 January 1873. Full details of the negotiations and Campbell's inducements have been given because of subsequent controversy (see pp. 122–8).

119. Knight to Campbell, 13 January 1873, India, Gen. Dept, Public Proceedings, entry no. 66. This file included two other encouraging letters from Campbell, but these crossed Knight's acceptance and thus could not have influenced it.

120. Great Britain, India Office Records, *Bombay Baptisms*, vol. 45, p. 474, and vol. 47, p. 85.

121. Ibid., *Bengal Baptisms*, vol. 147, p. 10, and vol. 154, p. 2.

122. Hilda (Knight) Kidd to the author, 26 August 1968.

123. George Knight to the author, 31 October 1982.

124. Great Britain, 16 and 17 Vic., c. 95.

125. For a general but informative description of modern Calcutta, see Geoffrey Moorhouse, *Calcutta* (New York: Harcourt Brace Jovanovich, 1971).

126. From a perusal of the newspaper files of the 1870s and 1880s, particularly the *Hindoo Patriot* and *Amrita Bazar Patrika*.

127. Daniel Houston Buchanan, *The Development of Capitalistic Enterprise in India* (New York: Macmillan, 1934), pp. 165–7. See also my '*White Mutiny': The Ilbert Bill Crisis and the Genesis of the Indian National Congress* (Columbia, Mo.: South Asia Books, 1980), pp. 105–14.

128. The bhadralok are described in Leonard A. Gordon, *Bengal: The Nationalist Movement, 1876–1940* (New York Columbia University Press, 1974), p. 7; Blair B. King, *Partner in Empire: Dwarkanath Tagore and the Age of Enterprise in Eastern India* (Berkeley: University of California Press, 1976), p. 5; and David Kopf, *The Brahmo Samaj and the Shaping of the Modern Indian Mind* (Princeton: Princeton University Press, 1979), p. 87.

129. The best description of significant Bengali-language newspapers is in India, Home Dept, Public Proceedings, October 1878, 143–61(B), 'List of Vernacular Newspapers Published in India'. The section on Lower Bengal, dated 24 November 1877, was written

by H.H. Risley. The government maintained two sets of periodic reports during the 1870s, the *Annual Reports of Presses Worked* and the *Reports on Native Papers* (titles and usefulness vary). Descriptions of the English-language papers may be found in histories of Indian journalism; two of the better ones are Natarajan, 1962, pp. 128–9, and Rangaswami Parthasarathy, *Journalism in India*, 4th rev. edn (New Delhi: Sterling Publishers, 1997), pp. 47–67.

130. *IE*, 21 June 1873.

131. Ibid., 31 December 1873, p. 68; March 1874, p. 211, and May 1874, p. 267, respectively.

132. Ibid., 31 October 1873, p. 57.

133. Ibid., Knight's alarm on this famine threat was shared by the *Friend of India* in Bengal and the *Times* in London.

134. *Memoirs of My Indian Career* (London: Macmillan, 1893), pp. 322–4. Northbrook belonged to the prominent banking family of Baring. For his version, see Bernard Mallett, *Thomas George, Earl of Northbrook, GCSI, A Memoir* (London: Longmans Green, 1908), pp. 82–8.

135. *IE*, February 1874, pp. 192–3.

136. Ibid., 30 March 1874, p. 257. In fact, the government was accused of wasteful extravagance because it had imported too much rice and about a fourth of it was left unsold. Lord Salisbury said Anglo-Indians felt it a mistake 'to spend so much money to save a lot of black fellows'. Salisbury to Northbrook, 21 September 1874, Northbrook Papers, MSS Eur. C144, 2, p. 55. The attitude that lost an empire.

137. Memo of 23 January 1874 in India, Gen. Dept, RAC Proceedings, pp. 1–5.

138. Arthur Howell, Office. Secretary, Govt of India, to Secretary, Govt of Bengal, 3 June 1875, in India, Gen. Dept, Public Proceedings, June 1875, No. 949.

139. Memo of 'J.B.R.' (probably John B. Roberts), 1 February 1874, in India, Gen. Dept, RAC Proceedings, June 1874, p. 10.

140. Hume, 3 February 1874, ibid. See Appendix B of the volume for substantial excerpts from Hume's memo.

141. Buckland, vol. 1, pp. 568–9.

142. Resolution of 11 May 1874, included in India, RAC Proceedings, June 1874, p. 10.

143. Ibid.

144. For a satiric sketch of Temple see Philip Woodruff (Mason), *The Men Who Ruled India* (London: Jonathan Cape, 1963 [1954]), vol. 2, pp. 60–3.

145. Knight to Temple, 9 September 1874, in India, Gen. Dept, Public Proceedings, June 1875, entry no. 66, p. 789.
146. Buckland to Knight, 20 September 1874, and Knight to Buckland, 2 October 1874, ibid., pp. 794–5.
147. *Indian Statesman* (Calcutta), 15 January 1875.
148. Knight to Buckland, 21 January 1875, in Public Proceedings, June 1875, entry no. 66, pp. 794–5.
149. Ibid. The idea of publishing two or more editions of a newspaper in different centres was not implemented in this instance, but it was successfully adopted by several Indian newspapers, including the *Statesman*, during the twentieth century.
150. Knight to Buckland, 1 February 1875, Public Proceedings, June 1875, entry no. 66, p. 798.
151. See p. 12. See preface on sources for a description of this 'history'. Another writer said the *Statesman* was begun 'with the co-operation of the Honourable Kristo Das Pal, Mr. Manmohan Ghose, and other Indian gentlemen'. Kiran Nath Dhar, 'Some Indian Economists', *CR*, 127 (253), July 1908, p. 429. No supporting evidence is given, and this article's accuracy may be questioned, as it gives the wrong starting date.
152. Knight to Buckland, 24 January 1875, Public Proceedings, June 1875, entry no. 66, p. 795.
153. *Indian Statesman*, 1 and 24 February 1875, as quoted in Benoy Ghose, *Selections From English Periodicals in 19th Century Bengal, vol. VIII: 1875–80, The Statesman* (Calcutta: Papyrus, 1981), pp. 20–1 and 45. In fact, Dawson never arrived.
154. *Brief History*, p. 13.
155. 24 February 1875, as quoted in Ghose, *Selections*, p. 45.
156. Ibid., 29 May 1875, as quoted in *The Statesman, An Anthology*, Niranjan Majumder (comp.), (Calcutta: The Statesman, 1975), pp. 19–20.
157. Buckland to Knight, 2 February 1875, in Public Proceedings, June 1875, entry no. 66, p. 798.
158. Ibid., 26 January 1875, in Public Proceedings, June 1875, entry no. 66, pp. 794–5.
159. Public Proceedings, June 1875, entry no. 66, pp. 796–7.
160. Temple to Northbrook, 10 February 1875, and Northbrook to Temple, 13 February 1875, both in Northbrook Papers, MSS Eur. C144, 17, pp. 45–6 and 27–8. .
161. Public Proceedings, June 1875, entry no. 66, pp. 797–810.
162. Arthur Howell, office. Secretary to the Govt of India, to 'The Secretary to the Govt of Bengal', 3 June 1875, in Public Proceedings,

entry no. 66, pp. 815-18. This apparently refers to the article 'Prohibition of Export', *IE*, 31 January 1874, pp. 147-9.

163. Memo of 24 February 1875, in India, Home Dept, Public Proceedings, February 1875, entry no. 260 (A).

164. H.H. Dodwell, 'The Relations of the Government of India with the Indian States, 1858-1918', in Dodwell (ed.), *The Cambridge History of India* (Delhi: S. Chand, 1964) [1932]), vol. 6, pp. 499-501; Edward C. Moulton, *Lord Northbrook's Indian Administration, 1872-6* (New York: Asia Publishing House, 1968), pp. 130-1. For a good account of the Baroda episode see chapter 5 by Moulton.

165. *IE*, 30 November 1874, p. 97.

166. Ibid., 30 January 1875, pp. 148-9.

167. Knight to Surgeon Major F.P. Staples, acting private secretary to the Lt Gov., 2 March 1875; Staples to Knight, 3 March, and Knight to Staples, 4 and 8 March 1875, all in Public Proceedings, June 1875, entry no. 66, pp. 804-6.

168. Knight to Staples, 13 March 1875, ibid., p. 808.

169. Ibid., 5 April 1875, p. 810.

170. *Friend of India* (Serampore), 15 April 1875, p. 371.

171. India, Military Records, L/MIL/9, #230/36-46. Colonel Osborn might well have been the role model for Kipling's 'The Man Who Could Write' in his *Departmental Ditties*. As with Boanarges Blitzen, his superiors, irked at his critical journalism, consigned him to 'a district desolate and dry'. Unlike Blitzen, though, Osborn got the message and responded by taking early retirement.

172. Knight to 'The Private Secretary to His Honour the Lieutenant-Governor of Bengal', 5 April 1875, Public Proceedings, entry no. 66, pp. 811-13.

173. Staples to Knight, 10 April 1875, ibid., p. 813.

174. Knight to Temple, 31 May 1875, enclosed in Northbrook Papers, vol. 17, pp. 215-16.

175. Knight to Staples, 13 April 1875, and Howell to 'The Secy to the Govt of Bengal,' 3 June 1875, Public Proceedings, entry no. 66, pp. 813-15 Howell was responding to the inquiry of the Bengal Government of 30 April, which had asked about dismissing Knight (ibid., pp. 785-6).

176. The council opinions are entitled India, Home Dept, Public Proceedings, June 1875, entry nos 65-7, 5 June 1875; they are included with the larger file cited above, though not in its overall pagination.

177. Ibid. Joshua Marshman had been the founding editor of the *Friend of India*.

178. Ibid.

179. Moulton, *Northbrook's Indian Administration*, chapter 5.

180. 1 May and 5 June 1875. Legally, the dismissal was by the viceroy, though on lines dictated by Lord Salisbury as Secretary of State. Northbrook and his council actually believed the Gaekwar guilty of the murder plot, but Salisbury insisted that there be no such imputation in the proclamation. Moulton, *Northbrook's Indian Administration*, pp. 160–70.

181. Public Proceedings, June 1875 (no sequential page numbers or date).

182. Howell, ibid., 3 June 1875, pp. 815–18.

183. Knight to Temple, 7 June 1875, and Knight to Staples, 16 June 1875 in Temple Papers, BL OIOC, F86, 115. See also Knight to H.J. Reynolds, Official Secretary of the Govt of Bengal, 17 June 1875, also in Temple Papers.

184. Northbrook to Hobhouse, 12 June 1875, and Temple to Northbrook, 19 June 1875, both included in Northbrook Papers, vol. 17, pp. 116 and 117, and 223–4.

185. Reynolds to Knight, n.d. but apparently 22 June 1875, Temple Papers, p. 115.

186. Woodruff, vol. 2, pp. 75–6. Francis G. Hutchins has written of the lingering suspicion and mistrust of outsiders (or 'interlopers') by Raj officials. (*The Illusion of Permanence, British Imperialism in India* [Princeton: Princeton University Press, 1967], p. 98). Bradford Spangenberg, examining the private papers of some officials, found them more concerned with personal careers than the well-being of the Indian people: 'Altruism vs. Careerism, Motivations of British Bureaucrats in Late Nineteenth Century India', in Robert I. Crane and N. Gerald Barrier (eds), *British Imperial Policy in India and Sri Lanka, 1858–1912 — A Reassessment* (Columbia, Mo.: South Asia Books, 1981), pp. 12–26.

4

The Making of an Imperial Critic, 1875–81

THE NEW VICEROY AND THE ROLE OF THE PRESS

Despite his harsh treatment by the Government of India and its subsidiary, the Government of Bengal, Robert Knight (Plate III) in 1875 retained his faith in the imperial ideal. He saw existing defects but also anticipated benefits, and he wrote:

To rule India according to the best and noblest English views is the only valid reason for the extension here of an alien power; to conduct our policy in accordance with the highest dictates of European humanity...by imposing on the Indians still suffering from ages of ignorance, disorder, tyranny and rapine, a higher and better law; to make the Indians the agents of their own regeneration,—these are some of the highest objects that can animate a Government or a nation....[1]

'Regeneration' included opportunities for a 'modern' (that is, European) education and a career in the official services. Indian Muslims usually declined these opportunities, so the government had to do more 'to supply the wants of higher class Muslims'.[2]

Knight's principles remained firm, but his mood differed from that of his *Times* years, probably due to his harrowing experiences of the previous decade. His approach was less often buoyant, more often sombre. Calcutta, was a political centre while Bombay was a commercial one; and Knight's editorial attention seemed to focus more on imperial issues, global as well as regional, and less on municipal taxes and provincial land revenues.

Plate III: Robert Knight. Courtesy *Statesman*, Kolkata

With the loss of his official job, Knight apparently relied entirely on his newspapers for income—his salary as editor, his dividends as shareholder—though no data is available. His family continued to live in Agra, where his youngest, Hilda, was born in 1875. In 1876 Edith, the second daughter, was married at the age nineteen to William N. Boutflower, a young man in the educational service.[3]

Even while pleading for his official job, Knight had consolidated his newspapers. The accounts for the first three months of the *Indian Statesman* showed a 'large and steadily increasing circulation' it was announced. It was already turning a profit and looking to expand. The directors arranged to purchase from Knight the *Friend of India* and the *Indian Observer* for the amount he had paid (unspecified, but presumably around Rs 20,000), and Knight agreed to take half the amount in Statesman company shares. The weeklies brought with them lists of subscribers and advertisers, along with 'a large staff of contributors'.[4] The directors also issued additional shares in the company to raise Rs 70,000 for office expansion and the purchase of new machinery.

The *Statesman* and *Friend of India* were jointly owned but produced by separate staffs until 1 January 1877, when they were merged into the *Statesman and Friend of India*. *Friend of India* was retained as the name of the weekly summary, which became the overseas edition for the 'home constituents'. William Riach, a young Scot who had gone to Calcutta in 1875 as a Doveton College mathematics professor, served as its editor in 1876.[5] He and Knight now shared editorial duties and presumably editorial views. This was announced in another promotional article, which began:

The large and rapid increase in the circulation of the *Statesman* necessitates our enlarging our machinery. The extreme pressure upon our advertising columns, has decided us also, as we have already intimated, to increase the size of the paper.... During the last few weeks only we have registered 600 new subscribers, a success wholly without precedent in Indian journalism.[6]

Knight also began a monthly *Indian Agriculturalist* on 1 January 1876, to provide 'a complete current record of everything that is being done, or attempted, in the provinces of the country, for the improvement of the husbandry of the people, and for the ascertainment and development of their mineral resources.'[7] His earlier *Agricultural Gazette* had been a part of the *Indian Economist* which had lapsed after the official purchase. In fact, in official hands the *Economist* itself soon withered and died. Knight again approached the government, presented his monthly as a valuable vehicle for the gathering, collating, and synthesizing of agricultural data, and again requested support in the form of official subscriptions. By mid-1878 there were 330 official subscriptions, at an annual cost of Rs 3960.[8]

Once again, this subscription policy was challenged in the Executive Council, and once again A.O. Hume came to the

defence of 'my friend Mr. Knight'. He urged the support of the
Indian Agriculturist, but only if Knight would agree to exclude
all political discussions and criticisms of the government. He
explained in a severe but incisive critique of the editor:

He is very sharp and clever in a small way, writes well at times, and is
far better read and educated than would at first be supposed....But he
altogether lacks [a sense of proportion]. He will slur an important point,
make a mountain out of a molehill,...will seize an idea, and run away with
it at such a pace that no adverse views can ever catch his mind up.[9]

Knight had 'about the best intentions and the worst judgment
of any man I know', he said, and described him as 'the kindest-
hearted man in private life, and would not, I believe, hurt a fly,
but he has a vile-tempered pen....'

The *Friend of India*, long identified with missionaries, now
became Knight's special vehicle. His evangelical drive had
gradually mellowed, and he pondered over the meager results
of the missionaries' labours. A Hindu newspaper claimed that
evangelicals did not understand the real nature of Hinduism
and should recognize 'the truth that is in Hindooism' before
they are qualified 'to recommend to Hindoos the truth that is
in Christianity'. Knight reprinted this and observed: 'Until our
Christianity can a little better stand this test of the precepts of
our Master—say in his Sermon on the Mount—we very much
fear we shall not soon overcome the world.'[10]

Meanwhile, Northbrook's council followed its ouster of Knight
from the government with a resolution on 8 July 1875, forbidding
ownership or management of the press by government officers,
to end any ambiguity or doubt on the matter.[11] Knight later
interpreted it:

Lord Northbrook wanted the absolute power to silence any pen in the
country that displeased him. He sent an express order to Mr. Knight
to cease all connection with the Press, even as a contributor; and
when it was pointed out to him, that he had no power to do so under
existing rules, he induced the Home Government to sanction this vital
change in them, while dishonestly and weakly professing that his
new Resolution was issued simply to 'make the existing orders on the
subject clearly understood....'[12]

He called it 'paltry trickery' by 'the feeblest ruler India ever had'.

However, the viceroy had larger worries. Early in 1874, when he had finished hardly two years of the customary five-year term, the British electorate had replaced his Liberal Party with the Conservatives under the imperialistic Earl of Beaconsfield (Disraeli). The assertive Marquess of Salisbury became the new Secretary of State for India. Though he and Northbrook assured each other that they could work together, significant differences soon appeared. Salisbury considered the viceroy and his council a branch of the British government and subject to orders from the cabinet, while Northbrook considered the Government of India a separate entity, obliged to protect the interests of India.[13] He resisted demands for the removal of India's tariff on cotton cloth and for a more forward frontier policy, especially in Afghanistan (see pp. 165–6). The Baroda case also rankled; Salisbury had embarrassed the Raj by overriding its decision. In September of 1875, Northbrook told Salisbury that he wished to be replaced at the end of that year, citing unspecified health and family concerns.[14] The Conservatives appointed Lord Robert Lytton, a more colourful and outgoing man with a diplomatic and literary background.

Knight tried to persuade the new viceroy to adopt a more open press policy than that of the departed Northbrook. The editor, as always, championed a free and critical press; even during the Rebellion he feared the emergency licensing act would suppress the 'watchdog' role of the newspapers.[15] The Raj, he often said, needed to open its meetings and explain its policies to the press; even his discussion of land reassessments in Surat district concluded by citing 'the folly of keeping such procedures from the public, until the time has gone by when criticism can be of any use....When will the Government learn the necessity of admitting the public to its counsels?'[16] As in 1859 and 1860, he said that an adversarial press was especially needed in an unrepresentative State (see p. 76); 'to expect the Indian press usually to support what the Government does, is to mistake its vocation altogether.'[17]

Two months after Lytton became viceroy, his private secretary, Owen Tudor Burne, sent a letter to nine leading editors (all European), expressing a wish for better government-press relations and allowing the press 'due facility' to obtain 'reliable' information on matters of public interest.[18] Knight replied with his fullest explanation ever of the need for a critical press within the British Raj.

The Government of India, he said, was necessarily a despotism, which made a free and critical press all the more essential as a check on officials. However, it needed some better way to explain the course of its proceedings, its views, purposes, and desires. An 'editors' room' had been tried, with informative releases made available to editors, but it had deteriorated into a sham, 'until the *pabulum* put on the table was not worth appropriating'. Knight proposed an official press bureau to review the press and provide needed information. It would be headed by a sympathetic man, not an official monitor and certainly not a censor, but more of a go-between,

a broad and genial man, endowed with prudence and plenty of commonsense, whose special office it would be to invite the confidence of every journal in the country and establish friendly relations therewith. It would be for him to communicate freely what information can be given them and to tell them frankly what it was deemed necessary to reserve.[19]

Was Knight angling for the job for himself? Perhaps. His old Bombay friend, Dr George Birdwood, proposed Knight as director. 'We intended nothing of the kind' he responded coyly [20] Lytton accepted the press bureau idea but delayed implementing it until April 1877, when the position of press officer (also called press commissioner) was created as a one-year trial, and the appointment went to Roper Lethbridge, of the Bengal Educational Service. [21]

By then Knight had resumed his role of angry critic. Instead of an improvement, he wrote, Lytton's 'anti-press' campaign had surpassed Northbrook's prohibiting resolution. The government, he said, had 'openly established an Inquisition, into the authorship of certain editorial articles' in the *Friend of India*, and had punished the author heavily. 'And yet it has never pretended that the articles were not true....'[22] The government had tried to silence those who knew where reform was needed, he asserted. 'Whoever has a wrong to redress or a right to assert, must be allowed to proclaim it, with a Government that conducts everything with closed doors, and contemptuously defies public opinion....'[23]

Admirers saw Knight as Bayard, the Peerless Knight of legend, charging into heroic battle against tyranny; to others, he appeared as Don Quixote tilting at windmills.

IMPERIAL POMP, IMPERIAL JUSTICE: DIVERGING VIEWS

Knight's critical eye surveyed the entire Indian landscape, beyond the problems of press and personalities. India, he acknowledged, needed British investment capital for development and diminished poverty. Indians who possessed wealth sank it into showy luxuries such as mansions, jewels, and fancy clothes, and so had little for 'reproductive use'. However, since the Rebellion European money had been pouring into India for factories and plantations, railways and irrigation works, and government bonds, with an annual interest given at twelve million sterling. This was paid in Indian products, so that India deceptively appeared to have a favourable balance of trade. 'India pays no political tribute to England,' he wrote, 'but this industrial tribute is larger than any the world has ever known.'[24]

He again blamed the poverty of the Bengal cultivators on the zamindari land settlement. Formerly hereditary local squires, the new zamindars were usually impersonal companies or disinterested agents and lawyers of remote landowners.[25] In the rest of British India, the Raj was the 'Great Landowner' but had never taken 'the least practical interest in the agriculture of the country, nor attempted to improve the condition of the millions of its tenantry.'[26] He urged creation of a Department of Agriculture to help.

Another problem was the restrictions and insults to which educated and talented Indians were subjected. Knight scolded his fellow Anglo-Indians for fighting every proposal to advance job opportunities and rights of Indians. Englishmen deny any possibility of Indians being their equal, he wrote, and consider the whole country British property, to be governed in British interests 'by that most indisputable of rights, the right of conquest'.[27] Therefore, Indians enjoy only those rights which Europeans allow them. He believed that India's future lay with the educated middle classes, and the Raj should encourage them and open career opportunities. Instead they were treated 'no better than Helots destined to remain hewers of wood and drawers of water' (mixing Greek and Biblical metaphors).[28] He reiterated these views in the *Friend of India* of 3 June and 19 August 1876, and the *Statesman* of 1 January and 6 February 1877.

Knight especially deplored the Conservative move to lower the age limit for the Indian Civil Service examination from twenty-one to nineteen in Britain, preceded by two years of British schooling. This was seen as a deliberate move to eliminate Indian entrants to the elite CSI for, as Knight said, 'no father will send his son across thousands of miles of sea to run the risk of a competitive examination at the age of sixteen or seventeen.'[29] An appointive system, he continued, risked becoming a patronage system; if good candidates are sought, they should be selected in a competitive test.

Knight particularly supported the middle-class college and university graduates of Calcutta, often ridiculed as 'Bengali Baboos' for their narrow learning, pompous airs, and quests for careers as clerks, schoolteachers, or *vakils* (solicitors or pleaders). Their stilted, sometimes comic 'Baboo English' amused Anglo-Indians (rarely fluent themselves in foreign languages). These scoffers included His Excellency the Viceroy, who wrote that 'the only political representatives of native opinion are the Baboos, whom we have educated to write semi-seditious articles in the native Press, and who really represent nothing but the social anomaly of their own position....'[30] Lytton claimed he had made 'a careful study of native character' in his first three months in India,[31] and he had concluded that India must be ruled through its 'natural leaders', the princes and other chiefs. He oozed contempt for the educated middle classes, whom Knight saw as the key to India's future; the viceroy contrasted them with 'the manlier races...which, if unrestrained by us, would soon grind the whole of Baboodom into powder.'[32]

LYTTON'S DURBAR

For the viceroy the way to hold India was to secure the loyalty of the traditional ruling princes,[33] and he saw his great opportunity when Queen Victoria assumed the title of Empress of India. When Beaconsfield steered the Royal Titles bill through Parliament in March of 1876, Lytton wrote to him that it would be 'ridiculous' to proclaim the new title merely through circulars when 'a few acts of liberality' would be received 'throughout the whole of India with energetic demonstrations of enthusiasm'. It would particularly give 'the great feudal aristocracy' of India an occasion 'to rally round the British Crown as its feudal head' and also rebut Liberal critics in Parliament. He unveiled his plan for a magnificent 'Imperial Assemblage' to dazzle the princes. Presentation of salutes and banners, he remarked, would be 'much more effective than any political concession'.[34] He admitted to Salisbury that 'your Council may pooh-pooh as trivial and silly, my proposal about the presentation of banners & c., and the institution of an Indian peerage,' but 'the further east you go, the greater becomes the importance of a bit of bunting'.[35]

With the cabinet's approval, Lytton proceeded with his elaborate plans and preparations for the assemblage to convene in the old imperial capital of Delhi on 1 January 1877. (Most writers call it the 'Delhi Durbar'.) The viceroy soon reported an enthusiastic acceptance from all the principal princes, 'including the nizam, who was considered most doubtful'.[36]

Hyderabad and its nizam might well have spoiled the party. By common consent it was foremost among the princely states (only the nizam was addressed as His *Exalted* Highness). In 1876, however, HEH was ten years old and relied on his regent and dewan, Sir Salar Jung, who had quarrelled angrily with the British Raj over its grasp of the Berar districts (see pp. 43–5). Hyderabad had always considered itself an independent ally of the British; nowhere did their treaties mention 'subsidiary' or 'paramount' status. Would the nizam and Salar Jung publicly acknowledge Victoria as Empress of India or stay aloof?

It was a dilemma for the dewan. He had helped the British by keeping Hyderabad out of the Rebellion, only to have the Viceroy, Lord Canning, declare Britain the 'paramount power' in India, heir to the collapsed Mughal Empire and its claims of allegiance. But had the nizams ever become sovereign, or had they always been titular feudatories of the Mughals? Whatever legal experts might say, the British in fact flaunted their power unrestrained, as though 'might makes right'. But they saw a potential challenger in the strong and shrewd Salar Jung.

Disputes arose, the first being the public acknowledgement of British sovereignty. Another was the peremptory seizure and retention of Berar by the Raj. A third grew out of the construction and financing of the Nizam's State Railway. The British marvel of rapid railway construction peaked in 1871 with the completion of lines linking their major cities, including those connecting Bombay and Madras at Raichur, on the south-western edge of the nizam's territory. In 1869 the Government of India had induced Nizam Afzal-ud-Daulah to commission his own railroad, linking Hyderabad city with this main line. Once he had committed, though, the devil appeared in altered details which boosted the final cost well beyond the estimated Rs 11 million and assured a steady financial drain on the nizam.[37] It far exceeded the resources (or prudence) of local moneylenders; a large external loan was needed. The Government of India would have gladly arranged it but would have required a first lien on Hyderabad's revenues, constricting its credit and freedom of action. This Salar Jung was determined to avoid.[38]

The Raj wanted Hyderabad (and every other princely state) to channel all outside business through its officials, starting with the court residents. It retained its perennial suspicion of all outsiders as persons beyond its control and thus potential troublemakers. Salar Jung, on the other hand, felt he was being bound (and sometimes slighted) by petty officials in Calcutta. If he could present his cases, particularly on Berar, directly to the statesmen and people of Britain, where he was remembered for his help in the Rebellion, they would be far better received. Therefore, during the 1870s he engaged several private agents who convinced him that they had the ears of influential officials, journalists, and other important persons.[39] One such was J. Seymour Keay, a money manager who had been Hyderabad head for W. Nicholls and Company, a managerial octopus whose far-flung clients happened to include Knight's *Statesman*. Keay was employed by Salar Jung in 1872, initially to raise funds in Britain for railroad construction. A joint-stock company was created which purchased the assets of the Nizam's State Railway and, as a private corporation, obtained the consent of the Secretary of State to market shares in London.

With a six per cent annual guarantee they were snapped up. The viceroy (Northbrook in 1875) had been bypassed; he angrily demanded that Salisbury never again give such an approval.[40]

Lord Lytton, during his first few months as viceroy, developed a dread of Salar Jung's strength and purpose. The dewan, he said, had arranged three personal appeals to Queen Victoria for restoration of the Berars. The 'best practical solution' of the Salar Jung problem, he wrote, might be 'the fall and removal from office of that Minister, if it can be effected by the spontaneous action of his own colleagues.'[41]

Lytton had nightmarish visions of Sir Salar building a hostile 'Mahomedan' power in central India, which would join invading Turks from Central Asia as the advance wedge of a Russian army. 'We can't afford to encourage the development of a strong Mahomedan state in the centre of our own power,' he wrote.[42] (Actually, the Turks and the Russians were the bitterest of enemies during the entire nineteenth century, and British policy since before the Crimean War had been to protect the Ottoman Empire against the Russians.)

Salisbury, who also seems to have considered all Asians simple-minded, replied that the Berars must never be restored to the nizam, because the rest of India would conclude that Britain had become a retreating, not an advancing, power. But he wanted to encourage Salar Jung's raising capital in England; it would soak up his surplus revenue and leave him in thrall to 'a host of inexorable creditors' who, in case of misgovernment, would press the Raj to bring Hyderabad under 'more direct control'.[43]

Salar Jung's next move was to visit England in the summer of 1876, ostensibly a social call on invitation of his friend, the Duke of Sutherland. It was a social success but a political waste, as officials would not negotiate. He returned to an India whose officials were abuzz with plans and preparations for the Imperial Assemblage and the proclamation of Victoria as Empress of India.

At first Salar Jung reportedly did not want the young nizam and himself to go to Delhi, but the nizam's family persuaded him to accept.[44] While in England, Beaconsfield had approved his submitting a new petition for return of the Berars, or so he had understood, but when he did so, the resident, Sir Richard Meade, refused to receive it and declared the issue closed.

Lytton even called this new petition an act of insubordination; he now demanded a letter from Salar Jung acknowledging in writing Victoria's sovereignty. When Sir Salar reached Delhi for the durbar, the viceroy told him that his letter was unsatisfactory and demanded that he change it. After several exchanges and attempts, the humiliated dewan submitted an acceptable text.[45]

The gorgeous pageant came off as planned: the speeches were spoken, the title was proclaimed, and the sixty-three princes who attended in person had their assigned interviews with the viceroy. The official historian declared that the event 'will stand out for all time as an epoch in the history of India'.[46] Salar Jung, responding for the chiefs of India, offered their 'hearty congratulations' to the queen and prayed for her long life and enduring prosperity.[47] The Delhi ceremony was echoed 'at every English Station and Native Court throughout the Empire'.[48]

Knight had tepidly supported the Imperial Assemblage. He recognized it as a display of political unification but questioned such extravagance at a time when famine raged in Bombay and Madras presidencies.[49] He wanted the Raj to reciprocate all that popular adulation with some boon or favour for the people of India (not just the princes). When none appeared, the editor simply exploded:

The Viceroy's proclamation speech has certainly disappointed us. The sentences are all well turned, the compliments sweetly honeyed and almost too profuse....We look in vain for any backbone of performance to give the speech substantial worth. It is a mere mellifluous river of words....

We are sick of seeing Britannia playing the part of a sweet-lipped, honey-tongued mistress, throwing caressing arms round the neck of India, and murmuring love-speeches and transcendental promises. Such 'fiddle-faddle, sweet flirtation' is unproductive, and tends to become disgusting....

We think we have had enough and more than enough of stars and ribbons, banners and medals, certificates of merit, and all such cheap and meaningless vanities....The people and Princes of India, are to be forever treated as children, to be put off with pattings and praises, and kept from sulkiness by such toys as stars and medals, and parchment certificates. It is not statesmanship: but Beaconsfield 'fireworks'.[50]

Soon after, the Conservative-led Parliament spurned Indian objections and enacted the lower age-limit for the CSI. The year-old Indian Association responded with a large public meeting in Calcutta on 24 March 1877. Speakers called for protests and petitions against this harmful action.[51] Knight was delighted that 'all sections of the native community have thrown aside for the nonce their differences and antagonisms, and stood shoulder to shoulder, and declared themselves with one voice.' This showed the promise of a future political life for all the people of India. He called the Indian Association a missionary group which was trying to send agents all over the country and establish branches in every important town. Its memorial to Parliament 'perhaps marks a new stage in the political development of India, the germ of a new power destined to grow till it becomes giant and irresistible for good or evil—the peaceful constitutional pressure of native public opinion on the British Parliament....'[52]

The immediate step was a pioneering political mission. An Indian Association leader, Surendranath Banerjea, toured the major cities of British India by the new railroads during the summer of 1877, addressing (in English) local activists and students, urging them to unite, organize, and work for all-India causes.[53] India's nationalist movement had begun.

If Lord Lytton even noticed these events, he never committed such notice to paper. During that same summer he and Meade, his Hyderabad agent, were busily plotting the downfall of Salar Jung. His letters refer repeatedly to the dewan's dubious and reluctant attitude, his clandestine talks with other princes, his training and equipping of a new military force in Hyderabad, his continuing intrigues in Britain through friends and agents, etc. It approached obsession: 'the sooner we suppress Salar Jung the better. He is the most dangerous man in all India, and, like a horse, or a woman, that has once turned vicious, thoroughly irreclaimable.'[54]

One tactic already used by the British was to build up Salar Jung's dynastic rivals, the *paigah* family, commanders of the household troops, whose head was called *amir-i-kabir*, or premier nobleman. Rafi-ud-din Khan, the amir-i-kabir in 1869, was made co-regent of the infant nizam along with Salar Jung, with whom he worked. But Rafi died in April of 1877, and his half-brother, Rashid-ud-din Khan (usually referred to by his previous title, *vikar-ul-umrah*), assumed the position of amir-i-kabir. Rashid, however, had a disreputable past, including an attempted bribe and/or swindle of the official British resident; the British had barred him from official functions.[55] He was also suspected of participating in an assassination attempt against the dewan. Salar Jung refused to accept this enemy as co-regent; he threatened to resign as dewan first. Lytton jumped for joy at this prospect ('A godsend, if we can force Salar Jung to resign on this question'[56]); he could dispose of his antagonist with no bloodstains showing. But Salar Jung stood his ground: he would neither resign nor accept the new amir-i-kabir as a partner.

After several months of increasingly-angry exchanges, the Government of India peremptorily proclaimed the amir not just co-regent, but co-administrator of the state. Meade asked authorization to remove Salar Jung from office. Salisbury responded by wire that if the dewan still refused to accept his new partner, he (Meade) should proclaim a new minister; 'Personal force should be avoided if possible, but you should take such precautions, military and other, as you may deem expedient.'[57] British officers in Hyderabad were alerted and summoned. Meade later reported to Lytton, 'I was quite prepared to carry out, if necessary, the minister's removal, and should have had no doubt of my full power to do so....I carefully explained to him exactly how the case stood, as regarded the action of the Government...'[58]

The minister did not yield until he had had a private conversation with the assistant resident, Major C.B. Euan Smith, who later reported that 'after much discussion, the Minister at last said that of course he was helpless, that he must yield....'[59] Exactly what Euan Smith said is not known, but Salar Jung inferred that he would be arrested, deported, and exiled if he did not yield (as the ex-Gaekwar of Baroda had been two years earlier). Faced with a virtual coup d'etat and perhaps his own imprisonment, Salar Jung surrendered and accepted the amir. He later explained that his sense of duty did not allow him to abandon the child-nizam. He feared the British might even have used this as a pretext to annex Hyderabad.[60]

So Lytton won: he humiliated his supposed adversary, forced him to bow to Victoria's sovereignty, and then forced him to accept his enemy as partner. Having thereby 'saved' the British

Empire, Lytton could mock the educated middle classes. Knight by contrast, understood that India's future lay with those young men, not with princes or their ministers, but he was drawn into this Hyderabad maelstrom by his hatred of injustice. Four years later he would reveal these facts, previously hidden in confidential files and private letters, endangering his newspapers and his personal reputation to champion the cause of an unappreciative Salar Jung.[61]

KNIGHT AND THE TORIES

Given Knight's acidic attack on the Imperial Assemblage, Lord Lytton might have marked him as another 'irreclaimable' enemy. Similarly, Knight's angry opposition to the lowering of the CSI examination age and the cruel treatment of Salar Jung should have soured him on Conservative rule. However, events were not so straightforward; it took three disputes in 1878–9 to open the gap between them: the cotton tariff, the Vernacular Press Act, and the invasion of Afghanistan.

Knight even wrote a deferential and supportive letter to the viceroy dated 17 July 1877, after having been his dinner guest. In it he lauded Lytton's 'sympathetic attitude toward the Press' and felt Lytton agreed with him that fears of a Russian advance toward India were 'most unworthy', and had 'profound contempt' for that notion as a part of the Conservative programme. He called Salisbury 'one of the strong men of whom our country can boast' and concluded:

frankly I am touched by your generosity towards the public press, and I am emboldened to address you thus, and Lord Salisbury has my profound and absolute respect. I am tired of Whig insincerities and weakness, and would have India long repose under the strong sympathetic rule we now have.

Though a Liberal, I hate 'party' men, and Conservative rule has always been the best rule India has had in my time, and I sincerely long for its continuance....[62]

This puzzling letter runs against the current of Knight's writing both before and after. There is no doubt about its authenticity; the letter is in Knight's handwriting, on the *Statesman* stationery. There are three possible explanations: first, Knight was dazzled and charmed by Lytton's amity after his humiliations by

Northbrook and Temple; second, Knight wanted something from the viceroy, perhaps an appointment. If he was eyeing that press commissionership, he was too late; Roper Lethbridge had received the permanent appointment two months earlier, and when he went on leave, Knight's old nemesis, C.E. Buckland, got the interim job. Third, Knight in his haste wrote the wrong date. It sounds as though he actually wrote it in July of 1876, when Lytton was newly arrived and disputes had not yet arisen. One can only speculate.

Knight's views on India's tariffs also shifted with time. What began as a question of economic principle became a question of fiscal prudence, then one of political assertion. Knight, with his classical liberal background, had been taught that tariffs and all other impediments to free trade were foolish if not outright immoral. In his 1866 speech to the Manchester Chamber of Commerce he agreed with the chamber's position that the Raj should repeal its tariff on imports of cotton cloth. He wanted India to close its custom houses entirely and rely on 'the one great and inexhaustible source of revenue in India—the land!'[63]

A decade later, though, neither the land nor its potential revenue appeared inexhaustible. Costs of governance kept rising, and local revenue officers were unable to squeeze higher yields from the cultivators, despite the exhortations of their superiors (and the *Indian Economist*). Knight complained: 'We have managed our finances so unintelligently in the past, and administered the land revenue in particular with such deplorable weakness, that we are no longer in a position to dispense with the custom house.'[64] Far from closed, the custom house was doing a brisk business in 1876–7, bringing in a needed £1,275,000.[65] Most of this, £811,000, came from the tariff on imported cotton cloth (essentially from Britain, presumably), although the rate had been cut to 5 per cent of piecegoods and 3½ per cent on cotton twist.[66] Knight clearly preferred this to the hated income tax, which he always considered unsuitable for India (see pp. 58–61).

Knight violated another dictum of Adam Smith when he argued that Indian cotton industries should receive some protection from British competition. Cotton cloth had historically been India's staple export to the lands of the Middle East and South-east Asia, sometimes East Africa and China, and, in the seventeenth and eighteenth centuries, even Europe.[67] British industrialization and mass production led to their capture of those export markets in the early nineteenth century, causing underemployment and poverty among Indian spinners and weavers. British millowners then invaded India's domestic market. Indian entrepreneurs tried to recapture a share of that market in the 1860s and 1870s, building their own factories to challenge the British imports.[68] Knight had long promoted economic development as the answer to Indian poverty, and he feared that if these pioneering enterprises were drowned in a flood of cut-rate imports, the setback would be a disaster. He admitted that this duty served to protect the products of the Bombay cotton mills, 'but we say it is a justifiable protection, while this new industry is in the stage of experiment.'[69]

British industrialists complained noisily about this new competition, and in 1876 Lord Salisbury was determined to remove a tax which he called 'wrong in principle, injurious in its practical effect, and self-destructive in its operation',[70] although most officials in India opposed the repeal. Knight saw this as a political challenge; he ascribed to the Secretary of State an 'imperious attitude toward the Government of India' and 'an exploit worthy of the perfection of despotism'.[71] He set out his view of imperial control:

We are quite prepared to give the paramount power to Parliament to control Indian affairs our fullest support, provided it be exercised through legitimate channels, but if Lord Salisbury's views were carried out in their entirety, the Indian Legislature would soon be reduced to the position of such 'wee' councils as Ceylon or Jamaica, which simply meet to pass the resolutions of the Colonial Office.[72]

Knight saw here the 'miserable weakness of Government by electric cable'.[73] The new technology had already changed the dynamics of imperial governance, but had it also changed their principles? Previous viceroys, he wrote, had stated that they were duty-bound to protect the interests of India. The viceregal council believed that the repeal of the cotton tariffs would hurt India. But Lytton's 'superior intelligence' insisted that there was no conflict of interest between India and Manchester.[74]

The dispute dragged on until 13 March 1879, when Lytton used his extraordinary powers to overrule the majority of his council and exempt certain categories of imported cottons from the tariff, costing India's treasury £250,000.[75] Knight's *Friend of India* was predictably outraged at the Tories. This nascent industry was so important for India's future, it said, that a 'wise and honest' government would have been more cautious in removing tariff protection.

But Lord Lytton's Government, we are sorry to say, is neither wise nor honest. It is a Government that lives, as Tory Governments ever do live, by pandering to privileges and to party necessities. We do not mean that Liberal Governments are free from this reproach, but the Tory has no shame in this respect, and does not know what 'uprightness' means.[76]

A mass protest meeting was held in Calcutta's Town Hall on 27 March to articulate and harness the anger. Sir John Strachey, finance member of the council, dismissed those protests and the 'foolish calumny' of blaming party politics. 'Popular opinion in India', he later wrote, 'had always, in regard to questions of fiscal reform, been obstructive and ignorant....'[77] Further exemptions from the cotton duties followed.

Imports of British cloth grew without the tariff, but Indian mills, far from collapsing, grew even faster.[78] The lost tax revenue faded as a fiscal issue, but the scorn of the Raj for public protests was remembered. The plight of those truly hurt, the cottage cotton-spinner and weaver, also reverberated as the anti-imperialist movement grew.[79] When Indians wanted to retaliate against the Bengal Partition of 1905, it was the mass boycott and destruction of British-made cloth that became their main weapon. When M.K. Gandhi, who had been a lad of ten in 1879, took charge of the nationalist movement, he made hand-spinning a daily duty of Congress members, and the humble *charkha* (spinning wheel) adorned the Congress flag. Lytton and Strachey were long gone by then but not forgotten.

The Vernacular Press Act was another measure through which Lytton and his Conservatives lost popularity while gaining nothing. ('Vernacular' means an indigenous spoken language, but the British loosely applied the term to all Asian language publications.) As explained earlier (see pp. 2, 19–20), Indian newspapers were usually small, with few news gathering resources. Therefore, they lifted articles from each other or from the nearest large urban papers, with their rough translations peppered with editorial comments.[80]

The Government of India, though scornful of Indian opinion, felt a need to know the messages of these often-obscure journals, particularly those who were spreading 'disloyal' or 'dangerous' sentiments. Therefore, in 1863 the imperial government ordered the provinces to compile, translate, and summarize the contents of their vernaculars. The Bombay and Bengal governments hired translators and published their summaries, leaving invaluable records of early public opinion. Other provinces, with fewer papers, did a skimpy and haphazard job.[81]

The newspapers of Bengal, watching developments in the Anglo-Indian press, saw in 1875 the start of a new and interesting member. Perhaps the first to cite this was the *Akbar-ul-Akhiar* of Muzafferpore, which wrote on 15 June that some English papers, especially the *Indian Statesman*, had been urging the necessity of government looking after poor whites.'[82] A sampling of the 1876 reports showed a growing awareness by the 'vernaculars' that they had a friend and anti-government critic in Calcutta:

1. *Sahachar*, Calcutta, 12 June: 'The proposal of our liberal-minded contemporary, the *Statesman*, to confer district judgeships on natives, has been severely condemned.... But the *Statesman* says the natives are by no means less qualified to discharge judicial duties most satisfactorily.'

2. *Bharat Mihir*, Mymensingh, 22 June, criticized the British for 'dishonest means', and continued: 'Our contemporary of the *Statesman* is revealing these artifices in his discussions about the public income and expenditures.'

3. *Som Prakash*, Calcutta, 27 November, noted Knight's efforts to have records published in controversial cases.

4. *Behar Bandhu*, Patna, 29 November, wrote of the *Statesman*: 'Blessed be this paper for its bravery, ever since its birth, in not having given the Ruler of Bengal, a moment for breathing time.'

5. *Qasid*, an Urdu weekly of Patna, 11 December: 'The *Statesman* is a truthful, free, just and good paper....'[83]

This was just the visible and specified tip of the iceberg. No one journal 'created' Indian public opinion, but Knight's paper clearly helped stimulate, stir, and focus it.

Earlier, officials had dismissed the 'vernaculars' as irresponsible but ephemeral, their editors as mischievous boys pelting mudballs or annoying insects not worth swatting. By the mid-1870s, though, some officials were worrying. William Digby, editor of the *Madras Times*, analysed the faults of Indian papers in a thoughtful article and foresaw the rise of a press which would be 'intensely nationalistic' and progressive.[84] Knight's *Indian Economist* ran a long article by Frederick S. Lely, a Bombay civil servant, attacking distortions in the Indian press and urging the government to issue an official gazette as an antidote. Knight endorsed this in a preface to Lely's essay, calling it 'a fatal mistake to assume that our Government can really commend itself to the people, by the force of its own merits, in the face of calumnies and persistent misrepresentations of the Native press.'[85]

Amrita Bazar Patrika, then a bilingual Anglo-Bengali weekly, seemed especially skilled at drawing blood. On the poisoning of Colonel Phayre in Baroda (see pp. 126–7), the *Patrika* asked whether it was a greater crime to poison an obscure colonel or to 'emasculate a nation'. This caught the eye of Lord Salisbury, who urged Northbrook to prosecute under the Indian Penal Code. But the viceroy rejected the idea, remarking that this was no worse than what English papers were saying. One official spoke of the difficulty of getting such a conviction from an Indian jury, while another noted that such a prosecution would cause greater excitement than the original attacks.[86]

When the more combustible Lytton became viceroy, he heeded officials who wanted a new law for press control. Drafted and circulated late in 1877, it was limited to publications in Asian languages, although Lytton remarked:

I cannot but attribute the extravagant improprieties of the Vernacular Press largely...to the bad example set to Native journalists by their English contemporaries in India. Indeed, however disloyal or profligate may be the Vernacular Press of this country, it is only European journalism in India that can seriously embarrass or weaken the Government.[87]

No names were mentioned.

Legislation was drafted, sent to the local governments for comment, then enacted on 14 March 1878, as 'emergency' legislation—Act IX of 1878. Under its terms any local magistrate or presidency police commissioner could determine 'seditious matter' or whatever would 'excite feelings of discontent' against the government or 'hatred and contempt' between different communities. A substantial bond could be demanded of the publisher and printer, which would be forfeited if the offence were repeated.

The Vernacular Press Act turned out to be a fumble and a farce from the beginning to the end of its short life. First, the terminology was so vague and the hazard of abuse by local police so great that a circular letter was sent out a week later, stating that no action was to be taken without the previous sanction of the viceroy.[88] Second, Sir Ashley Eden, Lieutenant Governor of Bengal, was so eager that he began enforcing the law retroactively. This was clearly illegal; the viceroy rebuked him, and he apologized.[89] Third, the law hit the wrong target. *Amrita Bazar Patrika*, the most obvious culprit, escaped its clutches by promptly dropping its Bengali columns (mostly advertising) and becoming an all-English weekly, while the only journal stopped by the law was a respectable Bengali weekly, *Som Prakash*.[90] Fourth, Gladstone denounced the act in his parliamentary campaign,[91] and it became a Liberal weapon against the embarrassed Conservatives. The Liberals won the 1880 elections and repealed the Vernacular Press Act. After the *Som Prakash* case there is no record of any attempt to enforce it, but the newspapers continued to lament loudly that they were 'shackled' and 'muzzled'. Buckland also claimed that in 1879 'the tone of the Native Press generally improved' because of the act.[92] However, a perusal of the *Reports on Native Papers* before and after imposition of the act discerned no weakening of rhetoric nor dodging of hot topics in their editorial comments. They still enjoyed twisting the lion's tail.

With Robert Knight's long championing of a free and critical press,[93] *The Statesman* should have fought vigorously against the Vernacular Press Act, but it did not. When this bill was suddenly enacted, Knight was away, touring upper India, and the acting editor was William Riach (see pp. 193-4).[94] Riach generally shared Knight's views, but his editorial leader of 16 March (written the day after passage of the act) voiced cautious approval of it; it called the vernacular press 'unflinchingly opposed to British supremacy in any shape or form' and that the government would have been foolish to ignore such a dangerous weapon.[95] This does not sound like Knight.

As other European papers (including the rival *Englishman*) began to criticize the new law, the *Statesman*'s support of it softened. A week after its passage, the paper warned the government not to ignore complaints of the vernaculars; a better approach would be to remove their grievances.[96] On 12 April it cautioned against overzealous enforcement of the new act; 'really treasonable and injurious writing ought to be suppressed, but we desire to be assured in every case where this act is enforced what the real character of the offence has been.' Then came the *Som Prakash* case, showing how the government could 'crush at a blow every vernacular paper in Bengal'.[97] The *Statesman* had come home.

In sum, Knight, despite his liberal background, had not been dogmatically anti-Tory in 1876. He even wrote that he thought the Conservatives better for India than the Liberals. However, as the Salisbury–Lytton programme unfolded, Knight perceived, on issue after issue, that theirs was not the path to India's progress, prosperity, or self-rule. The heavy-handed rule from Westminster was evident in the Baroda verdict and the repeal of the cotton tariffs; in their contempt for the rising middle class ('Bengali Baboos'), which fuelled the Vernacular Press Act as well as the reduced civil service opportunities; in the obsessive vendetta against Salar Jung, and, as will be shown, in the costly campaign against an imaginary Russian threat. He would vent it all in his London paper in 1879.

IMPERIAL DEFENCE AND FAMINE FINGER-POINTING

Despite his misadventures, Knight in 1878 still considered the British Empire a benevolence for those fortunate enough to nurse its nourishing bosom. Mistakes were made, and foolish and corrupt men sometimes attained high office, but mistakes would be corrected, and the foolish and corrupt would be replaced by the wiser, abler, and more principled. In fact, the duty of the conscientious journalist was to expose those failings as frequently and vigorously as necessary. For instance, he reminded readers of the 'shame and dishonour' staining Britain and its queen in the abuse of Salar Jung: 'The English people desire to see just rule in India, and the Government, in its strength and power, will not rule justly. There is but one way of correcting the evil, and that is by exposure....'[98]

Knight's call of conscience surmounted the borders of India. In 1872 he denounced the British governor of Jamaica who had hanged a popular political leader, and his parliamentary defenders.[99] In 1875 he condemned the 'hasty, inconsiderate, and unauthorized' intervention by the Governor of the Straits Settlements in the local disorders in the State of Perak, which opened the way for British dominance of the Malay Peninsula (on urging of the businessmen of Singapore).[100] In his first editorial days, in 1857, Knight had disparaged the British occupation of Persian lands (see p. 29), and he often revisited the blundering 1839–40 invasion of Afghanistan.

The Raj would have feared any strong power approaching the borders of India. Despite their public bravado, the British saw India as a tinderbox awaiting any outside spark. The 'Russian menace' had replaced the 'French menace' well before their march through Central Asia in the 1860s.[101] Their conquest of the Khanate of Khiva in 1873 took them to the edge of Afghanistan and upset Whitehall, where Disraeli and Salisbury took charge in 1874. Lytton responded with his persecution of Salar Jung, whom he fantasized as plotting a pro-Russian Muslim revolt (see p. 153).

Knight, as usual, scoffed at this 'almost insane dread' and saw 'no danger to India from the Russian advance, but that which our own childish folly is by itself creating.'[102] Order in India might be upset, not by real Russians, but by the Foreign Office panic at imaginary ones, 'coming down in immense hordes from the North and bringing with [them] the intervening Mahommedan States to sweep us into the sea.'[103] Three months later, he even approved the Russian approach:

We believe that Russia has about that much serious thought of invading India as we have of storming St. Petersburg, and that our attitude on this subject must be a source of constant amusement in the inner circles of the Russian court. We further hold that Russia has as true and legitimate a mission in Central, as we have in Southern Asia;...and that, viewed rightly, her advance is a real gain to civilization and to humanity....[104]

Afghanistan, with its militantly independent tribes, had a well-earned reputation of ungovernability, but the mid-1870s saw a relatively effective and respected ruler, the Amir of Kabul, Sher Ali. The amir watched the Russians edge closer from one side, the British from the other. He tried to maintain Afghan independence by neither favouring nor alarming anyone. He declined to receive a British mission at Kabul, much less a permanent court resident (who implicitly would control his external relationships). Such a move, he said, would upset his proud and excitable subjects. This stand satisfied Northbrook, but not his proud and excitable successor. Lytton was confident that he could outwit a 'half-barbaric' Afghan to gain a British advantage.[105]

Knight lacked access to the diplomatic dispatches and private correspondence, but he saw what was happening. He wrote:

At this very moment we are contemplating another advance into Affghanistan [sic], and trying to persuade the Amir of Cabul to permit us to send a force to Kandahar and Herat. Parliament knows nothing of it, and the country is in imminent danger...of getting involved in Affghanistan, the result of which no one can foresee.[106]

Actually, Knight himself did foresee a repetition of the futile 1839 invasion and 'the massacre of the forces that were the instruments of our sin.'[107]

British policy was keyed to stopping the Russian invasion of the Ottoman Empire, then approaching Istanbul and the Turkish straits. Their military advance was anticipated in Central Asia as well as the Balkans. Knight, whose interest and understanding of frontier matters was stimulated by his friend, Colonel Osborn, continued to ridicule such 'Russophobia'.[108]

As stated, Knight went on tour early in 1878, leaving Riach in charge of the *Statesman*. He went to examine the state of military readiness, or to check reports of the onset of famine, or to spend some time with his maturing family in Agra, or all three. Nothing infuriated Knight as much as official indifference to starving masses. He had seen such aloofness at the grand Imperial Assemblage in Delhi, where famines extant in Madras and Bombay presidencies were discussed, in the words of the official historian, 'to lay down general principles of policy, to guard against rash impulses which are often at work under the pressure of such calamities.'[109] Knight stands convicted of such rash impulses. The British as landlords, he wrote, were taking £21 million annually from 'the poor toiling millions, who mutely appeal to us not to allow them to die of hunger when their crops have been burnt up.' Warmongers who were ready to spend £100 million a year to fight Russia 'assure us that we shall all be "bankrupt" if we save these poor creatures alive, who give us their toil, and sweat, and blood, for a mouthful of food and a rag round their loins. It is *cant* to talk about the cost of relief, and cost only....'[110]

When Knight reached Agra on 11 February 1878, he received a letter from William R. Cornish, the Madras sanitary commissioner, who had organized medical efforts during the Madras famine. In a personal inspection the doctor found that many in the Agra area had died and others were in advanced states of starvation, and he called the overall situation worse than that of Madras.[111] Knight, in several scathing letters from Agra, reported that Indians had been dying by the tens of thousands in December, January, and February, and that no significant relief works had been opened until 20 January, when many were already too weak and sick to qualify as workers. He blamed the government of Sir George Couper, Lieutenant Governor of the North-Western Provinces, for suppressing the facts; most local officials had seen the situation and reported it. 'The chords of their humanity have been keenly touched,' he wrote. 'Surrounded by the dying and the dead, they have sent in appeal after appeal to their superiors, in every possible tone—angry, piteous, sarcastic, economical and sanitary.' They were answered with denial, disbelief, and even censure. His last letter concluded: 'We failed in Madras lamentably; we have now failed here, with far less excuse than there; and to acquit Sir George Couper's administration of the blame is impossible to those who know the facts.'[112]

Knight's accounts evoked a storm of denials and disputes. (The usual British response was a shrug, that famines are caused by monsoon failures, often a part of life in India, or perhaps a clever quip, that droughts must be blamed on the gods and not the British.) But it was gradually accepted that the Raj needed some more farsighted and systematic programme of famine relief. A Famine Commission, headed by General Sir Richard Strachey, was appointed later in 1878 and spent two years deliberating the appropriate use of state shipment of grains into a stricken region, remission of revenue collections, prompt opening of public works projects, distribution of raw grains, creation of public kitchens, emergency medical facilities, etc. Its report was accepted by a new Viceroy, the Marquess of Ripon, who rejected the views of a Malthusian minority, that famines were a natural and necessary check on population growth.[113] The Indian Famine Code gradually evolved from this report, including directions to local officials to report regularly on weather conditions, crop prospects, local market prices on staple grains, etc. Famine was not banished from India until a century later (the 'green revolution'), but after 1878 no government dared to appear dormant or negligent when warning signs had been reported. Some of Knight's reports and accusations might have been off-target, but he hit his main target, the British conscience.

Meanwhile, the Russian invaders of Ottoman Turkey had extorted the Treaty of San Stefano from the helpless sultan. Lord Beaconsfield declared its imposing terms unacceptable, and Britain prepared to defend the Turks against the Russians, as it had in 1854–6. Russia also began to prepare a Russian mission pushed into Kabul and obtained a treaty from Sher Ali.[114] Britain was seized with patriotic enthusiasm, and war was expected. Seven thousand Indian sepoys were shipped to a camp on Malta in preparation. The *Statesman* warned against the proposal to recruit and train 'hundreds of thousands of Indian troops upon which the Jingoes [that is, rabid superpatriots] count so confidently.' For one thing, India could not afford such an army. For another, it would create a constant fear of mutiny:

it is preposterous and impossible. A hundred thousand native troops poured into India, flushed and excited by a recent victory over an European foe, would mean the end of our rule at once; while the disbanded relics of a defeated army, scattered over the country to tell of our reverses, would mean the same.[115]

War was averted, however, by Bismarck's mediation at his Congress of Berlin in June and July of 1878. The Russian mission was withdrawn from Kabul. The crisis might have passed there also, but Lytton was determined to use the opportunity to secure the British position on the approaches to India. He sent a mission to Sher Ali to obtain a treaty giving Britain control of the amir's foreign relations. This mission was stopped at the frontier and refused entry into Afghanistan. Lytton called this an insult and demanded an apology. He wrote to the Secretary of State that 'the Ameer's policy was to make fools of us in the sight of all Central Asia and all India.'[116] Knight had a keener analysis:

Without the slightest right to do so, we send an armed Mission to invade the Amir's territories;...we send an armed force into the territory of a Prince who is as completely independent of us as France or Germany— knowing full well that he wishes no relations with us whatever....and when he refuses to allow our Mission to advance, we declare ourselves 'insulted' and affirm that an 'affront' has been put upon us that can only be washed out in Affghan blood....It is a course of fresh insanity and fresh guilt that we are entering upon, and will end in disaster and shame.[117]

Even Beaconsfield and Salisbury tried to restrain their headstrong viceroy by insisting that he should await a response from Sher Ali.[118] Not knowing this, Knight blamed the Tory government for seeking war, for demanding that the amir 'surrender his independence altogether and become a mere vassal or feudatory of the British Empire'.[119] Did building an empire require such forms of immorality and self-indulgence? Sooner or later, he wrote, man will realize that brute force does not pay off. An empire built on force, which ignores moral laws, will perish and be forgotten.[120]

The reply from Sher Ali arrived and was immediately declared unsatisfactory; it contained no apology. Therefore, an armed force had to be sent to Kabul, 'to guarantee the Ameer his absolute independence'. Knight raged: 'The most repulsive part of this most repulsive business has been the varnish of morality by which the projectors have attempted to conceal its real character.' Robbing the amir of his independence and his dominions must not be called robbery but 'protecting' him against the Russians. It is not called a war of conquest but a 'vindication of outraged honour'.[121]

War was declared on 21 November, and British forces invaded Afghanistan through three mountain passes. Sher Ali fled (and soon died in exile), and his son and successor, Yakub Khan, signed the Treaty of Gandamak in May 1879, promising the British what they wanted: a permanent resident at the court in Kabul and to conduct all foreign relations in accord with British policy. Sir Louis Cavagnari, the new resident, assumed his post in July. On 3 September the Afghan army mutinied and massacred Cavagnari, his staff, and his entire escort. British forces marched back into Afghanistan but were practically besieged in their forts. The Afghan countryside, so quiet a year earlier, was alive with insurgents.[122] The Tories' 'forward policy' to secure India lay in shreds.

Before this drama played out, though, Robert Knight had set out on his own 'forward policy'. The Afghanistan and cotton tariff issues had convinced him that the Raj had deteriorated into an extension of the British government, with narrow and selfish British interests setting its policies. Someone had to inform British statesmen and voters of the injustices being done to Indian taxpayers, princes, peasants, middle classes. *The Statesman* needed a London edition!

THE LONDON *STATESMAN* AND SALAR JUNG

England was the seat of power for the 'Government of India', and in 1878 Knight decided to return there to change imperial attitudes and structures. He said that he had been asked to stand for a Parliamentary seat; 'If I go into the House I will make it "warm" for our Foreign Office.'[123]

Knight had intended to found a London journal on his previous visit, in 1865, but financial setbacks prevented it. This time, one month after the start of the Afghanistan invasion, he had completed the prospectus for a London *Statesman*, 'awaken the conscience of the English people to the real character of our rule in this country'.[124] In this letter to Salar Jung he claimed the 'full approval' of Gladstone and other Liberal leaders, and he then made his pitch:

It is almost useless for me to go on writing in India as I have done for the 20 years past. The Government simply becomes more despotic every year, and less capable of dealing with the condition of the people....

I feel sure that in London, we could awaken a conscience amongst the people that would put an end once for all to the injustice, oppression,

neglect, and cruelty with which all classes from the native Prince down
to the ryot are now treated by our Government without hope of redress.
The Statesman here has become a valuable property but it has cost us Rs
1,00,000 [sic] and I want you to help me start this London paper. It would
injure the scheme, if it were to be known that any native gentleman
was assisting me but our financial agents here Mesr. Nicholls & Co.
could manage the matter entirely. What I wish you would do is lend
me at a mild rate of interest—say 8 percent, Rs 10,000 or 20,000, for say
three years. That money need only be deposited with Nicholls & Co. as
brokers in any name you liked, and they would be responsible for its
repayment....

P.S. If you have any hope at all of getting justice done to the Nizam,
believe me it is through our influence with Mr. Gladstone, and the great
Liberal leaders who will soon be in power.[125]

The dewan, who had been humiliated by Lytton and Sir Richard
Meade a year before, wanted to avoid further difficulties. He
wished Knight success but declined to finance the paper because
should it become known, 'it would be very disastrous to me'.[126]
Nonetheless, Knight pushed ahead with his plans and somehow
obtained initial financing. Riach was again left in charge of the
Calcutta paper, and in London he would rely on his old friends,
Colonel Osborn and Major Evans Bell, along with his son Paul.[127]
Bell, who represented the Indian princes in London (see pp. 40–
1), was later described by Knight as 'that old and valued friend of
the people and native Princes of India'.[128]

The move to London allowed Knight to rejoin his family from
Agra. The Knights took a house at 11, Haroldstone Road, Earl's Court,
South Kensington.[129] According to the census data, the residents of
the house were Robert and Catherine; their oldest daughter, Alice,
who was then 23; William, seventeen; Raymont, fourteen; Philip,
ten; Duncan, eight; Mabel ('Bonnie'), seven; Imogen, five; and
Hilda, three. Edith, the second daughter, had married, and the two
oldest sons, Paul and Robert Jr, having finished school, were most
likely working and living elsewhere. Hilda's recollections many
years later included a lot of political talk by her father at meals. 'I
often heard him talk about how much he admired Mr. Gladstone,'
she said.[130]

The first London *Statesman* was published on 29 November
1879. Knight called his weekly 'a teaching power', to counter the
deceitful official version of the Raj successfully and benevolently

ruling India. Englishmen trusted with despotic power, he wrote, 'have too often succumbed to its corrupting influences,' believing that because they had a mission to elevate and improve the people of India, they might 'dispense with those moral laws without which no elevation of character is possible.' He quickly warmed to the task:

We have come from India to protest against the ruinous self-complacency in which our countrymen are steeped....People of this country have no conception of the misery through which the people of India have gone in the last few years. And...*it is our rule* that is the cause, either directly or indirectly....[131]

He fired heavy barrages of rebuke at the Afghan War, expressing 'the true history of the crime into which the Ministry has betrayed us...against the wretched people of Afghanistan in this second war upon them'.[132] The massacre of Cavagnari and his mission had occurred just a month before, and the news was still being digested. Knight again wrote of the absurdity of a Russian invasion of India through that disordered and forageless country. He urged the rapid removal of the remaining British garrisons there:

it is ridiculous to say that, having broken down the government which formerly existed, we are bound to remain until a new one has been organized. It is our presence in Afghanistan that is the cause of the anarchy prevailing there, and until the cause is removed, the anarchy will continue. Any government which is set up under our patronage, will be knocked down immediately on our withdrawal from the country....[133]

But there was hope on the horizon: Gladstone! 'He is emphatically the great Christian statesman of the century....Whether Mr. Gladstone is returned for Midlothian, or beaten by the powerful and sinister forces arrayed against him there, he is still—happily for England—the Coming Man!'[134]

In later issues Knight expanded upon these themes. He approached a blanket condemnation of imperialism: 'Was any people in the world ever yet governed wisely by strangers and aliens, the great mass of whom regard their exile with impatience, and long to get it over, while engrossing to themselves every position of dignity, influence, and emolument...?' Better to return the land to native rule than 'treating India as a vast preserve for our sons and nephews to make their fortunes in'.[135]

Knight also wrote an informative letter to the *Times* on poverty in India. Yes, prices of agricultural produce were three or four times what they had been in 1840, because a vast export trade had arisen and bid them up, thus impoverishing the urban population. The old East India Company bonds had been retired (finally!), but 'private remittances' (goods, profits, salaries) were far higher: in all, £20–25 million in 1880 as against £3–5 million in 1840. 'the condition of the masses under our rule has deteriorated steadily', he wrote. 'It is not taxation *per se*,...but the disintegration of everything caused by our rule.'[136]

What impact did Knight's journal make? It must have helped stir opposition to the Tory ministry. The editor claimed that in two months it had already created a sensation, and that five officials had written to the *Times* to counter it.[137] Gladstone told his advisor, Lord Granville, of a 20 December article asserting that events foreseen in Afghanistan had been treated as unforeseen to cover up blunders,[138] Another reader lauded the *Statesman's* understanding of the lot of the Indian peasant. He called it 'a journal edited by a good man—sometimes called in India 'the melancholy pessimist'—who, for a quarter of a century, has been striving to obtain equitable rule for England's greatest dependency.'[139]

However, Knight needed money, and he again pleaded with Salar Jung for help:

Our expenses are heavy, and I cannot afford to carry on the paper for any great length of time unless the people and Princes of India help me by contributing liberally as subscribers. Thus you should take copies of the *Statesman* for all your officials and for your schools. No one will blame you for doing this. We have already nearly 1,000 subscribers in India, but we ought to have 3,000.[140]

Two days later he proposed another tactic: subscriptions bought by Indians should be sent to MPs and other public men in Britain. He told the dewan: 'It would be of no use for you to hire an agent here or to spend a *lakh* of rupees. It is public opinion only that will insist on your being treated with the honor and consideration overdo [*sic*] you.'[141] Two weeks later he pleaded for 200–300 subscriptions, foreseeing great imperial reforms:

For the first time in the history of our rule, is there now an opportunity of making the leading men in Parliament and the reading public of

England, acquainted with what our rule really is....If the Princes and People of India will but help *now*, we will change the whole system of English rule within a year or two.[142]

He added in a plaintive postscript: 'If I were a rich man, I would not ask anyone's help in my work.'

This time Salar Jung granted his request and sent him a draft for £280, for two hundred subscriptions. Knight thanked him but noted a new problem: the weekly was too much work, and a change to a monthly was being contemplated. 'My health moreover is feeling the strain of the paper very much.'[143] The last issue of the weekly *Statesman* was that of 28 February 1880. Knight later wrote: 'It has pleased God that my health has been declining ever since I came home. This indeed was the paramount cause of changing the weekly into a monthly paper....'[144] Since he did not describe the symptoms, it is not known whether his illness was due to nervous strain and exhaustion from overwork or the onset of malaria-based ills which would (apparently) take his life a decade later.

GLADSTONE'S VICTORY AND KNIGHT'S SETBACK

The *Statesman* of London resumed as a monthly journal in June 1880. During the four-month interval Gladstone and the Liberals had indeed won the sweeping electoral victory which Knight had anticipated. He crowed in triumph at the ouster of the Beaconsfield ministry:

The *Statesman* was established in London to be a protest against that divorce between politics and morality which characterized the statesmanship of the late Ministry....The profound conviction of our own mind is, that 'Righteousness exalteth a nation'; and that a course which is morally wrong, can never be politically right.[145]

Four months of muffled grievances burst forth in this hundred-page issue: the blunder of the Afghanistan invasion, the deceptive reports by the Conservatives of war financing, the danger to the Raj of its overstrained finances, and the Raj itself:

In speaking of what we call 'our' Indian Empire, we generally overlook the two hundred millions of human beings who are its natural and rightful possessors, and to whom, one day, that Empire will have to be restored....British rule in India is nothing more than this—that a huge horde of British officials collect the taxes, imprison and hang the natives...and are heavily paid for doing so.[146]

A new worry was ecologically-caused famine in India, due to a century of levelling the forests of Oudh for fuel and the salinization (*reh*) caused by the construction of the Jumna Canal, which Knight said had ruined agriculture in the Delhi territory.[147] Once-pure wells had become polluted by river waters.

He also denounced aggression elsewhere in the empire. The Zulu War in South Africa was called 'a national crime....[a]s unnecessary as it was unjust'.[148]

In letters to Salar Jung, Knight predicted great improvements:

Our turn is now coming for the institution of a wiser and juster rule of India than has ever yet been seen. I cannot tell you my feeling of indignant shame at the treatment which you *personally* and H H The Nizam as a Prince have received at the hands of our Foreign Office in India. Having Mr. Gladstone's ear and the confidence of the great Liberal leaders, I will take care that the quarrel about the Berars, and the petty insults offered to yourself, are fully known and understood.[149]

By the end of 1880 'we shall have a Royal Commission to change the whole system of our Indian Government,' and he even hoped to direct this commission.[150] But once again he needed money. The paper, he explained to the dewan, had already cost about £2000, of which he had received £1200 from India. He pleaded:

I wish you and Travancore and Jeypore who are all my personal friends would still help me to meet my heavy expenses here. [The maharaja of Jaipur had promised, and he of Travancore had already lent him £80.] I ought to have £5–6,000 by the end of October to enable me to finish my work here.[151]

Salar Jung sent him another £200. Knight, in thanking him, remarked that he expected to return to Calcutta shortly, leaving Colonel Osborn to run the London paper for a few months.[152]

Knight also sought appointment to the viceroy's Legislative Council. Gladstone, in forming his new ministry, had named the Marquess of Hartington his Secretary of State for India and the Marquess of Ripon Viceroy. As Ripon was preparing to leave for India, Hartington wrote to him:

Mr. Gladstone has, I believe, written to you about Mr. Knight, who wants to be a Member of the Legislative Council at Calcutta....I have not seen him, but have read some of his writings. He appears to be very clever and energetic, and to possess a large knowledge of Indian questions. But he is evidently extremely impulsive, and I should think unscrupulous....he had written to the Maharajah of Travancore asking for money in support of his newspaper....it proves that all his zeal in the cause of the Native Princes and their subjects is not absolutely disinterested....He would be troublesome, I should think; but if you want to admit active, well-informed and able outside criticism, he would probably supply it.[153]

Ripon replied, 'I will consider Mr. Knight's claim to be a Member of the Legislative Council at Calcutta, but I confess I do not much fancy the idea.'[154]

This was neither the first (see p. 41) and nor the last talk of Knight being in the pay of princes; J.G. Cordery, who had succeeded Meade as resident in Hyderabad, wrote matter-of-factly that the *Statesman* had been in Salar Jung's pay.[155] However, there is no available evidence to support such an assumption. Knight's requests to Salar Jung and the Maharaja of Travancore were for one-time subsidies to launch and maintain his London paper, clearly not a part of any ongoing arrangement. As noted, Knight had severe financial problems, but when he sought help, he considered it as support for his truth-revealing mission, as though his paper were a noble public cause.

EXPOSURE AND REACTIONS

Knight's high hopes for a new imperial structure and a significant personal role were swiftly smashed. The London *Statesman*, on 1 October 1880, published its extensive exposé of the exploits and intrigues of Rashid-ud-din Khan, now the amir-i-kabir but usually referred to as the *vikar-ul-oomrah* (or *wikar-ul-umrah*)— the antagonist whom Lytton and Meade had forced on Salar Jung. (Knight, writing to the dewan, called it 'Bell's admirable article')[156] The piece was the second of three entitled 'Restoration of the Berars'; the first, dated the previous July, traced the British takeover of those Berar districts in 1853.

The feud between the family of Salar Jung and that of the amir-i-kabir was a struggle for power and influence in the nizam's court. Rashid, the hotspur half-brother of the previous amir, had been implicated in that assassination plot against Salar Jung and in a comic-opera intrigue to swindle the nizam out of a packet of gold coins as a bribe to allow the dismissal of Salar Jung, which *The Statesman* described in gossipy detail.[157]

However, the priority shifted in 1874, the article continued, as the Raj, irked at Salar Jung's independence and his persistent pleas for return of the Berars, promoted his rival, the amir. When the amir died in 1877, they were left with his soiled successor, Rashid. Said *The Statesman*: 'He had robbed and deceived his master; he had insulted the British Government and slandered its representative. But now he was fully available for the discomfiture of Salar Jung....' The paper blamed this 'mischief' on the Hyderabad residency and its Calcutta superiors: 'We charge Lord Lytton's Foreign Office with this crime, and demand an inquiry into the facts.'[158]

The Establishment struck back. Knight was preparing to return to Calcutta when he was stopped by court summons. A criminal libel suit, based on the 1 October article, had been filed against him in the name of the amir-i-kabir. However, it was probably the work of J. Eldon Gorst, barrister, MP, and Conservative Party functionary, who represented the plaintiff in all subsequent hearings.[159] (During the ten weeks between the publishing of the article and the filing of the lawsuit, the amir was probably in Hyderabad and unfamiliar with British legal procedures; Barrister Gorst was on the spot.)

The case was transferred to the Queen's Bench (from Police Court), and Knight anticipated presenting a sensational defence, with witnesses from Hyderabad or even an investigating commission, to show the 'influence of evil' of the amir. But such a defence would take significant funding, and he had none. Through his Calcutta paper he appealed to 'the people and princes of India' to contribute to a Statesman Defence Fund: 'Such an opportunity of bringing home to the conscience of England the faults of our Government of India under the late regime, that they shall be made impossible in the future, may never occur again....'[160] He wrote to Salar Jung that he must ask old friends such as the maharajas of Indore and Travancore to help set up a fund, and he asked the dewan to please wire him £500.[161]

The reply which Knight received must have stunned him. Salar Jung saw danger in the lawsuit, not just for Knight but for himself, because of his link to the editor. He wrote:

You are well aware that ever since I have known you it has been far from my desire to encourage you in bringing Hyderabad affairs before the public....neither directly nor indirectly have I been any party to the publication of the article on which the libel was based...[as] this case concerns my colleague, approved by the British Government, the Resident, and the Calcutta Foreign Office, my position prevents my being mixed up with it at all, as I ought not and cannot come into collision with those authorities....

When you first asked me, as you may remember, on your first starting the Statesman as a weekly journal, to afford you some pecuniary aid in your undertaking, I felt very loath to refuse you, not merely as the editor of a paper, but as you were my personal friend....It was therefore a relief to my mind to be able on two later occasions, when you appealed to me for aid in your difficulties, to meet your wishes as far as was in my power. I hope that my having thus come to your aid did not lead you to think that I wished you to give any special prominence to Hyderabad affairs, or indeed to publish anything concerning them. I cannot think that you can have had this impression....[162]

The dewan concluded by saying that he hoped Knight would take nothing amiss and that their friendship would continue. However, there is no record of any further communication between the two.

THE BATTLE WITH MEADE AND THE LIBERAL REJECTION

Even before a hearing, the libel suit filed on behalf of the amir hurt Knight badly. It ended his relationship with the cautious Salar Jung. It also cost him whatever chance he might have had for a Legislative Council seat, as Ripon wrote: 'With respect to Mr. Knight's wish to be a Member of the Legislative Council, it would be, at all events, quite impossible to think of him in that position until the trial now going on in London has been brought to an issue.'[163] Meanwhile, the dispute and lawsuit became a topic of lively interest and comment in the Indian press. Several papers carried Knight's appeal for funds, and supportive meetings and fundraisers were held in India.[164] The Anglo-Indian papers generally treated it all as amusing gossip.

The case was heard 2 February 1881. A Mr Waddy and a Mr Besley, representing Knight, asked that the charges be dropped. They said there was no question of criminal libel, as there was no intent to disturb peace. As for a civil action, the defendant had to be able to defend himself, and this would require archives and witnesses (such as Salar Jung) who could not be brought from Hyderabad. The case could only be properly heard in India. The presiding officer agreed and entered a *nolle prosequi* on 3 June, discharging Knight.[165] Never one to back away from a fight, Knight promised the allegations would be reprinted in Calcutta for further action. However, the amir-i-kabir died on 12 December 1881, which ended his lawsuit.

The third part of the 'Restitution of the Berars' series appeared in the 1 July 1881 London *Statesman*. This one (presumably still written by Evans Bell) took the dispute up to date, assailing the behaviour of General Sir Richard Meade and his staff at the British residency. The fifty-page essay also blasted the Hyderabad Contingency Force as 'an utter scandal for the extravagance of the pay of its officers' and its opulent lifestyle, all at the expense of the nizam (pp. 433–5).

It told a lurid story of the events of 1877: how Rashid-ud-din had usurped the title of amir-i-kabir, shoving aside the nephew to whom it had been bequeathed; how Lytton's government had rehabilitated Rashid as a check against Salar Jung; how the residency staff (especially Major Euan Smith) had helped Rashid seize estates belonging to his nephews; and how the dewan's refusal to accept Rashid as co-regent was overcome only by the threat of 'his arrest and deportation to Madras on a special train, on the Nizam's own State railway'.[166] (The only angle missed was the role of Salisbury as the chief wirepuller.)

Fast and furious flew the denials. Meade, who had just retired to England, heatedly denied the accusations and asked Hartington how he could vindicate himself. The new Liberal officials immediately and instinctively leapt to his defence, even though he was a legacy from their Tory predecessors. 'The charges against Sir R. Meade are so libellous that it seems almost necessary for him to prosecute Knight,' wrote Hartington. 'I do not suppose you believe there is the slightest foundation for charges of the character which are made by Mr. Knight.'[167]

Ripon replied that he felt there was 'not a word of truth' in Knight's charges against Meade. The viceroy wanted criminal libel charges placed against Knight, 'whose accusations are sufficiently serious to justify and require the prosecution of the person who makes them.'[168]

Thomas Henry Thornton, Meade's former aide, called the article 'full of outrageous misstatements' and abounding in 'disgraceful innuendoes and other productions of malevolent bazaar gossip'. Thornton described the editor as 'a prolific writer of some ability, especially on economical subjects, and may be credited with a certain amount of genuine sympathy with the Princes and people of India; but he was the ready dupe of slanderers and not very scrupulous in his methods.'[169]

In the House of Commons questions were put to the Secretary of State on 11 August about the *Statesman's* disclosures and whether an independent inquiry would be made into the allegations. Hartington replied that the article 'contained a series of most violent attacks upon the conduct of the Government of India'. It was the government which had appointed the wikar and not Meade, yet the latter was charged with 'misconduct and actual corruption' he said. Meade, informed of the article, had told him that many of the statements were falsehoods and others were 'gross misrepresentations'.[170]

Hartington then asked the viceroy which official papers could be reproduced; 'I am told that most of Meade's reports, discussing, as they do very freely, Sir Salar Jung's conduct and character, could not possibly be published.' However, he had also heard that 'almost all of the most confidential papers are already in the hands of the enemy [!], having been obtained by the treachery and bribery of some native official.'[171]

Ripon sent the requested papers home but admitted that he had found some 'very curious revelations' in them. For instance, Meade had originally opposed the appointment of Rashid-ud-din as co-regent and was practically forced by Lytton to recommend it. 'What will happen if this comes out?' he wondered.[172] Hartington and his Council of India decided not to allow Meade to sue for libel.

Knight's credibility was badly hurt when Salar Jung denied that he had been physically threatened or forced to accept the amir.[173] the *Times of India* commented: 'The impetuosity and exaggeration of the Editor of the London *Statesman* have long been proverbial in Indian journalism,' and this flat contradiction would 'shake our faith' in his list of indictments.[174] Knight insisted that Salar Jung had believed it, and in fact he had said so (see Chapter 4). Since the resident had 'full permission to proceed to any extremities,' his duty lay in submission. Moreover, officials had not denied the graver charges: 'Give us the opportunity of putting Lord Lytton and Sir Richard Meade...into the witness box, and then Sir Salar Jung,' said Knight, 'and we will *show* that the charges are true....'[175] The editor had fought long and hard for the dewan and his cause of the Berars, but when he needed vindication, Sir Salar chose to deny it.[176]

Meade, for all his outrage, must also have known that the *Statesman's* account (which acknowledged that he had been following orders from Calcutta) was correct, but that proof lay deep within the confidential archives. Lytton and Salisbury, who had directed the *coup*, kept silent publicly.[177] Their Liberal successors covered up for them. Ripon warned the Secretary of State to take a 'very reserved attitude' in the Commons regarding 'Knight's unscrupulous proceedings'.[178] Hartington was asked in the Commons on 23 February 1882 whether, as promised the previous August, he had obtained the views of the Government of India regarding the *Statesman's* allegations against Meade. The Secretary acknowledged that a report had been received in October that, in the opinion of that government,

it was conclusively proved, by papers in their possession, that...Sir Richard Meade had acted under orders, and in entire accord with the wishes of the Government of India, and...that they retained an entire and unshaken confidence in his integrity and honour; and that they consider the imputations of corrupt conduct brought against him in the articles in question to be without foundation....[179]

Hartington thus gave a ringing endorsement of Meade's character and actions without addressing the specific question of the truth or accuracy of the *Statesman's* charges. Meade, he added, had sought legal proceedings so that he could refute the charges, but the court might require confidential papers connected with the episode, which was not in public interest. However, a backbencher, D.R. Onslow, asked if the report might be published, so that 'the public might see that the Government had gone into the matter, and the conclusion at which they had arrived'. No, replied Hartington, 'that course would be inconvenient, as the Report that was sent home contained confidential papers which it is not desirable to publish.'[180]

Knight pursued the matter once more, two years later, in a complaint to Sir Louis Mallet, Permanent Undersecretary of State for India, whom he knew. Mallet explained candidly:

The position of the Secretary of State is very helpless. He receives a statement such as yours, and it makes a due impression, but of course he cannot act except through the Government of India....He therefore refers the matter to Calcutta, and the reply, whether the Viceroy be Northbrook, Lytton, or Ripon, is certain to be the same—that Sir R. Meade is a man of highest character and most excellent judgment, and he reports that there is no foundation whatever for the statements in question. So we are thrown back, and we are in a worse position than before, because after that the Government of India is committed, and any further doubt is an insult that the Viceroy personally resents.[181]

Knight published the letter, which angered Ripon at Mallet for writing such an 'improper' letter and at Knight for breaking a confidence.[182]

The London *Statesman* ceased publication after September of 1881. The final issue carried a cannonade against the Government of India for policies of secrecy which had deceived not only the public and Parliament, but the India Office and even the Secretary of State. The truth had been concealed on issues such as Afghanistan, relations with the princes, and outbreaks of famine. 'Freedom of the Press is a dangerous absurdity,' he admitted, 'under a system of secret and irresponsible administration such as exists in India today....'[183]

In more hopeful days Knight had envisioned his periodical as an enduring part of the London journalistic scene, but in addition to the financial drain, it had lost its purpose. That purpose had been justice for Hyderabad and Salar Jung, but the dewan had shunned Knight's aid. Its purpose had been the triumph of Gladstonian Liberals, but even when empowered they protected the imperial establishment and considered Knight 'the enemy.' Above all, its purpose had been the reform of the Indian Empire into an engine for the enlightenment and improvement of its subject peoples through liberal principles, economic development, and a Christian conscience, and this vision was fading. The Raj could be no more benevolent than the men running it.

NOTES

1. *Friend of India* (Calcutta) (hereafter *FOI*), 5 August, 1876, pp. 708–9.
2. Ibid., 11 September 1875, p. 836.
3. Bengal, *Register of Baptisms, Burials, and Marriages*, vol. 156, p. 189.
4. Prospectus published in *Indian Statesman*, 29 May 1875, as quoted in Benoy Ghose, *Selections From English Periodicals of 19th Century Bengal*, vol. 8 (1875–80), *The Statesman* (Calcutta: Papyrus, 1981), pp. 101–3.
5. *The Statesman* (Calcutta), 17 November 1876, as quoted in *The Statesman, An Anthology* (hereafter *Anthology*), compiled by Niranjan Majumder (Calcutta: The Statesman, 1975), p. 31; S.C. Sanial, 'History of Journalism in India—V,' *Calcutta Review* (hereafter *CR*), vol. 127, July 1908, pp. 386–7n.
6. *Statesman and Friend of India* (hereafter *Statesman*), 4 January 1877.
7. *FOI*, 29 January 1876.
8. Memo of 'J.B.R.' (John B. Roberts?), 2 December 1878, in India, Revenue, Agriculture and Commerce Dept, General Proceedings, December 1878. (Found in Lytton Papers, E218/142B, pp. 549–61.)
9. Memo of Hume, 30 July 1878, ibid. For a fuller presentation of this memo, see Appendix B.
10. *FOI*, 3 July 1875.
11. India, Home Dept, Public Proceedings, August 1875, entry no. 6, Res. entry nos 19–1134.
12. *Statesman*, 22 January 1877, as quoted in *Anthology*, p. 35. If Knight here overstated the viceroy's annoyance with the press, Northbrook just as clearly understated it when he wrote, 'I hold strongly to not noticing what is said in the papers, an old Whig tradition and I believe a wise one.' Bernard Mallet, *Thomas George, Earl of Northbrook, G.C.S.I., A Memoir* (London: Longmans, Green, 1908), p. 87.
13. Mallet, *Thomas George*, pp. 90–1.
14. Edward C. Moulton, *Lord Northbrook's Indian Administration, 1872–76* (New York: Asia Publishing House, 1968), pp. 258–72.

15. *Bombay Times*, 3 July 1857.
16. An 1870 *Indian Economist* (hereafter *IE*) article, reprinted as *The Land Revenue of India, Is It Being Sacrificed or Not?* (Bombay: Thacker, Vining, ap. 1870), p. 23. A copy may be found in the Yale University Library, bound into College Pamphlets, vol. 51, entry no. 20.
17. *Statesman*, 11 July 1876, as quoted in *Anthology*, p. 28.
18. Letter of 7 June 1876, Papers of Owen Tudor Burne, MSS D951, 27.
19. Knight to Burne, 31 July 1876, ibid. See Appendix A for a fuller text.
20. *Statesman*, 3 February 1877.
21. India, Home Dept, Public Proceedings, October 1878, pp. 127–9 (A).
22. *Statesman*, 3 February 1877.
23. Ibid., 24 October 1876, as quoted in *Anthology*, p. 30.
24. Ibid., 10 September 1875, as quoted in Ghose, *Selections*, pp. 122–3.
25. Ibid., 14 March and 4 August, 1876, as quoted in Ghose, *Selections*, pp. 132–3 and 144.
26. Ibid., 10 April 1877. Knight and other critics ignored the substantial construction of irrigation canals under British rule.
27. Ibid., 28 September 1876, as quoted in *Anthology*, pp. 29–30. This editorial was demonstrably the work of Knight since it refers to 'demands addressed to ourselves...in the last twenty years'.
28. Ibid., 16 July 1876, as quoted in *Anthology*, pp. 25–6. This was borne out by an 1882 survey of the first 25 years of graduates of Indian universities. Of those contacted, roughly half had entered the public services, and all but a handful had been restricted to minor careers as clerks or *munsiffs* (petty hearings officers), with few judges or magistrates. Many others had become schoolteachers or *vakils* (legal pleaders), with very few barristers. Extracted from India, *Report of the Indian Education Commission*, as quoted by Anil Seal, *The Emergence of Indian Nationalism, Competition and Collaboration in the Later Nineteenth Century* (Cambridge: University Press, 1968), pp. 357–60.
29. *FOI*, 4 November 1876, pp. 994–5. See also *Statesman*, 1 January 1877. Earlier, Knight had opposed lowering the age ceiling from 23 to 21, preferring more mature recruits.
30. Lytton to Salisbury, 11 May 1876, Lytton Papers, MSS Eur. E218 (hereafter LP), vol. 23, p. 149.
31. Lytton to Disraeli,, 30 April 1876, LP, vol. 23, p. 123. This is a prime example of what later writers would call 'Orientalism'.
32. Lytton to Lord George Hamilton, 22 January 1877, LP, vol. 19, pp. 51–2.
33. Ibid. However, that same letter also shows Lytton wanted to deceive or beguile the princes: 'they are easily affected by sentiment,

and susceptible to the influence of symbols to which facts very inadequately correspond.'

34. Lytton to Disraeli, 30 April 1876, LP, vol. 123, pp. 120–4.
35. Lytton to Salisbury, 11 May 1876, ibid., vol. 18, pp. 149–50. For an incisive study of the Assemblage as a device to install a hierarchical (and manageable) order in India, see Bernard S. Cohn, 'Representing Authority in Victorian India', in Eric Hobsbawm and Terrence Ranger (eds), *The Invention of Tradition* (Cambridge: Cambridge University Press, 1983), esp. pp. 179–81.
36. Lytton to the Queen, 11 September 1876, ibid., p. 455.
37. Bharati Ray, *Hyderabad and British Paramountcy, 1858–1883* (New Delhi: Oxford University Press, 1988), p. 146. Two insights into these murky matters are to be found in Ray, *Hyderabad*, pp. 132–64, and Vasant Kumar Bawa, 'Salar Jang and the Nizam's State Railway, 1860–1883', *Indian Economic and Social History Review* (henceforth *IESHR*), 2(5) October 1965, pp. 307–40.
38. Ray, *Hyderabad*, p. 146.
39. For abundant detail on these agents, see Harriet Ronken Lynton, *My Dear Nawab Sahib* (Hyderabad: Orient Longman, 1991), pp. 159–70.
40. Ray, *Hyderabad*, pp. 144–8; Bawa, 'Salar Jung', *IESHR*, pp. 316–22. Hyderabad sources spell the company 'W. Nicol'.
41. Lytton to Sir Richard Meade (official resident in Hyderabad), 2 May 1876, LP, vol. 23, pp. 127–8. He wrote the same thing on the same day to Salisbury. Ibid. p. 131.
42. Lytton to Meade, 11 May 1876, ibid., pp. 154–5.
43. Salisbury to Lytton, 16 February 1877, LP, vol. 4, entry no. 3.
44. Bawa, 'Salar Jung', *IESHR*, p. 187.
45. Lytton to The Queen, 23 December 1876–10 January 1877, LP, vol. 19, pp. 6–7.
46. J. Talboys Wheeler, *The History of the Imperial Assemblage at Delhi, Held on the 1st January, 1877* (London: Longmans, Green, Reader and Dyer, 1877), pp. 1 and 68–70.
47. Ibid., p. 88.
48. Ibid., p. 124.
49. *FOI*, 2 September 1876, p. 799.
50. *Statesman*, 6 January 1877. To the credit of the British, they never shot or poisoned the angry editor, arrested or deported him, or seized his presses. But this was because of his colour; they did retaliate against mouthy Indian editors, as the next section will show.
51. Surendranath Banerjea, *A Nation in the Making, Being the Reminiscences of Fifty Years of Public Life* (London: Oxford University Press, 1927), p. 44.

52.　*Statesman*, 27 March 1877.

53.　Banerjea, *A Nation in the Making*, pp. 44–50. Transliterations of this Bengali name vary in spelling. I have used that of the man's autobiography.

54.　Lytton to Salisbury, 2 July 1877, LP, vol. 19, p. 558. Harriet Lynton attributes Lytton's festering fears of Salar Jung to his own background of personal insecurity; pp. 185–6.

55.　India, Foreign Dept, Secret Proceedings, December 1879, entry no. 328, memo of Thomas H. Thornton, 13 June 1877.

56.　Lytton to Salisbury, 2 July 1877, LP, vol. 19, p. 558. For Meade's viewpoint see Thomas Henry Thornton, *General Sir Richard Meade and the Feudatory States of Central and Southern India* (London: Longmans, Green, 1898), pp. 322–8.

57.　Meade to Lytton and Salisbury to Meade, both 23 September 1877, Salisbury Papers, Reel 11682, Bundle 20 (2). The new cable enabled the secretary of state to bypass the viceroy.

58.　Lytton to Salisbury, 23 September and Meade to Lytton, 26 September 1877, LP, vol. 32, entry no. 31.

59.　Note by C.B. Euan Smith, 25 September 1877, in Meade to T.H. Thornton, Officg Secretary, India, Foreign Dept, 624P, p. 28, entry no. 374.

60.　Salar Jung to John Fleming (one of his agents), 20 August 1878, Salar Jung Collection, Andhra Pradesh State Archives, Misc. File, Letter 632, as quoted in Ray, *Hyderabad*, p. 89, and Lynton, *Nawab Sahib*, pp. 211–12.

61.　See pp. 176–8.

62.　Knight to Lytton, 17 July 1877, LP, vol. 31.

63.　Pamphlet 'Speech on Indian Affairs Delivered Before the Manchester Chamber of Commerce, on 24th January, 1866', pp. 14–17. See also Chapter 3.

64.　'Manchester and England: A Protest Against Sir John Strachey's Financial Statement in the Legislative Council of India, Dated 15th March 1877' (Calcutta: Thacker, Spink, 1877), reprint of some 1877 *Statesman* editorials, pp. 8–9.

65.　John Strachey, *India, Its Administration and Progress*, 4th edn (London: Macmillan, 1911), p. 193. Sir John was finance member of Lytton's council.

66.　*IE*, 5 (8), March 1874, p. 211.

67.　K.N. Chaudhuri, 'European Trade With India,' in Tapan Raychaudhuri and Irfan Habib (eds), *Cambridge Economic History of India*, vol. 1 (Hyderabad: Orient Longman, 1984 [orig. edn Cambridge: University Press, 1982]), pp. 401–2; Haripada Chakraborti, *Trade and Commerce in Ancient India* (Calcutta: Academic Publishers, 1966), pp. 236–8.

68. K.N. Chaudhuri, 'Foreign Trade and the Balance of Payments (1757–1947)' and Morris D. Morris, 'The Growth of Large-scale Industry to 1947', in Dharma Kumar (ed.), *Cambridge Economic History of India*, vol. 2, pp. 842–3 and pp. 668–71, respectively.

69. *IE*, 5 (8), March 1874, p. 211.

70. Strachey, *India*, pp. 190–1.

71. *FOI*, 3 June 1876, pp. 482–3.

72. Ibid., 6 May 1876, p. 387.

73. *Statesman*, 18 April 1877.

74. Ibid.

75. Strachey, *India*, pp. 194–5; Lady Betty Balfour, *The History of Lord Lytton's Indian Administration, 1876 to 1880, Compiled From Letters and Official Papers* (London: Longmans, Green, 1898), pp. 482–4.

76. 28 March 1879, p. 269. Compare this with Knight's letter dated 17 July 1877, praising the Tories.

77. Strachey, *India*, p. 194.

78. Morris, 'Growth of Large-scale Industry', p. 576.

79. According to Morris, 'Growth of Large-scale Industry', p. 669, it was actually the expansion of the Indian mills which ousted the hand-spinners, not the British imports.

80. For a graphic (and demeaning) description of the vernaculars of the Punjab and North-Western Provinces, see 'Memo on the Vernacular Press for Upper India, 1876–77', in India, Home Dept, Public Proceedings, August, 1879, pp. 1–2.

81. The Bengal series is entitled *Reports on Native Papers* (hereafter *RNP*); titles from the other provinces vary slightly. For a thoughtful and helpful study of the Indian press in the 1870s, see Uma Dasgupta, *Rise of an Indian Public, Impact of Official Policy, 1870–1880* (Calcutta: Rddhi, 1977), esp. Chapter 1.

82. Bengal, *RNP*, week ending 3 July 1875.

83. Bengal, *RNP*, weeks ending 17 June, 1 July–9 December (for #3 and #4), and 16 December 1876, respectively.

84. 'The Native Newspapers of India and Ceylon', *CR*, vol. 65, 1877, p. 392.

85. *IE*, 30 November 1874.

86. India, Home Dept, Judicial Proceedings, April 1878, entry no. 203–6(A).

87. Statement of 20 December 1877, in India, Home Dept, Public Proceedings, October 1878, entry no. 127–9(A). However, Lytton said almost the exact opposite—that the vernaculars were the real danger—a few months later, to justify exempting the English-language papers. India, Proceedings of the Legislative Dept, March, 1878, pp. 52–3.

88. India, Home Dept, Judicial Proceedings, April 1878, entry nos 236–40(A).

89. Eden to Lytton, 21 April 1878; included in India, Home Dept, Judicial Proceedings, April, 1878, entry nos 236–40(A).

90. India, Home Dept, Public Proceedings. March, 1879, entry no. 221–2(A) and April, 1880, entry nos 115–16(B). *Som Prakash* had aroused Lytton's ire with a remark about British threats to Afghanistan.

91. See for instance his speech of 5 December 1879, in St Andrew's Hall, Glasgow, reproduced in W.E. Gladstone, *Midlothian Speeches 1879* (Leicester: University Press, 1971), p. 201.

92. C.E. Buckland, *Bengal Under the Lieutenant-Governors*, 2nd edn (Calcutta: Kedernath Bose, 1902), pp. 718–19.

93. In fact, one editor wondered why 'he of the independent and plainspoken *Statesman*' was not considered disloyal, but 'native editors' who wrote in similar style were. *Sambad Prakash*, 20 August, 1877, as reported in *RNP*, Bengal, week ending 1 September 1877, p. 9.

94. S.C. Sanial, 'History of Journalism in India—V', *CR*, vol. 127, July 1908, p. 386n.

95. *Anthology*, p. 44.

96. 22 March 1878, as quoted in Dasgupta, pp. 290–1.

97. *FOI*, 28 March 1879.

98. *Statesman*, 1 July 1878.

99. *Indian Statesman* (Bombay), 11 July 1872.

100. *FOI*, 27 November 1875.

101. The classic account is John Howes Gleason, *The Genesis of Russophobia in Great Britain, a Study of the Interaction of Policy and Opinion* (Harvard: University Press, 1950).

102. *FOI*, 11 September 1875, pp. 833–4.

103. *FOI*, 18 September 1875, p. 853.

104. *Statesman*, 7 December 1875, as quoted in *Anthology*, pp. 21–2.

105. Even a classic pro-British textbook is highly critical of Lytton's policy and largely blames him for the debacle which followed. P.E. Roberts, *History of British India, Under the Company and the Crown* (3rd edn completed by T.G.P. Spear) (London: Oxford University Press, 1952 [1st edn, 1921], Part II), pp. 431–41.

106. *Statesman*, 2 February 1877.

107. Ibid., 26 April 1877. See also Roberts, p. 434

108. See for instance *Statesman*, 16 April, 1 June, 2 July, and 1 October 1877.

109. Wheeler, p. 95.

110. *Statesman*, 2 February 1877.

111. Ibid., 18 February 1878. See also ibid. 22 April 1878.
112. Ibid., 1 and 2 April 1878. In an earlier letter he blamed district officials for concealing the facts of the famine, but this view must have changed. The rival *Englishman*, which accepted the official version, was charged by Knight with 'free use of a bucket of editorial whitewash' (1 April 1878).
113. H. Verney Lovett, 'The Development of Famine Policy', in H.H. Dodwell (ed.), *The Cambridge History of India*, vol. 6, (Delhi: S. Chand, 1964 [1922]), pp. 300–6; S[arvepalli] Gopal, *The Viceroyalty of Lord Ripon, 1880–1884* (London: Oxford University Press, 1953), pp. 178–9.
114. Roberts, *History of British India*, pp. 437–40.
115. *Statesman*, 1 July 1878.
116. Lytton to Cranbrook, 23 September 1878, LP vol. 20, p. 676. See also Roberts, *History of British India*, pp. 438–41.
117. *Statesman*, 2 October 1878.
118. Roberts, *History of British India*, pp. 441 and 451.
119. *Statesman*, 2 November 1878. He had earlier sharply criticized Lytton's leadership and judgment; ibid., 23 October 1878.
120. Ibid., 2 November 1878.
121. Ibid., 4 November 1878.
122. Roberts, *History of British India*, pp. 441–5.
123. Knight to Salar Jung, 17 July 1878, Salar Jung Collection, Personal Papers, Accession #604, Andhra Pradesh States Archives. The Parliamentary candidacy never materialized.
124. Knight to Salar Jung, 20 December 1878, Salar Jung Collection, acc. no. 605.
125. Ibid.
126. Salar Jung to Knight, 3 January 1879, Salar Jung Collection, acc. no. 715.
127. Knight to Salar Jung, 2 April 1880, Salar Jung Collection, acc. no. 733.
128. *Statesman* (Calcutta), 4 September 1883.
129. Great Britain, General Register Office, census data from 1881; Hilda Kidd to the author, 26 August 1968.
130. Interview with Hilda Kidd, 21 August 1968.
131. Ibid., p. 2.
132. Ibid., p. 11.
133. Ibid., p. 6.
134. Ibid., p. 3.
135. *Statesman*, 14 February 1880, p. 370.
136. *Times* (London), 1 December 1879, p. 5.

137. Knight to Salar Jung, 3 June 1880, Salar Jung Collection, acc. no. 730.
138. Agatha Ramm, ed., *The Political Correspondence of Mr. Gladstone and Lord Granville, 1876–1886* (Oxford: Clarendon Press, 1962), vol. 1, pp. 105 and 105n.
139. Samuel Baildon, *The Tea Industry in India* (London: W. H. Allen, 1882), p. 181.
140. Knight to Salar Jung, 18 December 1879, Salar Jung Collection, acc. no. 716. This letter bore an imprint of '332 Strand', presumably the *Statesman's* London office.
141. Ibid., 20 December 1879, Salar Jung Collection, acc. no. 717.
142. Ibid., 3 January 1880, Salar Jung Collection, acc. no. 730.
143. Ibid., 27 February 1880, Salar Jung Collection, acc. no. 731.
144. Ibid., 2 April 1880, Salar Jung Collection, acc. no. 733.
145. *Statesman* (London), June, 1880.
146. *Statesman*, June 1880, p. 17.
147. Ibid., pp. 77–82.
148. Ibid., 1 December 1880, p. 640.
149. Knight to Salar Jung, 2 April 1880, Salar Jung Collection, acc. no. 733. See also 6 August, 1880, Salar Jung Collection, acc. no. 736.
150. 27 August, 1880, Salar Jung Collection, acc. no. 737.
151. Ibid.
152. 22 November 1880, Salar Jung Collection, acc. no. 739.
153. Hartington to Ripon, 17 December 1880, Ripon Papers [hereafter RP] BL, Add. MSS 43510, #39 of 1880.
154. Ripon to Hartington, 6 January 1881, RP, #1 of 1881.
155. Cordery to Ripon, 30 January 1884, RP, BP 7/6, 1 of 1884, entry no. 39.
156. Knight to Salar Jung, 31 December 1880, Salar Jung Collection, acc. no. 746.
157. pp. 448–66. The story was that the British resident, Col Cuthbert Davidson, allegedly sought a bribe to approve dismissal of Salar Jung, and so a woman disguised as Mrs Davidson was given a packet of gold coins from the nizam. But Davidson never knew of plot or packet, never got it, and when he learned of the plot, denounced it and Rashid-ud-din as its author. As fantastic as this sounds, it was later confirmed by Lynton (*Nawab Sahib*, chapter 5, pp. 92–9), who mined archives closed in 1880. Bell and Knight seem to have had their own sources of information.
158. Ibid., p. 466.
159. Knight to Salar Jung, 12 December 1880, Salar Jung Collection, acc. no. 740, and 24 December 1880, acc. no. 743; *Statesman* (Calcutta),

3 February 1881; Lynton, pp. 165–6 and 169. Gorst's hostility toward Salar Jung is shown in his journal article, 'The Kingdom of the Nizam', *Fortnightly Review*, vol. 35, n.s. January–June 1884, esp. 522–4. Lynton also attributes the lawsuit to Thomas Palmer, a disgruntled ex-agent of Salar Jung.

160. *Statesman* (Calcutta), 3 February 1881.

161. Knight to Salar Jung, 31 December 1880, and 28 January 1881, Salar Jung Collection, acc. nos 746 and 774.

162. Salar Jung to Knight, 13 January 1881, Salar Jung Collection, acc. no. 773.

163. Ripon to Hartington, 19 January 1881, RP, BP7/3, entry no. 4.

164. See for instances the *Delhi Gazette*, vol. 1 February 1881, and in retrospect Surendranath Banerjea's *Bengalee*, 1 February 1890.

165. The full transcript of the hearing was reproduced in *Statesman* (London), 1 July 1881, pp. 394–403.

166. *Statesman* (London), 1 July 1881, p. 465.

167. Hartington to Ripon, 5 August, 1881, RP, BP7/3, entry no. 39.

168. Ripon to Hartington, 26 August 1881, RP, entry no. 42. He also warned the Secretary of State against the Wikar-ul-Umrah, 'a stupid, blundering, and not very clean-handed individual.'

169. Thomas Henry Thornton, *General Sir Richard Meade and the Feudatory States of Central and Southern India* (London: Longmans, Green, 1898), pp. x and 351–2.

170. *Hansard's Parliamentary Debates*, 3rd series, 264, cols 1526–8. Meade never seems to have specified which of those statements he was calling 'falsehoods'.

171. Hartington to Ripon, 12 August 1881, RP, entry no. 40.

172. Ripon to Hartington, 1 October 1881, RP, entry no. 49.

173. *Times* (London), 5 September 1881

174. *Times of India*, 9 September 1881.

175. *Statesman* (London), 30 September 1881, pp. 579–80.

176. Lynton explains that a chastened Salar Jung had determined to smooth relations with the Raj and work within its limitations; pp. 210–15.

177. The *Hansard* and the *Times* indices show no mention. Lytton gave two long speeches in Manchester, 1 and 2 February 1882, in which he defended almost all of his Indian policies, but on Hyderabad and Salar Jung and the *Statesman's* accusations there was not a word, judging from the *Times* accounts.

178. Ripon to Hartington, 27 January 1882, RP, entry no. 6. For other expressions of his enmity toward Knight, see Ripon to Hartington, 26 August 1881, #42, and 24 February 1882, #12.

179. *Hansard*, vol. 266, col. 1372, for 23 February 1882.
180. Ibid., col. 1373. That ended any official enquiry, but rumours persisted. Two years later, Wilfred S. Blunt, globetrotter and writer, reported that Gorst, no less, had told him prosecution of the *Statesman* 'was dropped in consequence of representations from the Calcutta Foreign Office that a scandal would be created,' and Meade 'would have come out badly'. *India Under Ripon, A Private Diary* (London: T. Fisher Unwin, 1909), p. 84.
181. *Statesman*, 17 February 1884.
182. Ripon to Earl of Kimberly (who had succeeded Hartington as Secretary of State), 24 February 1884, RP, 5, pp. 42–4.
183. *Statesman* (London), p. 683.

The Making of a Statesman Elder, 1881–90

THE *STATESMAN* MORTGAGE AND THE PAIKPARA RAJ

While Robert Knight was fighting for his reforms and his London paper, he almost lost his Calcutta *Statesman*. Under the editorship of William Riach, the paper several times made news instead of merely conveying it. A brief sensation, an article by Evans Bell that jewellery worth Rs 36,000, belonging to the estate of the late maharaja of Mysore, had mysteriously vanished from the British residency at Mysore in a likely burglary.[1] Officials seemed less concerned with catching the thief than with discovering who had leaked the secret reports of the crime. They fastened the blame for this to the residency's Indian *sheristadar* (record keeper), who was promptly fired. He sued to recover his job, but in vain.[2]

An earlier flare-up came on 5 July 1879, when William Riach, annoyed at the inanity of official press releases, described one as 'fatuous flapdoodle'. C.E. Buckland, then acting press commissioner, snapped back that since the editor scorned his releases, he would 'desist from so troubling you', and ordered the *Statesman* stricken from all distribution lists. A chastened Riach asked the viceroy for help; in a 28 July letter to Lytton's private secretary, G.H.M. Batten, he admitted having ridiculed the press commissioner. 'A public servant, paid for by public revenue, is liable to public criticism,' Riach explained, 'and I regard ridicule as one of the most effective weapons of criticism.' But 'fatuous flapdoodle' might have been 'peculiarly offensive', and so he withdrew the remark and expressed his regret. He promised to keep 'offensive ridicule' out of the *Statesman*.[3]

The near-loss of the *Statesman* came on 10 February 1881, when Roberts, Morgan and Company, as solicitors for an (unnamed) mortgagee, seized possession of the newspaper property. The London paper had been a financial drain, but this default may have been caused, not by the *Statesman's* debts, but by the bankruptcy of Nicholls and Company, managing agent for the paper and perhaps also a shareholder. Once again, information on the early ownership and financing of the *Statesman* was apparently destroyed beyond recovery.[4]

Paul Knight had already been sent back to Calcutta to help with the management, but apparently it was Riach who took the lead. He contacted Indra Chandra Singh (sometimes transliterated as 'Sinha'), an heir of the immensely wealthy and prestigious Paikpara Raj family, zamindars with a huge mansion in the Belgatchia area, north of Calcutta, and many estates and other properties. Indra Chandra, a high-minded young man, was reportedly learned in both Hindu classics and modern subjects, and at one point sponsored a Hindu reform effort.[5] The Paikpara Raj took out a first mortgage on the *Statesman*, thus preventing its sale to outsiders and saving it for the Knights.[6]

As mortgagee, the Paikpara estate had ultimate control of the *Statesman's* business affairs. Knight later wrote that he was not the legal proprietor as long as that mortgage remained unredeemed,[7] and it was not redeemed during his lifetime. He disliked the arrangement and apparently blamed Riach for the financial mess. A rift between them was created. Hilda Kidd recalled hearing as a young girl that her father felt that he had been let down by an 'untrustworthy partner', a 'Mr. Reeack'.[8] Why Knight felt this way is not known; it would appear that Riach had saved his newspaper for him.

There is no evidence of editorial control by the mortgagee, although Knight's disparaging remarks about zamindars seem to have disappeared after 1881. Trailokya Nath Chatterjee, manager of the Paikpara estate, became an influential figure in the *Statesman* management, and staff members considered him to be a supportive and friendly presence in the years which followed.[9] But once again, Knight had violated a prime law in Anglo-India, taking a position subordinate to a 'native'.

THE RETURN TO CALCUTTA

Robert Knight and his family returned to Calcutta in April of 1883, one-and-a-half years after the disappointment of the London *Statesman*. Perhaps he had been ill again or depressed, or a combination of the two. The snubs he had received from those he had championed could have depressed anyone. His only known writing during this span was a pamphlet denouncing the British invasion and occupation of Egypt in 1882. He was appalled that the conscientious Gladstone should have launched it ('Is there no way that conscience and honesty and true wisdom can suggest, by which to get back into the path from which we have wandered?'[10]) He proposed that instead of smashing the nationalist insurgency led by Colonel Achmad Arabi, the British should negotiate an agreement with 'Arabi Pasha' under which they would temporarily guard the Suez Canal and private British property.[11]

When Knight resumed writing, his editorials often took a cynical and world-weary approach, compared with the enthusiastic and optimistic reformer of earlier decades. He did not immediately recover the editorship of the *Statesman*. Riach wrote that there was 'not the slightest possibility' of their serving as joint editors, without explaining.[12] Apparently there were some backstage manoeuvres before Knight took control. Riach thereupon left India; he later joined the staff of the *Scotsman* of Edinburgh.

Knight's family moved into the top floor of the Statesman building at 3 Chowringhee, and there they lived until 1890. Hilda in her last years retained some recollection of those times. She remembered her father as a man of medium height and gentle voice, an informal man of 'great kindness'. She told an interviewer, 'I never heard him raise his voice, never.'[13] She remembered regular discussions of politics and the latest news dispatches. Her father was a retiring man, devoted to his work, never much involved with clubs or lodges or the social whirl. Her mother sometimes went to viceregal balls, escorted by one of the sons, or even alone![14] Hilda recalled her mother as a slender woman of medium height whom she never saw 'out of temper'. She wrote: 'My mother and father were both very fond of music, and they both sang and played the piano.'[15]

The Knight children—eleven in number—were growing up and going their several ways. Edith, as mentioned, had married William Nolan Boutflower and was living in Allahabad. Alice, the oldest, married B.R. Harrington, an engineer, in 1885. The two eldest sons, Paul (Plate IV) and Robert Jr ('Rob') (Plate V), joined the *Statesman*, with Paul as the business manager. The third son, William Hugh, studied law in London, then became a barrister in Calcutta, where he was popular and successful. The fourth son, Raymont, studied at the University of London,

Plate IV: Paul Knight. Courtesy *Statesman*, Kolkata

Plate V: Robert Knight (Jr). Courtesy *Statesman*, Kolkata

then passed the Indian Civil Service exam and joined the judicial branch in Bombay Presidency, where he was assigned to Sind. The two youngest sons, Philip and Duncan, were in school in England during all or some of the 1880s. The three youngest girls, Imogen, Emily ('Bonnie'), and Hilda, were tutored at home; Hilda remembered a French governess.[16] In sum, the Knights were a large and close-knit mid-Victorian family; neither Robert's unusual political views nor his financial difficulties interfered with their normal Anglo-Indian bourgeois lifestyle.

Even after his losses Knight was ready to seize the crusader's lance and gallop into combat. The Calcutta to which he returned in 1883 was riven by the angry quarrel over the Ilbert Bill (see next section). Also upsetting to many was the imprisonment of Surendranath Banerjea, the nationalist leader, for a disrespectful (and inaccurate) comment about a High Court judge in his weekly *Bengalee*. Knight, in a public show of support, escorted Banerjea's wife to the prison for a visit and later wrote a series of articles condemning the sentence.[17]

One editorial essay attributed Indian poverty, not to laziness or a lack of resources, but a lifestyle of scanty demand for consumer goods, that until the well-to-do classes 'appreciate more keenly the true uses of money, to surround themselves with the comforts, conveniences, and elegancies of life,' the country could never become wealthy, since there was insufficient demand for products of indigenous industry.[18] (Contrast this with his earlier editorial deploring extravagant spending on mansions, jewellery, and elegant clothing, rather than investment in productive industries.)

In another, Knight showed a rare sensitivity, well ahead of his time:

There are two expressions in incessant use, that we dislike so much that we always strive to avoid them...'half-caste' and 'the natives'. Observers of our columns may have noticed, that we uniformly write 'the people'... 'The native' suggests to an English ear...the idea of a savage people, and the term 'half-caste' is so constantly used opprobriously, that no public writer should ever use it, when he can avoid it.[19]

However, Knight also launched vindictive attacks based on past grudges. Sir Bartle Frere, who had encouraged the Bombay speculative bubble twenty years earlier, was blamed for that, for the Second Afghan War, for jailing thousands of indigo-growers in Bengal, the Zulu War in South Africa, etc.[20] Sir Richard Temple was accused of 'creating a race of private landlords' while he was chief commissioner of the Central Provinces in the 1860s and giving away land rights belonging to the state and the ryots.[21]

This is also the likely explanation of his criticism of Roberts, Morgan, and Company, the firm of solicitors which had seized the *Statesman* on behalf of the mortgagees in 1881. A dispute grew out of a tawdry trifle in which a Miss Pigot, principal of a female orphanage for the Church of Scotland, was accused by a missionary of 'immoral' behaviour (unspecified) at a church picnic. In the lawsuit which followed, corroborative testimony against Miss Pigot was introduced through what the *Statesman* called 'the manipulation of the lawyers'. These lawyers, Roberts, Morgan and Company, thereupon sued Knight for libel, claiming that he had accused them of suborning perjury. Knight denied that his article could have been so interpreted, but agreed to a statement that he 'unreservedly expresses his regret' if his words were misconstrued.[22] This retraction amused Knight's adversaries such as the pro-government *Pioneer* of Allahabad; it chortled: 'The Vulgar Boy of the Calcutta Press has already resumed his favourite pastime of mud-throwing.'[23]

Despite these foibles, the *Statesman* was generally growing and building. It began a weekly *Overland Summary* on 1 January 1884, summarizing the week's news in India for European readers, intended as replacement for the deceased London *Statesman*. It was 'prepared especially for the use of Parliament, the leading Home Journals, and the Mercantile body.'[24] On 27 August 1884, it carried this triumphant notice: 'The Statesman has the largest circulation of any newspaper in India.'

THE EXPLOSIVE ILBERT BILL

Gladstone and his Liberals never even attempted the kind of radical reform of the British Empire that Knight had envisioned. (In fact, their 1882 invasion and occupation of Egypt showed how bipartisan imperial policy could be.) However, Lord Ripon, Gladstone's man in India, brought a distinctly different approach to the Raj from the hawkish and egotistical Lytton. The troops were withdrawn from Afghanistan. The Vernacular Press Act was repealed. Measures to extend and develop local self-government were promoted vigorously by the new viceroy. But he became best known to history through that trivial amendment to the Criminal Procedure Code called the Ilbert Bill.

The agitation against the Ilbert Bill was a contrivance of leaders of the Anglo-Indian community, apparently centred in the Calcutta bar, who wanted to cut down Ripon and the movement to expand the political rights and roles of Indians. Instead, they created a monster which threatened the Raj with a European insurrection, which in turn stirred an angry nationalist and anti-imperialist reaction among Indians.[25]

The bill was designed to resolve an administrative problem and remove a racial disability. That handful of sturdy Indian youths who had passed the ICS examinations had been rising through seniority into responsible offices such as district magistrate and sessions judge, but they lacked legal authority over Europeans within their jurisdictions. C.P. Ilbert, legal member of Ripon's council, drafted and introduced his bill to remedy that disability.

The newspapers served as the vehicle for this contrived agitation. Before any opposition surfaced in India, the *Times* (of London) ran a dispatch from Calcutta which claimed that the government had 'suddenly sprung a mine' on the European community. It forecast intense opposition, then sounded the alarm and urged resistance.[26] The *Times* correspondent in India was a Calcutta barrister, J.C. Macgregor.[27] His message was cabled back to India, where most (though not all) Anglo-Indian papers picked up this drumbeat of panic. Their editorials and letters columns were soon filled with outspoken and angry expressions of European feelings about their Indian neighbours. Protest meetings were held in towns around India. The capstone came at a 28 February meeting (only 26 days after the introduction of the bill) at Calcutta's Town Hall, where eminent Anglo-Indians emoted on the horrors which awaited any British woman who fell into the clutches of a Bengali magistrate.[28]

Rival newspaper, *Englishman* led this howling pack, but the *Statesman* dissented. It welcomed the Ilbert Bill and at first said that it expected no illiberal opposition.[29] When that opposition arose, the *Statesman* called it 'simply ridiculous' and even suggested a broadened bill which would include deputy magistrates.[30] The paper scoffed at fear of the British Raj not protecting the British from its own magistrates.[31] Ripon stoutly defended his bill at a Legislative Council meeting, which showed that the bill would never be defeated 'by empty declamation, vulgar abuse, or even threatened mutiny'.[32]

Educated Indians angrily read the insults being heaped on them. In Dacca a Bengali barrister, Lalmohan Ghose, said Indians should respond to this outrage by forming a new national organization to work for national interests.[33] From Simla, Allan Octavian Hume, recently retired from high office, wrote a circular letter to the graduates of Calcutta University, saying that their response should be to organize and work for the regeneration of India.[34] This began the chain of events which created the first Indian National Congress in 1885 (see p. 216).

When Knight replaced Riach at the editorial helm, the *Statesman* took a more moderate, even a diffident view of the Ilbert Bill. His ambivalence showed in a rambling, two-part editorial on 3 September 1883. On the one hand, he said that the bill should not try to eradicate racial distinctions; not only should Europeans have their own traditional judges and judicial systems, but so should Indians, instead of having a European judiciary forced on them. On the other hand, those Indians who had earned positions in the CSI deserved to be entrusted with all the rights and powers of Englishmen. European agitators were to blame for antagonizing Indians who supported the bill, 'but we are not going to flatter the native by telling him we sympathize with or approve his attitude towards the Bill, for we do not...' Instead he proposed a 'right of transfer'. Let concerned Europeans seek out a judge or magistrate of their own race, however distant, but let Indians do the same. He would even have broken it into provinces: Bengali officials in Bengal, Punjabis in Punjab, etc., as far as possible.[35]

By November, it was obvious that most Anglo-Indians, including officials, opposed the bill, many frantically, and even those on the Legislative Council wanted to kill or drastically amend it. A face-saving compromise was sought. Some took up Knight's ideas, and one councillor, James Gibb, said he would talk to the editor, whom he had known in Bombay. 'He is a queer character,' Gibb wrote, 'with some real good at bottom, but eccentric and at times very violent'.[36] Ripon apparently ignored this advice.

Knight's diffidence had disappeared by then. The original bill had no principle, he wrote, but its opponents had one: that no Indian, however well qualified, should ever be allowed to judge a European. If Ripon should concede that, 'he will deserve to have every badge of honor that he wears torn from him, and to be stricken off the rolls of the peerage as a disgrace to the English nobility'.[37]

On that point the viceroy stood firm under severe pressure. Planters and other European settlers flocked into Calcutta for the winter social season, many of them wielding guns and snorting defiance. When Ripon returned to his capital from his tour on

1 December, he was hissed and spat at in the streets—by his own countrymen![38] Could the public order be maintained, he then worried? Would British troops fire on their own countrymen if ordered? If Indian sepoys were brought in and ordered to fire, would this touch off a nationwide race war? Whatever the outcome, it threatened disaster for the Raj.[39]

Knight criticized the viceroy, but he was furious at the agitators. They were 'excited youngsters...who have neither age, nor experience, nor culture enough, to make them know that what they are demanding is impossible.'[40] When Ripon held his viceregal levee, most Europeans boycotted it; Knight, who usually abstained, this time pointedly attended and introduced his son Paul to the viceroy.[41] Knight stood up for Ripon when he most needed support.

Flouting public opinion never bothered Knight; he again recalled that long-past instance:

It is now 27 years since the editor of this paper, stood absolutely alone of the whole Anglo-Indian Press, by the side of Lord Canning in the terrible days of the mutiny. We remember, as it were but yesterday, when we went into the office day after day at the old *Bombay Times,* to find our table piled high with letters from indignant subscribers, telling us to 'stop the paper'....no Englishman living ever encountered such a storm of popular wrath, as was poured out upon our head....we had then as journalists to 'look hellfire in the face,' and the baptism has served us in good stead. We have never flinched since. It is no use for excited and foolish men to write to us, telling us peremptorily to 'stop the paper' or 'stop the advertisements'. They would spare themselves the trouble, if they knew how 'infinitely little' in our eyes such reprisals are.[42]

Knight also turned intermediary; he urged Ripon to confer with leaders of the responsible opposition, organized as the European and Anglo-Indian Defence Association, and explain to them why the principle of the bill must be maintained.[43] He wrote to the viceroy that if the government endorsed Knight's 'right of transfer', the head of the association would support this as a compromise.[44] (As usual, Ripon did not acknowledge or respond to Knight.) The association leaders feared that their young rowdies were getting out of control.[45] There was even a scheme to break into Government House, kidnap the viceroy, and deposit him on an outgoing steamer.[46]

To Knight the Ilbert Bill was 'an act of criminal carelessness, like that which leads a man to light his cigar in a powder factory'.[47] He blamed it for the rise of 'an extreme party' on each side: the extreme English, who want to humiliate the Indian by never allowing him to try an Englishman, and the 'extreme native section', which wants to 'humiliate' the Englishman by forcing him to answer to an Indian magistrate.[48] He vigorously condemned both parties.

Indian papers rejected the 'right of transfer' plan as reducing the bill to a sham and were disappointed that Knight was pushing it. He may be 'an ardent friend' of the people of India, said *Amrita Bazar Patrika*, but he loved his own countrymen more.[49]

Decision time approached, and the city thronged with planters spoiling for a fight. The 'right of transfer' proposal, though acceptable to the Defence Association, was rejected by the viceroy. Since a majority of the Executive Council opposed the bill as drafted, they offered another compromise at the session on 21 December: that Europeans tried by district magistrates and sessions judges have the right to trial by jury (which under pre-existing law would have a European majority). Shuttle negotiations with the Defence Association produced its acceptance, and so Ripon, while ready to fight, decided that compromise was wiser.[50] He approved. A monster protest rally was cancelled. The crisis passed.

The accord nearly collapsed as Ripon again failed to realize the importance of a prompt and full public explanation of his actions. The Defence Association put its own 'spin' on the announcement and proclaimed it a 'concordat' between the government and the association, a 'completely satisfactory settlement' in which the State had conceded the principles for which the European community had been fighting.[51] Supporters of the bill were stunned. Knight wrote: 'The Viceroy is most unlucky. It was with a sort of dazed feeling that the city learned yesterday morning, the terms of the "capitulation" of the Government, to the demands of the European Defence Association....'[52] Rural magistrates, he said, would be stripped of their law-enforcement powers, since they would be subject to juries of British planters, engine-drivers, etc. He even urged Indians to rise in protest against this 'abject capitulation'.[53] Osborn wrote from London that the accord had been received 'with no little disgust' by supporters at home, that Ripon appeared 'weak and vacillating' and should resign his office.[54]

Ripon was furious. He issued an official and more accurate version of the compromise.[55] He explained to Gladstone and others in England how little he had really conceded. But not until the Legislative Council meeting of 7 January 1884, did Ripon explain publicly how judicial arrangements and other safeguards would prevent miscarriage of justice.[56] Europeans saw how illusory their gains were; they would still be subjected to a 'black face' on the bench. Even Knight then changed his mind: 'The concessions which the Government has made are happily far less grave than we had feared....It is Lord Ripon who triumphs after all, and we are heartily glad it is so.'[57]

But first impressions are lasting, and most histories still identify Ripon as the man who gave way on the Ilbert Bill.

THE RAILROAD ROBBERY AND
THE WHISTLE-BLOWERS

Even as the Ilbert Bill reached its threatening climax, Knight and his *Statesman* were sucked again into the murky whirlpool of Hyderabad. Salar Jung died unexpectedly, reportedly of cholera, on 8 February 1883. His antagonistic co-regent, Rashid-ud-din Khan, the amir-i-kabir, had preceded him in death on 13 December 1881. The family feud passed on to the next generation. Salar Jung was succeeded by his eldest son, Mir Laik Ali, who took the title of Salar Jung II and claimed the office of dewan. This was rejected by the Foreign Office in Calcutta which, finally rid of one troublesome Salar Jung, did not want a second. Rashid was succeeded as amir by his son, Kurshed Jah, but the role of the Paigah family was weakened by an internal quarrel over properties and influence between Kurshed Jah and his cousin, Bushir-ud-Dowlah.[58] Knight saw Laik Ali as the great hope for the future of Hyderabad: 'He inherits, it is said, his father's great qualities and his high character, while giving proof that he possesses...the firmness and fearlessness which his father lacked.'[59] After some dithering, authority was fragmented by the British: Laik Ali was named joint state administrator with the *peshkar,* an elderly Hindu official, and a council of regency was created, presided over by the nizam and consisting of Kurshed Jah, Bushir-ud-Dowla, and the peshkar.

One mess which Salar Jung left behind was the Nizam's State Railroad (see pp. 152–3). The railroad had been designed by the British to meet British needs, and for Hyderabad it had been a steady loss since its opening in 1874. A line to the north of the city of Hyderabad, to the towns of Warangal and Chanda and their nearby coal fields, might have changed that, but Salar Jung had been unable to procure the needed investment capital. This was due, at least in part, to the hostility of Lord Lytton and the Conservatives. By 1880, though, the mood had changed, and the Liberals wanted to encourage British investments and enterprises in India, supposedly to help its economic growth.[60]

In 1881 Salar Jung accepted the proposal of a shady newcomer to his service, whom Knight quickly mistrusted—Abdul Huq (or Huk, or even Hak).[61] Huq had developed relationships with officials at the British residency and, perhaps through them, investors and agents in Bombay and London. Representing the dewan he struck a deal with a British agent in Bombay in which a syndicate would buy the existing railroad from the nizam for Rs 20 million, the nizam would then finance construction of the northern line, and the syndicate would receive a 99-year concession of all mineral rights in Hyderabad. This would include the gold and diamond deposits as well as the extensive coal fields.[62] Ripon and the Government of India rejected this as too risky and costly to Hyderabad. Negotiations resumed; Huq visited England, where he favourably impressed Lord Hartington.

The death of Salar Jung produced a regency council without the strength or shrewdness to block Huq. In December of 1883 an elaborate deal was struck and approved by the Raj. Under it a new company would buy out the Nizam's State Railroad for £1,666,000, but the nizam would take £500,000 of that in company shares. He also had to buy out the shareholders of the old company at £625,000 and guarantee a five per cent annual profit (for which £200,000 was deducted in advance). Abdul Huq, though negotiating as a Hyderabad official, secretly deducted £83,000 for himself as a 'sales commission'.[63] An associate of Huq's, William Clarence Watson, received £100,000 from the railroad for 'promotional expenses'.

Just when the financial stars were all aligned, a whistle-blower appeared: J. Seymour Keay, former Hyderabad banker, former agent of the late Salar Jung, and freelance entrepreneur. Keay wrote to the viceroy, with a copy to the *Statesman*, that the proposal would inflict a 'crushing financial injury' on the Hyderabad treasury, between the five per cent guarantee and the interest payments on a construction loan, while the anticipated gains from that Chanda extension rested on 'unfounded assumptions'.[64] Knight commented: 'We have long had a profound distrust of the whole business as a mere job of the "promoters,"' that both the nizam and the British investors were likely to be swindled. And he saw in it a covert scheme by the residency staff.[65] However, the rest of Calcutta was obsessed that month with the climax of the Ilbert Bill battle and the danger of a 'white mutiny'; the Hyderabad railroad deal was silently signed on 27 December 1883.

This was also the time that Knight chose to fulfil his 1881 promise to tell the people of India the *whole* Hyderabad story, as he had to readers in England. Beginning on 21 December, a century of tawdry linen was strung out across eight rambling articles within sixteen days, an indictment of British encroaching, bullying, cheating, and exploiting the dynasty of the nizams and their officials. He blamed the Parliamentary whitewash of Sir Richard Meade on the influence of Northbrook, who had appointed him resident.[66]

Some of these articles were accompanied by pieces attacking the political mess of 1883 which, they said, centred on the British residency in Hyderabad and its corrupt officials. After Meade's retirement in 1881, three residents served there in two years, and so the man who really ran the residency was the first assistant resident, Major G.H. Trevor. However, the major's position had been compromised. His brother had been appointed tutor to the nizam, but lacked teaching qualifications. Rather than disappoint the major, Salar Jung gave his brother a lucrative, do-nothing sinecure, the *Statesman* explained. After seven years of doing practically nothing, much of that time on furlough in England, the brother decided to retire on a generous pension, which the regency council promptly doubled. In this way the major became their prisoner, subject to blackmail.[67]

The newspaper cited a further lesson in practical political science. Both 'the tool and terror' of the residency, and therefore of the state, was that railroad entrepreneur, Abdul Huq. Huq had placed one brother as police superintendent and another as cantonment magistrate, and therefore he knew all the secrets of both court and residency. 'There is not a native subordinate in the Residency who is not under his orders,' it said. 'No dispatch from the Government of India to the Residency, however secret or confidential it may be, is 24 hours in the Residency, before Abdul Huq or his brother has read it.'[68] Knight then wrote to the House of Commons, urging an investigation of the railroad scam and the role of Abdul Huq, to 'save the young Nizam from the ruin which impends over him and his State....'[69] Such a parliamentary inquiry was held, with devastating results, but not until 1888 (see pp. 225–6).

The editor disliked the railroad deal for other reasons. He cited Egypt, where European investments had led to military occupation, and predicted that it would introduce 'a whole host of English adventurers into the Nizam's service, all expecting large salaries and great consideration for condescending to serve a native prince at all.'[70]

Lord Ripon publicly ignored this tumult, but he happened to visit Hyderabad at that time to celebrate Nizam Mahbub Ali Khan's coming of age (that is, eighteen) and the end of the British-imposed regency. The young man, who impressed Ripon with his intelligence, asked for approval to appoint his close friend, Laik Ali, as dewan.[71] The viceroy consented.

Ripon also used the occasion of his visit to inquire closely into the affairs of the residency, and his findings corroborated Knight's main assertions down to the details. He found in Hyderabad 'a mass of intrigue and corruption which it is not easy to exaggerate'. The city was full of shady Europeans, living off the nizam or some noble, claiming vast influence with high officials at the residency or in Westminster. 'The whole place is an Augean Stable which it will take a real Hercules to cleanse,' he wrote.[72] The first example he gave was that of Major Trevor's brother and his sinecure; if only his pension had not been doubled, 'the ugly color which has been given by the Statesman to the transaction would have been without excuse'.[73] His second example was the old peshkar, who admitted falsifying the account books to hide Hyderabad's deep debts. One nebulous withdrawal of Rs 82,000 went, indirectly, to J. Eldon Gorst (who had prosecuted Knight in 1881) for his writing and influence-peddling on behalf of the peshkar.[74]

Ripon seemed more concerned to trace the leaked secrets of the *Statesman* exposé of wrongdoing than to punish the wrongdoers. Hyderabad leaked like a sieve, and the viceroy's inquiries identified two spigots as Captain Claude Clerk, tutor of the nizam, and Colonel Hastings Fraser, military secretary of the residency, along with a regular the *Statesman* correspondent, a former Foreign Office clerk named Sylvester.[75] These might have given that paper some credibility with Ripon, but Knight remained an untouchable to him; neither the editor's political support nor his incisive revelations ever won the viceroy's favour. When one official urged Ripon to publicly contradict Knight's 'mischievous calumny' against Meade, the viceroy answered that the government could not refute 'every wrong newspaper assertion,' and advised him to 'leave Knight and his inventions to go to the father of all such things'.[76] When Knight sent him some secret documents which allegedly proved that the Chanda railway scheme had been forced on the regents by Abdul Huq and the residency, the viceroy (through his secretary) rejected them, claiming he had already been offered them and they proved no such thing.[77] Knight replied that Ripon had intimated that he wished to see the papers, and so the *Statesman* had paid Rs 5600 for them, which the government had never reimbursed.[78]

Knight was disgusted when, at a special durbar on 22 March 1884, Laik Ali (now officially Salar Jung II) fully endorsed Abdul Huq's railroad deal and declared he was completely satisfied with the arrangements, and the nizam rewarded Huq by ennobling him for his successful negotiations.[79] Sylvester heard that Ripon himself, on his recent visit to Hyderabad, had urged the nizam to fully and publicly embrace the Chanda railroad scheme, while Cordery, the resident, had requested the ennobling of Huq 'to prop the waning credit of the scheme'. Furthermore, Huq had arranged the grant of all Hyderabad mining rights to his railroad friends.[80]

Knight later published excerpts from a secret memo by Colonel Fraser (probably the same one he had sent to Ripon), which purportedly showed that Salar Jung I had been forced to accept the Chanda extension plan. The real purpose of the project, he observed, apart from giving Abdul Huq £80,000, was 'to provide a lot of retired Civilians in London, with large salaries at the expense of the Nizam's treasury, under the pretence of their acting as a Board of Directors'.[81]

But the editor was bitterly disappointed in the new dewans fulsome endorsement of Abdul Huq. He wrote to Claude Clerk:

To my great grief I hear the saddest possible accounts of the young Nizam and the Diwan alike. Their excuse of course is their youth; but are there no elder men near them to guide State affairs aright?...

At present I have almost ceased to take interest in the position. I had all of the proof in my hands of the scoundreldom of Abdul Huq...then that fatal memorandum of the young Diwan's appeared justifying and condoning all.[82]

Knight also asked Clerk about 'the true financial position' of Hyderabad. He feared that vague references to 'concealed assets' in the railway prospectus meant the secret transfer of those mining rights. The young dewan needed a chance 'to govern the State wisely and with success. If they have no desire themselves, it would be obtrusive nonsense, for me to concern myself with their affairs any further....'[83]

By mid-1884 Knight's discouragement and weariness were evident. Was the Indian empire producing only exploitation and swindles? Whatever came of 'the moral and material progress' of the Indian people? However, the last word was yet to be heard on Abdul Huq and the great railroad robbery (see pp. 225–6).

CRITIC OF THE EMPIRE AND CIVIL SERVICES

Knight's encounters with officialdom provided mounting evidence of its faults—instinctive opposition to reforms, neglect of mass poverty and famine, crude and callous treatment of the princes, concealing public information from the public, and, most basic, the attitude that the empire existed to provide career outlets for 'civilians', but not 'natives'. (Kipling later glamorized this as 'The White Man's Burden'.) The Raj appeared, as Hume remarked, as a 'great cruel blundering machine....even the driver being incapable of directing its course.'[84] Yet without a bureaucratic mechanism, how could an empire function?

Knight also noted grievances such as ryots driven from ancestral forest lands in Assam, 'the rights of the people being trampled upon with positive contempt'.[85] He deplored the annual flight of officials to remote hill stations, not just each summer, but for up to nine months a year.[86] He chided 'the heaven-born officials who have administered Indian affairs so successfully, that 90 per cent according to Mr. Hume are worse fed, worse clothed and worse off in all respects than they ever were under native rule.'[87] When famine was reported in Murshidabad district of eastern Bengal, the 'civilians' ignored it:

The simple fact is that the heartless civilian tradition—that 'the people are accustomed to starve'—still pervades the whole mind of the Government in these periods of distress. Not an order is issued that is not a covert warning to the district officer not to 'do too much'....It is not until the road sides begin to be strewn with the corpses of the people that the Government really wakes up to its responsibilities.[88]

Knight frequently attacked the exploitation of princely states by 'civilians'. He said the treatment of Hyderabad and Mysore illustrated the two types of British misrule. In one, Hyderabad, all real power and all corrupt influences 'emanate from the Residency'. Mysore (like Hyderabad, a large and historically important state in south India) suffered the consequences of state rule through foreigners. The Raj had replaced the maharaja's officials with some ninety Englishmen, who caused 'the unsettlement and disintegration of everything native'. The state had been restored to the (nominal) rule of its young maharaja in 1881, but it was still 'filled with Englishmen who are holding positions and receiving emoluments that properly belong to the people'. Earlier treaties had been ignored and 'degrading' restrictions imposed, 'a dishonor and a disgrace to a Christian nation,' Knight fumed. 'We become false to ourselves, false to our civilization in doing so, and rightly deserve to lose the supremacy we morally forfeit by such conduct.'[89]

And how did the high-minded Ripon feel about this? Did it even matter?

He is surrounded by experts whose traditional methods, conventional morals, and system of administrative secresy [sic] have robbed them of all sense of honor and conscience, and he is helpless in their hands....

We sometimes wonder whence the remedy will come. We believe it can be looked for, from representative assemblies only.[90]

On economic development, another passionate interest, Knight castigated official incompetence and narrow-mindedness for restraining India from 'the natural and vast progress it would have made' had the government pushed railway extensions forward.[91] At least Liberals favoured State construction of the rails. Knight said that conservative officials such as Sir Alfred C. Lyall, Lieutenant Governor of the North-Western Provinces, would pour tax money into frontier wars but wanted railroads built by private enterprise: 'The legitimate business of the State is—war. The work of railway extension is the work of the English merchant or wealthy native.'[92]

The official mind generally disbelieved that indigenous persons ('natives') could add to the quality or effectiveness of governance. Knight chided A. Rivers Thompson, Lieutenant Governor of Bengal, for refusing to consider Indians for clerkships in his Opium Department. The pretence that they were unqualified for such routine jobs was 'too impudent to be maintained by the most thorough-going civilian conservative,' he wrote.[93] He once proposed a 'very radical reform' of the services in which a portion of the deputy, assistant, or under-secretaryships would be filled by Indians, so that 'a real knowledge of the people, and an element of real sympathetic feeling with the people, might be introduced into the Secretariat.'[94] This was not taken seriously—not until the approach of independence.

Self-serving officials and their private associates knew many ways to exploit an empire, but even principled statesmen could be swept away by political pressures and passions. Gladstone (whom Knight had hailed as 'the great Christian statesman of the century' in 1879) disappointed many by launching the invasion and occupation of Egypt in 1882. The editor wondered

how this great statesman who had moved all England against the Afghan war, could ever have plunged into the Egyptian crime....The influence of the bondholders headed by Mr. Goschen, and represented further by the Barings in the person of Lord Northbrook, and the Rothschilds in Lord Rosebery, with the intensely warlike spirit of the Court, blinded Mr. Gladstone as to the course he was pursuing.[95]

The further plunge into the Sudan and the losses there to the Mahdists filled 'the measure of the nation's wrath with a Ministry that has betrayed every promise and falsified every hope, upon which it was borne into office.'[96]

In India it was the Foreign Office in Simla which was blamed for mischievous adventurism on the frontiers. Knight wrote that even an innocuous commercial mission into isolated Tibet was converted by the Foreign Office into an armed expedition by an 'escort' of several hundred soldiers, a show of force.[97] Ostensibly, these were thrusts in that 'great game' with the Russians.

Knight scoffed at the danger of a Russian invasion of India, as he had for thirty years. Russia, he said, would never get trapped in a costly and profitless war in Central Asia when it faced a real menace in Europe in the expansive German Empire.[98] However, war threatened briefly when a Russian force drove Afghan troops from the disputed border village of Panjdeh on 30 March 1885. Knight accused the Foreign Office, especially its Boundary Commission, of deliberately trying to provoke a war with Russia by pressing Abdur Rahman, the Amir of Kabul, to stake his questionable claim to Panjdeh.[99] From his editorial pulpit he pontificated:

When the historian comes to pass a verdict on this quarrel, he will not mince his language as to our course. It has been unscrupulous and shifty throughout, while it has brought calamity upon the amir and disgrace upon ourselves. We sometimes wonder what these semi-savages must think and say of us, and our pretensions to high morality....[100]

While the press and politicians of London and St Petersburg stoked these fires, it was the 'semi-savage' amir who decided to relinquish his claims to Panjdeh rather than see his nation turned into a bloody battleground by Britain and Russia. The crisis passed. The *Statesman* was also impressed by the Afghans' love of freedom: 'It is absolutely certain that whoever is the first— Englishmen or Russians—in attempting to force the Afghans under the yoke, will make that people an ally and friend of the other.'[101] The Russians learned this lesson a century later.

On the eastern side of India, half of Burma had been annexed by British India after earlier wars, but the king of Upper Burma rejected British commercial and diplomatic demands. The British sent a flotilla up the Irrawaddy River which seized the capital at Mandalay and the royal family in December 1885, abolished the monarchy, and annexed the State.

Knight protested with his customary vigour, finding 'no moral justification whatever' for such a breach of international law. Moreover, the unfortunate Burmese would be consigned to the clutches of the Raj's Foreign Office:

we know nothing more instructive, or more humiliating, than the mass of special pleading which makes up the bulk of our Foreign Office records of its dealings....Having been condemned to read a whole library of these records in the last thirty years, we avow our absolute conviction that no Foreign Office in the world could produce such a record of chicanery, special pleading, and to describe it by a good old Saxon word—rascality.[102]

He recalled the takeovers of princely States in India, such as Oudh:

We begin by abolishing their Prince and reducing his Court, with its multitude of dependents, to beggary. We follow it up by abolishing the whole indigenous machinery of domestic administration, by appointing Englishmen to every office whatever that is either important or lucrative....The people may henceforth be policemen, or private soldiers, or chowkidars [watchmen], but no more. They practically become hewers of wood and drawers of water to us....[103]

Along with the illegality and immorality of annexing Upper Burma, Knight foresaw costly administrative problems, such as 'reducing to order the 99 Shan States or tribes of the interminable forest-clad valleys, gorges, and plateaux which they people'.[104] He feared a continuous grass-roots insurgency, such as the French were then facing in Tonkin.[105] The real purpose, Knight wrote, was the vision of making the Irrawaddy a channel of British trade with populous western China. Therefore, Burma had to be occupied and all armed resistance suppressed. 'If the Burmese people and tribes along the border prove intractable,...the country is so sparsely populated and the distances so great, that military occupation will be all that is practicable.'[106]

Moreover, annexation would bring Britain into direct confrontation with China, which also claimed lands along that undefined border. To European politicians 'China' meant the decaying and near-helpless Ch'ing empire, but Knight peered deeper and saw a future rival more dangerous than Russia:

Does anyone really suppose that with a people like the Chinese, the Western nations will for an indefinite term of years maintain their present superiority over them in arms, equipment, or possible even valour? For ourselves, we have for many years steadily regarded China as the Power we have eventually to dread in this country: and the belief grows upon us.[107]

War, like misgovernment and exploitation, was not an inevitable outcome of imperialism to Knight, but the linkage grew, crowded upon him and enraged him. 'The callous wickedness of the human heart is never so clearly seen,' he wrote, 'as in the utter frivolity with which the idea of war is nursed and encouraged, till it breaks into flame.'[108] A war is the work of a few individuals, he said, seldom an entire nation. It is not needed to prove a nation's courage or 'manliness'. He predicted:

The time is certainly not distant when war between civilized nations will cease....No cause can be more sacred than that against war and oppression and cruelty....War for purposes of national aggrandisement, call it by whatever name we please, is crime. Lord Beaconsfield's war upon Afghanistan, in search of a scientific frontier, was pure and simple crime....[109]

Knight was making many insightful forecasts—elected legislatures, Afghan resistance, the rise of China, dangerous border disputes— but the imminent end of war was not among them.

SELF-GOVERNMENT AND THE START OF THE CONGRESS

As early as 1859 Robert Knight had called for some sort of representative government for India, and he returned to the theme from time to time (see pp. 51 and 110). It was an abstract principle rather than a specific political design, but it was a principle which included meaningful participation of Indians. This was quite radical for 1859, when embers of the Rebellion still smouldered. It was not the universal suffrage direct-democracy which independent India adopted less than a century later, but in 1859 no nation on earth had such a democracy, Britain included.

Knight believed this could be developed within the broad reaches of the British empire. The British North American Act of 1867 had created an essentially self-governing dominion within the empire; while Canada was vastly different from India, it did show the feasibility of home rule schemes. Australia and New Zealand were slowly inching toward home rule, and some crown colonies had local or provincial legislative councils; why not India? In fact, India had had some vaguely representative municipal councils (such as the one in Bombay) for some time. A few Indians had been appointed to serve on legislative councils since 1861, and laws by Lord Mayo as viceroy and later Ripon had promoted local self-government—tokens, perhaps, but also pointers. Knight noted the public participation in the Calcutta Municipality Bill discussions in 1876 and said he had no doubt that 'the day is fast coming when a far more complete system of self-government must be conferred on such a community.'[110]

In 1884 he suggested reconstituting Britain's House of Lords on an empire-wide basis: 'The opinion is rapidly gaining strength that if the empire is to have any permanence, a Chamber must be created where its affairs can be impartially and adequately discussed.'[111]

These were his hopeful and cheerful moments. More often he lamented India's lack of self-government and its rule by 'strangers and aliens'. This mood produced a sad summary of the viceroyalty of Lord Ripon, whom he had sometimes admired:

His Viceroyalty is drawing to a close, and already bids fair to be characterized as a period of great promise and insignificant results....Lord Ripon will leave India, as he found it, bound hand and foot in the fetters of official tyranny, and the overthrow of bureaucratic power used primarily and chiefly for selfish ends...will merely devolve on another Viceroy.[112]

When a physician warned that Calcutta risked a massive cholera epidemic because the slum dwellers of city and suburbs neglected 'simple sanitary precautions', Knight turned the tables. He said the people had been pleading for years for decent water and waste facilities, but the Secretary of State in London refused to authorize a construction loan and the taxes to pay for it. 'We have been 37 years in India,' he continued, 'and have failed to this hour to discover what power the people have. Our system of rule denies them all power, and the world has seen the fierce anger and scorn with which Lord Ripon's mild attempt to vest them with certain powers, has been met....'[113]

However, that 'anger and scorn' of the anti-Ilbert Bill campaign stirred a group of educated Indians to organize and work for India's political revival and strength. The first Indian National Congress convened in Bombay in December 1885. The proceedings were carried out in a democratic manner, and the very first resolution passed asked for a royal enquiry into the administration of the Government of India.[114] The *Statesman* sent no staff reporter but picked up the accounts of the neighbouring *Indian Mirror*, which included summaries of the speeches and resolutions.[115]

Knight apparently never attended a Congress session, but he was a sympathizer and supporter from the start. In the months that followed, he reiterated the Congress's criticisms of the Raj (which largely matched his own). He chided those British who were resentful or fearful of Indian interest in public life; this had been the real purpose in establishing the Raj. Would it be more honourable, he asked, after a century of English rule, that the people were cowed and depressed, and dead to all ambition? He still felt 'the brightest page in England's history will be her regeneration of the East....'[116]

To welcome the second Congress meeting in Calcutta starting 26 December 1886, the *Statesman* rolled out the editorial red carpet. The city's deep interest, it declared, showed that educated Hindus wanted to share responsibilities with the British.[117] Knight urged the Congress to focus on the problem of mass poverty in India, but also on introducing a representative principle into the existing provincial legislative councils. There should be no real opposition, he claimed, because the existing government

consists of men who have no interest in the country, but that which is ephemeral and adventitious, and that arises from an honorable desire to do what, as foreigners, they believe to be best for the people. No purity of motive...can possibly stand in the place of that interest which the people themselves feel in their own affairs....[118]

The Congress accepted these ideas, without mentioning a method for achieving them, such as elections. The editor hoped that with legislators representing their interests, the Indian people would become happy partners in the British empire. The government, without abdicating any authority, could 'popularize the Councils so as to make them thoroughly representative in character, and responsible in the eyes of the people for measures passed thereby, and thus reconciling them for an indefinite period to British rule as their own national rule....'[119]

Preparations began for the third annual Congress, scheduled to be held at Madras at the end of 1887. The *Statesman* noted several local meetings at which delegates were chosen. One at Aligarh, on 6 December, was chaired by the secretary of the Aligarh Institute; six delegates were named for the Madras Congress, including two Muslims. Similar meetings were held at Kanpur and Lucknow, chaired by Muslims, and mixed delegations chosen.[120] Knight emphasized Muslim participation, having previously noted and regretted the reticence of some Muslim leaders. (He had expressed a special sympathy for Muslims, whose 'deep religious feelings,' he felt, handicapped their pursuit of modern education.)[121]

After that third Congress, Knight requested an interview with the viceroy, Lord Dufferin, to discuss the annual congresses 'and the growing demand of the people for Representative Councils'.[122] Such councils would strengthen the government, he explained; they would serve as a check on rogue mufassil officers, they would give popular support to the Raj in its negotiations with Westminster, and they would defend Indian interests when they clashed with those of Britain (as in the cotton tariffs and the costs of the Afghan war). Such councils would need the right to question government ministers, since 'it cannot be healthy or conducive to good government' to operate in complete secrecy. The existing councils, said Knight, should either be reformed 'or some new body altogether should be devised for consultative or deliberative functions'.[123]

Although there is no record of a response by the viceroy, either by letter or personal interview, he must have liked Knight's ideas, for he sent similar proposals to Westminster. There they were stopped by Salisbury and his Tory ministry.[124] Dufferin's successor, Lord Lansdowne, altered the provisions slightly and received Westminster's approval for what became the Indian Councils Act of 1892.[125]

Under its terms the legislative councils were expanded and given authority to question the ministers, as Knight had urged. The additional members were chosen by what was called 'election'; for the provincial councils, candidates were 'elected' by certain 'selected constituencies'—municipalities, universities, trade associations, etc.—and the names sent to the governor general for 'nomination' (that is, appointment). For the Imperial Legislative Council, each of the four large provincial councils 'elected' one of its own non-official members.[126] This advance was enough to jolt empire loyalists, though never enough to satisfy Indian nationalists. Even so, it showed that the Raj could be moved. One of its movers was Robert Knight—although he did not live to see the new law.

FURTHER FIGHTS: THE TENANCY BILL AND THE BURDWAN TRIAL

December 20, 1883: Looked in on Knight, editor of the 'Statesman,' who gave me his views on the decadence of English morality, which he dates from the first Afghan war. He has been useful in exposing many of the official iniquities here, and takes, as it seems to me, generally just views....[127]

—Wilfred Scawen Blunt

By 1883, Robert Knight was famous enough in India and beyond, that a freethinking traveller and journalist such as Wilfred Scawen Blunt might well seek him out. Whether Knight's views were liked or not, no one denied his candour and courage. However, Knight in his late years was drawn into a wide range of issues, and 'English morality' could not always guide him.

Might criteria of morality be altered by 'situational ethics'? After the issuance of the mortgage to a zamindari estate—the Paikpara Raj—in 1881, snippy remarks about the parasitical Bengal zamindars seem to have disappeared from Knight's columns. Now they were presented as conscientious managers of local estates who were forced by Cornwallis into the ruinous Permanent Settlement of 1793, and many were unable to meet the heavy revenue demands of the Raj. Therefore, he wrote, '[a]ncient families of the provinces, who had survived all of the oppressions of our predecessors, disappeared one after another under the cast-iron despotism of a rule resistance to which was hopeless....'[128]

The rival *Pioneer* jibed that the *Statesman*'s new approach must have been dictated by its mortgagees, but Knight credited his views to his lifetime study of land tenure questions and cited the writings of radical economist Henry George and the Muslim concept of *khiraj* to dispute the claims of cultivator-ownership of land.[129]

The immediate issue was the Bengal Tenancy Bill (also called the Rent Bill), intended to provide cultivators in Bengal-Bihar with improved occupancy rights and other protections. Such protection as they had retained in the 1793 settlement had been whittled away by zamindars and other landlords over time. They had a long train of grievances, and Ripon, upon arrival in India, determined on remedial legislation. He studied the matter carefully during 1881;[130] rural rights, relationships, and usages were a thorny thicket of variances and vagueness. Proposals were drafted in 1882, and, following the procedures of the day, the folders, bound in their traditional red tape, were circulated among the councillors, secretariat, and affected local officers for opinions and comments. (This procedure was so elaborate and involved that it gave 'red tape' the bad name which it retains to this day.) Further delays ensued when some of Ripon's key provisions were rejected by Hartington and his Council of India.

An approved Tenancy Bill was first introduced into the Legislative Council in 1883, but by then Ilbert's Criminal Procedure Code Bill was absorbing nearly all attention and energy. In December the Tenancy Bill was withdrawn and a commission appointed for further inquiry. Knight approved of this: 'Our sympathies are all with the ryot, as they have been throughout our journalistic life; but our judgment at present is against the Bill,' which he said would upset landlord-tenant relations.[131]

His opposition had hardened by the summer of 1884, when the amended bill was produced and sent through its procedural gamut. He fired a fusillade of argument against it: the bill was 'a palpable and gross violation' of the 1793 settlement; it would strip the zamindar of his property and give it to the ryot; rents which were too low would allow 'careless husbandry' and wasted resources; the bill falsely assumed that the zamindar was oppressing the ryot, etc.[132] Ripon, whose term as viceroy was expiring, drafted a watered-down bill but left final action for his successor, Lord Dufferin. Dufferin and his council promptly passed the bill early in 1885.

While the Raj was imploding from the Ilbert Bill, local self-government, and the Tenancy Bill, none of which helped India's economy, Knight bemoaned official inaction on proposals that could have, such as railroad extensions, bimetal currency, and rupee development loans. 'We used sometimes to reflect with bitterness how we would have changed it all,' he recalled, 'but we have long reconciled ourselves to mere remonstrating against it.'[133] He attended a conference on India's economic distress, which concluded (once again) that the basic problem was the density of population crowding and straining the land, and the solution was alternate employment, that is, industrial development. But the government was doing nothing to help it.[134]

Later, the editor presented a proposal: Why not collect the land revenue in surplus grain instead of demanding cash? Government agents could receive it at a set price (he suggested one rupee for 25 seers, roughly 62 lbs) and ship it to Britain. This would kill four birds with one stone: the ryot could pay his taxes without borrowing from the usurious moneylender, the grain market would be steady and reliable, the 'home charges' would no longer drain India's specie, and the people of Britain would have a set source of cheap grain.[135] A fertile idea, but sown on barren ground.

Rural poverty remained, and Knight, observing the 'squalid wretchedness' of the countryside in 1886, feared that it was worsening. In two extensive articles he re-examined but rejected his old familiar reasons: Poverty was not to be blamed on the land revenue, nor the home charges, nor the lack of an export market (which had gradually eased with time); it was not even overpopulation and lagging development, though these contributed. Instead

we are more and more disposed every year to attribute the general poverty to the legislative action which has broken up and utterly disintegrated the whole framework of rural society, and left it a ruin.

Ancient rights, privileges, and usages are all abolished, and the interests they represented made over to the trading and banking classes, under decrees of our civil courts....[136]

So the basic cause of Indian poverty, he now said, was this unfair 'redistribution of wealth...and the practical denial of justice' by the courts, through ignorance and the unsuitability of British legal institutions to Indian wants and needs.[137] Perhaps this was a bitter aftertaste of the Tenancy Bill squabble, or perhaps it showed the inroads made by age, illness, or disappointment. It was a strange stance for a man who had begun his career as an eager liberal social reformer.

Another once-fervent hope, for mass conversions to Christianity, was also fading. He remained confident that the Indian people, 'so sensitive, so thoughtful, so intellectual,' would not continue forever 'bathing in the waters of the Ganges or believing in the black stone in Mecca'. But British missionaries could not convert India; like other Anglo-Indians 'their utter inability to contract friendships with the native population' restricted their role. No spiritual movement would succeed in India, he concluded, if its evangelists were 'the salaried agents of a Missionary Society located in a foreign land'.[138]

Another awkward religious problem was the 'ecclesiastical establishment'—the Church of England in India, headed by the Bishop of Calcutta, required by the Charter Renewal Acts of 1813 and 1833. The Raj's earlier patronage of Indian religions (see p. 62) had been phased out, and only official Christianity was being financed by Indian taxpayers. This offended Knight's sense of fair play. He felt that the government should treat all major religions equally and so recommended dissolving the Anglican establishment.[139]

CALCUTTA'S PROBLEMS

In his Bombay days Knight had been passionately involved in civic affairs (see pp. 102, 110–12). He no longer had that personal participation after his move to Calcutta, but he retained his concern. Calcutta, like almost every metropolis, had an expanding population and overstretched municipal facilities. As in Bombay, the city fathers quarrelled over an equitable and effective means of raising revenue. As in Bombay, Knight urged the levying of a broad-based indirect tax, an octroi or customs duty on essentials, instead of fastening the burden on the house owners (see p. 72).

In 1884 he wrote a series of twelve articles in the *Statesman* on civic financing. He depicted a man who had invested his wealth in stocks making a comfortable tax-free income while his neighbour, who had invested instead in rental properties, was bereft through municipal rates atop the interest payments on his mortgage.[140] Moreover, Calcutta needed 'an army of tax-gatherers' to collect the rates and serve the demands and distress warrants.[141] All taxes are resisted, he added; the merchant, the official, the zamindar 'are positively content that Calcutta should be a dung-heap and a cess-pool rather than pay one sixpence'.[142] An income tax, theoretically the fairest, would in India's situation be impossible to levy equitably or collect effectively.

Knight proposed a balanced package of taxes: from the public, an octroi of 1½ per cent on basic necessities brought into the city; from merchants, a light transit tax, such as two *anna*s on a bale of cotton; and, from the imperial government, a small share on the goods which it marketed—Rs 10 on each chest of opium, one rupee on each *maund* (about 28 lbs) of salt, and a share of the *abkari* (liquor license) revenue. With such income the city corporation could float bonds to fund the much-needed public works projects, and within a decade the *bustee*s (huts), dungholes, and crowded thoroughfares could be replaced by 'a well-laid-out city, with broad streets, avenues of trees, water-channels, and green play-grounds all over it'.[143]

The editor reminded his readers of his plan at least twice during the following months.[144] But the reprinting of these articles by the *Statesman* thirteen years later must have meant that the powers-that-were, were not persuaded and the problems remained.

THE BURDWAN LIBEL CASE

In 1886 Knight was again accused of defamatory writing and prosecuted on a criminal libel charge, and again it became a *cause célèbre*. The Maharaja of Burdwan, a prominent and wealthy princeling and zamindar of West Bengal, had died childless in 1885. The Bengal Board of Revenue, acting as a Court of Wards, appointed as managers of the estate Thomas DeB. Miller, an estate official, and Bun Bihari Kapur, a member of the family, while the family arranged a posthumous adoption. The next year the *Statesman* ran a series of articles accusing the two managers of 'criminal misappropriation' of estate funds.[145]

In the Burdwan case, as elsewhere, Knight had relied on confidential informants. Journalists often try to develop such sources, but they must discern shrewdly their accuracy and reliability. In this case he denied indignantly that wanton or reckless charges had been made. 'We took very unusual pains to make sure that we were not being misled,' he wrote.[146]

Knight's trial began on 21 July 1886 at the Criminal Sessions Court. After a 'protracted and harrassing trial,' the jury voted to acquit, six to three. However, the presiding judge, Justice James O'Kinealy, refused to accept the verdict and ordered the case retried.[147] Thomas Miller died before the retrial at the next session, but the case was pursued by what Knight called 'a clique of hostile Anglo-Indians'.[148] Among them was J.C. Macgregor, the barrister/journalist who had first stirred the anti-Ilbert Bill panic (see p. 200). Knight claimed the prosecution was 'carried on by a knot of private Englishmen (officials and lawyers) who are dishonest to be known, but who have the *secret* support of the Government, I fear. They want to crush the *Statesman*, and thought to terrify the whole press by doing so....'[149]

If old enemies appeared, so did old friends, notably the Bengalis. His counsel for the trial was W.C. Bonnerji, then Congress president. A public meeting was held, with Surendranath Banerjea speaking and a fund raised for the defence.[150] *Som Prakash*, the Calcutta weekly, declared: 'If he is convicted for this, the evil purpose of the Government will become evident.'[151]

Two friends of Knight, George Yule and Sambhu Chunder Mookerjee, arranged a compromise settlement in which the *Statesman* printed a retraction and apology, and the libel case was dropped. Mookerjee later wrote that he had induced Knight to apologize 'for charges which, inspired as they were by good faith and a love of justice, were nonetheless entirely wanting in solid foundation.'[152]

And this was the verdict of a friend.

On a lighter note, while the Burdwan case was festering and Knight was lamenting rural poverty, he received a letter: 'Yours is the most socialist paper I know in India. You are ever advocating the cause of the poor against the oppression of the rich and powerful.' To which Knight responded: 'If this is Socialism, we are glad to be tinctured with it....We have been called a good many things in our lifetime, but never socialists that we remember before.'[153]

FINAL YEARS: ILLNESS AND DEATH

Knight's unspecified medical problems, perhaps stemming from malarial infection, had forced him to shut down the London *Statesman* in 1880 (see pp. 174 and 195). They may have caused his year of silence in 1882. From 1887 he was in 'failing health', according to his own paper, and had been advised to return to England, but he held on as editor.[154] Ill health probably contributed to the despair which showed in an 1887 letter to Sambhu Chunder Mookerjee: 'while I try to speak the truth from my heart, I feel so keenly my shortcomings from my own ideal, that I am very weary of the efforts and would fain never write another line from my sense of the rasping tone in which my nature expresses itself.'[155]

Mookerjee, a friend of his late years, called the editor 'a finished public man—of great knowledge and wide experience of affairs. For reading he had a passionate thirst. His collection of books, especially on finance, currency, statistics and cognate subjects, was one of the rarest.'[156] He later wrote:

Knight and I differed on many questions of home and foreign or outside politics. He was a man of strong likes and dislikes....He could not bear the Mussalmans....For all that, we loved each other with the highest esteem. Hundreds, if not thousands, of letters passed between us. He asked my opinion on every difficulty, political or personal. His was the only European table at which I sat with the family as one of them. Friendship got the better of my Brahmanic prudence.[157]

Knight developed a correspondence with D. Mackenzie Wallace, Dufferin's secretary, who also mentioned the editor's illness and hoped for his recovery.[158] Knight was still full of ideas; he urged the government to promote construction of a railroad through the Khyber Pass to Istanbul, 'giving the intervening territories the humanizing influence of travel,' in cooperation with the Russians and the Amir of Kabul. Wallace, in reply, cited some practical problems, such as the cost.[159]

Knight was at least cheered by the vindication of his earlier campaign against Abdul Huq, crooked minister of the Nizam of Hyderabad (see pp. 205-7). In October 1885, Secretary of State Lord Randolph Churchill and his India Council discovered the massive commission of £83,000 which Huq had deducted from the proceeds of the nizam's sale of railroad shares (and had negotiated as a minister) in 1883. Churchill chided the Government of India; had *he* known of this, he would never have approved the deal. He was told that '[r]umours that some such transaction had taken place reached us in the spring of 1884; but the source of our information was untrustworthy, and was not of such a nature as to make official action possible.'[160] (Did that sneer mean they read about it in the *Statesman*? If so, Knight had the last sneer.)

Meanwhile, Abdul Huq (now called Sirdar Diler Jung) and his British associates were scaling new financial heights. They formed the Hyderabad (Deccan) Company (also called the Hyderabad Deccan Mining Co.) on 1 January 1886 and personally obtained the concession of all Hyderabad mineral rights from generous State officials for a pittance ('as my reward for my great services to the State,' one partner later testified.)[161] The partners then sold the concession to their company for £850,000, of which Huq got £120,000. Huq also persuaded the nizam to invest £120,000 in the company, but instead of sending the order to the London stock exchange, he pocketed the entire amount and gave the nizam some of his own unissued shares. He even charged an additional £11,000 to cover any speculative price rises during the non-sale.[162] When this was discovered, in April of 1888, the furious nizam dismissed Huq from his service and demanded (and received) the return of his funds.[163]

These candid disclosures were made at the hearings of a Select Committee of the House of Commons which began on 1 June 1888. Whether they stemmed from Knight's request for such hearings, made four years earlier (see p. 207), is not known.

Although his revelations of 1883-4 were essentially confirmed, even that weary cynic sounded shocked at the effrontery of the mining concession and the swindle of the nizam.[164] Ripon had killed an earlier version of the concession in 1883, but it had been secretly revived after his departure. Knight reiterated his old object lesson:

Had this mining scheme been honestly confided to the public, it would have been impossible to carry it through. So successfully was it guarded from public knowledge, that no one ever heard of it until a few months back....There is no remedy that we can see but the establishment of some kind of representative assemblies, in which the Government shall be liable to interpellations.[165]

No one at the Parliamentary hearing shared Knight's shock or outrage, although J.D. Mayne, counsel for the Hyderabad government, complained of 'fraud' and 'bribery', and Sir Horace Davey, counsel for Abdul Huq, admitted he could not justify 'either legally or morally a transaction in which an agent for purchase sells his own property secretly to the Government'.[166] Cordery, resident at Hyderabad since April 1883, used most of his testimony to explain how little he knew of what had happened around him: he had not had 'the remotest conception' that Abdul Huq was a partner in the railroad company, nor that he had received a large sales commission from that company, nor that the mining concession had any connection with the railroad company, nor that its directors had retained that £850,000; had he known this last, he would have 'questioned it'.[167]

The Select Committee concluded that the concessionaires had injured the state through their great gains from the concession, obtained through their partner, Abdul Huq. But no one spoke of criminal proceedings; their only remedy, far less radical than Knight's, was 'more effective and direct British assistance' to princely states.[168] Just a slight squeak in the imperial machinery!

As for Abdul Huq, he showed no signs of contrition; he even had the further effrontery to seek restoration of his position with the nizam (which was rejected). Laik Ali (Salar Jung II), who had endorsed and supported Huq, was accused by the nizam of misuse of public funds and neglect of duties. He resigned as dewan in 1887, allegedly because of 'ill health'.[169]

DEATH OF KNIGHT

In 1889 misfortune befell Robert Knight. His oldest child, Alice Harrington, had been stricken with rheumatic fever and gone to the Isle of Jersey for recovery. Her three-month-old son, Robert, died. Her sister, Edith Boutflower, joined her with her own four children.[170] Colonel Osborn, Knight's longtime friend and London correspondent, died while playing tennis.[171] Then his youngest son, Duncan, who had recently passed the Indian Civil Service examination, died in London on 19 November 1889, also apparently of the effects of rheumatic fever.[172] Robert, in Calcutta, sent the news to Catherine, vacationing in Darjeeling, that 'our little Dun is dead'. He told her: 'Try dearest to bear it, for all our sakes—and for mine especially, as I will for yours. You know that I view early death as a dignity of God's love to the young, but the blow strikes very deep, and we must help each other to endure it, now that it has fallen upon us.'[173]

Robert himself was wracked with pain from 'complications of the liver and other complaints,' as Mookerjee wrote:

That the end could not be put off long was anticipated....The change to Darjeeling had done him some good, but the benefit did not continue, and he had to be brought down to Calcutta, but his condition was not regarded as quite so critical, and it was even hoped that a change to England might bring him round. It had accordingly been decided that in March he should return home.[174]

However, Catherine wrote in the family ledger: 'Dear Robert passed away,' at 5:40 a.m., on 27 January 1890, at the age of 64 years, ten months, and seventeen days. She wrote to 'the best beloved' that 'I will be with thee in trouble.' A poem followed: 'Ah! Sweet, the world grows old....'

NOTES

1.　*Statesman*, 7 April 1880. The loss had actually been reported in 1874; perhaps its news value in 1880 was that the chief commissioner who reported it was Sir Richard Meade (before his Baroda and Hyderabad episodes).

2.　Note of James D. Gordon, former chief commissioner of Mysore, 14 March 1881, and Ripon to Hartington, 19 December 1881, both included in India, Political and Secret Letters, Materials #149 of December, 1881.

3. The entire correspondence is reproduced in S.C. Sanial, 'History of Journalism in India—V', *Calcutta Review* (hereafter *CR*), vol. 127, July 1908, pp. 386–91. Some later writers blamed (or credited) Knight for that act of *lèse majesté*, but he had left for London by then.

4. This response was received from the *Statesman* managers, the Knight family, and the Paikpara family. The data in this paragraph came from Sanial, 'History of Journalism', 387n; *Thacker's Bengal Directory* for 1878, and the notice in the *Statesman* of 10 February 1881.

5. H.W.B. Moreno, *The Paikpara and Kandi Raj* (Calcutta Moreno, 1919), pp. 45 and 50–2. The author wishes to acknowledge gratefully the assistance of Dr Ujjal Ray on this section.

6. Sanial, 'History of Journalism'. He says Indra Chandra became 'virtually their proprietor', but it was actually a joint family ownership in the Indian tradition.

7. Knight to Henry Primrose, private secretary to Ripon, 17 April 1884, Ripon Papers (hereafter RP), Add. MSS #43635.

8. Hilda Kidd to the author, 26 August 1968.

9. N.A., *A Brief History of the Statesman* (Calcutta: Statesman, 1947), p. 12.

10. 'Egypt: a protest against the war, with suggestions as to the course the Ministry should follow' (London: W.J. Johnson, 1882), p. 10.

11. Ibid., p. 11.

12. *Statesman*, 30 April 1883.

13. Interview with the author at Eastbourne, 21 August 1968.

14. Ibid., also Hilda Kidd to the author, 26 August 1968.

15. Ibid.

16. Ibid.; interview, 21 August 1968.

17. Surendranath Banerjea, *A Nation in the Making, Being the Reminiscences of Fifty Years of Public Life* (London: Humphrey Milford–Oxford University Press, 1927), p. 78.

18. *Statesman*, 7 December 1883. The filed copy was marked 'Town Edition'; other editions might have run it a day earlier or later.

19. Ibid., 4 December 1883.

20. Ibid., 6 December 1883. Another such piece ran 18 December 1883.

21. Ibid., 28 August 1884.

22. Ibid., 20 Sept 1883, and 27 November 1883.

23. As quoted in the *Statesman*, 3 December 1883.

24. *Statesman*, 18 December 1883.

25. For the full story of the Ilbert Bill and its consequences, see Edwin Hirschmann, 'White Mutiny', The Ilbert Bill Crisis in India and the Genesis of the Indian National Congress (Columbia, Mo.: South Asia Books, 1980).
26. 5 February 1883.
27. Ripon to Northbrook, 5 March 1883, Northbrook Papers, vol. 3, pp. 40-2.
28. Statesman, 1 March 1883, or 'White Mutiny', Appendix C.
29. 5 February 1883.
30. 7, 9, and 14 February 1883.
31. 24 February 1883.
32. 12 March 1883.
33. Hindoo Patriot (Calcutta), 9 April 1883, pp. 173-4.
34. William Wedderburn, Allan Octavian Hume, CB (New Delhi: Pegasus (India), 1974 [1913]), pp. 50-2.
35. Statesman, 5 September 1883. The administrative complexities implied would have been staggering.
36. Gibb to Ripon, 18 November 1883, RP, BP7/6, 2 of 1883, #160b.
37. Statesman, 1 December 1883.
38. Englishman (Calcutta), 3 December 1883.
39. Steuart Bayley to Ripon, 6 December 1883, RP, BP7/6, 2 of 1883, #180c.
40. Statesman, 4 December 1883.
41. Ibid., 6 December 1883; Pioneer, Allahabad, 7 December 1883.
42. Statesman, 5 December 1883.
43. Ibid. For reiterations and amplifications, see his Statesman editorials of 7, 10, and 12 December 1883.
44. Knight to Primrose, 13 December 1883, RP, Add. MSS #43634, p. 78.
45. Times (London), 4 December 1883, p. 5.
46. C.E. Buckland, Bengal Under the Lieutenant-Governors (Calcutta: Kedarnath Bose, 1902), p. 787.
47. Statesman, 8 December 1883.
48. Ibid., 14 December 1883.
49. 20 December 1883.
50. Ripon to Kimberley, 22 December 1883, RP, BP7/3, #81, pp. 313-7; Ripon to Auckland Colvin, 20 December 1883, Ibid., BP7/6 (vol. II of 1883), #139a; European and Anglo-Indian Defence Association, Proceedings of the Meetings of the Council, Commencing from 29th March 1883 to 30th June 1887, now held by the United Kingdom Citizens' Association, Calcutta.
51. Englishman, Statesman, and every other major newspaper, 22 December 1883.

52. *Statesman*, 23 December 1883.
53. Ibid., 28 December 1883.
54. Ibid., 23 January 1884.
55. *Englishman*, 23 December 1883.
56. India, *Proceedings of the Legislative Council*, vol. 23, pp. 58–70. For instance, a judge could appeal an unjust acquittal by a jury.⁵
57. *Statesman*, 9 January 1884.
58. The most coherent and comprehensive account of this tangle is Ray, pp. 104–6.
59. *Statesman*, 30 December 1883.
60. Bharati Ray, *Hyderabad and British Paramountcy, 1858–1883* (New Delhi: Oxford University Press, 1988), pp. 152–3; Tara Sethia, 'Railways, Raj, and the Indian States: Policy of Collaboration and Coercion in Hyderabad State', in Clarence B. Davis and Kenneth E. Wilburn, Jr, eds, with Ronald E. Robinson, *Railway Imperialism* (New York: Greenwood Press, 1991), pp. 112–13.
61. The shadows even hide his biodata. Sethia (p. 114) says Huq began as a trooper in the British Indian army, then was 'loaned' to Hyderabad as a police officer but quickly promoted to home secretary. Ray (p. 207), however, identifies him as Hyderabad's public works and mines minister. The *Dictionary of Indian Biography* (p. 2) calls him the son of a small Deccan chieftain who joined government service in Bombay. Knight wrote that Meade and Assistant Resident G.H. Trevor had hired him to spy on Salar Jung. *Statesman*, 29 January 1884.
62. *Statesman*, 4 April 1884; *The Statesman*, 17 May 1888, as quoted in Syed Mahdi Ali, comp. *Hyderabad Affairs* (Bombay: Times of India Press, 1883–6), vol. 10, pp. 124–5, and 13 May 1888, as quoted in Mahdi Ali, *Hyderabad Affairs*, vol. 10, pp. 107–12.
63. J.G. Cordery, in testimony to a Parliamentary committee. Great Britain, Commons, First and Second Reports of the Select Committee on East India (Hyderabad Deccan Mining Company), 7 of 1888, (London: Eyre and Spottiswood, 1888), pp. 185–7. For further detail, see Sethia, 'Railways, Raj', pp. 113–16, and Ray, pp. 152–63. For the exposure, see pp. 225–6.
64. *Statesman*, 13 December 1883.
65. Ibid., 13 and 14 December 1883.
66. *Indian Statesman* (weekly edn), 22 January 1884.
67. *Statesman*, 30 December 1883.
68. Ibid., 1 January 1884.
69. *Indian Statesman*, 29 January 1884.
70. Ibid., 12 February 1884.

71. Ripon to Kimberley, 6 February 1884, RP, Indian State Papers, BP7/3. #7.
72. Ibid.
73. Ibid.
74. Ibid. One product of this arrangement seems to have been the critical *Fortnightly Review* article already cited (see Chapter 4).
75. Bayley to Ripon, 22 February 1884, and John G. Cordery (the resident at Hyderabad) to Ripon, 24 February 1884, both in RP, BP7/6, 1 of 1884, #63 and 64A.
76. Ripon to Alfred C. Lyall, 1 March 1884, RP, BP7/6, 1 of 1884, #67.
77. Knight to Primrose, 17 April 1884, RP, Add. MSS 43635, p. 17; Primrose to Knight, 26 April 1884, ibid., p. 136a.
78. Knight to D. Mackenzie Wallace, private secretary to Lord Dufferin (who succeeded Ripon as viceroy), 24 April 1888, Wallace Papers, MSS Eur. F130/46d. However, his newspaper was later reimbursed by 'Mr. Keay', Knight to Primrose, 7 June 1884, RP, Add. MSS 43635, p. 37.
79. Mahdi Ali, *Hyderabad Affairs*, 1883, vol. 9, p. 528.
80. *Statesman*, 3 and 4 April 1884.
81. Ibid., 5 February 1885. See also 11 April 1884.
82. Knight to Clerk, 10 June 1884, Claude Clerk Papers, MSS Eur. D538/13, f615.
83. Ibid., 18 June 1884, ibid., f621. Actually, that mining concession had been granted to a separate but associated company in a separate but associated deal (see pp. 225-6).
84. Hume to Ripon, 4 March 1884, RP, BP7/6 (1 of 1884), #87a.
85. *Statesman*, 2 April 1886.
86. Ibid., 5 June 1884.
87. Ibid., 1 June 1884.
88. Ibid., 20 May 1885.
89. Ibid., 6 April 1884.
90. Ibid. This proposal will be aired in the next subsection.
91. Ibid., 8 January 1884. Actually, the Ripon administration promoted railroad construction as famine protection. S[arvepalli] Gopal, *The Viceroyalty of Lord Ripon, 1880-1884* (London: Oxford University Press), pp. 180-5.
92. *Statesman*, 5 April 1884.
93. Ibid., 26 August 1884. Knight had also sought better use of, and compensation for, uncovenanted Europeans in the civil service. *Bombay Times*, 6 March 1858.
94. Ibid., 6 June 1884.
95. Ibid., 4 June 1884

96. Ibid., 8 April 1884.
97. Ibid., 28 May 1886.
98. Ibid., 5 February 1885.
99. Ibid,. 13 June and 10 November 1885. Virtual repetitions have been omitted. Knight often reiterated editorial themes, with his later language tending to grow stronger and more vehement.
100. Ibid., 16 June 1885.
101. 7 September 1886.
102. Ibid., 25 December 1885.
103. Ibid.
104. Ibid.
105. Ibid., 22 December 1885.
106. Ibid., 4 September 1886.
107. Ibid., 22 December 1885. 'This country' which China might some day threaten meant India.
108. Ibid., 6 September 1884.
109. Ibid., 16 October 1885.
110. *Friend of India*, 1 April 1876, p. 279.
111. *Statesman*, 4 November 1884.
112. Ibid., 1 April 1884.
113. Ibid., 31 January 1885.
114. R.C. Majumdar, 'The Indian National Congress', in *British Paramountcy and Indian Renaissance*, Part II, vol. 10, *The History and Culture of the Indian People* (R.C. Majumdar, gen. ed.), (Bombay: Bharatiya Vidya Bhavan, 1965), p. 537.
115. *Statesman*, 2 January 1886.
116. Ibid., 3 June 1886.
117. Ibid., 23 December 1886.
118. Ibid., 24 December 1886. Did he actually think there would be no 'real opposition'?
119. Ibid., 4 January 1887.
120. Ibid., 10 December 1887 (weekly edn).
121. Ibid., 7 February 1885.
122. Knight to D. Mackenzie Wallace, private secretary to Dufferin, 6 February 1888, Wallace Papers, MSS Eur. F130/46b.
123. Ibid.
124. Penderel Moon, *The British Conquest and Dominion of India* (London: Duckworth , 1989), p. 887.
125. Great Britain, 55 and 56 Vic., ch. 14.
126. Courtenay Ilbert, *The Government of India*, 2nd edn (Oxford: Clarendon Press, 1907), pp. 115–19.
127. Wilfred Scawen Blunt, *India Under Ripon, A Private Diary* (London: T. Fisher Unwin, 1909), p. 92.

128. *Statesman*, 26 August 1884.
129. Ibid., 3 September 1884,
130. Gopal, pp. 190–5. See also Lucien Wolf, *Life of the First Marquess of Ripon* (London: John Murray, 1921), vol. 2, pp. 84–9.
131. *Statesman*, 21 December 1883.
132. Ibid., 12 September 1884 and 31 January 1885.
133. Ibid., 11 April 1884.
134. Ibid., 1 January 1884.
135. Ibid., 3 June 1884.
136. Ibid., 11 and 12 May 1886.
137. Ibid.
138. Ibid., 8 February 1885.
139. Ibid., 5 January and 2 November 1884, and 18 October 1885.
140. The articles were reprinted in *Statesman* beginning 21 October 1897, when the city faced a similar crisis. They were then reprinted separately and entitled 'The Condition of Calcutta', pp. 1 and 2.
141. Ibid., p. 6.
142. Ibid., p. 13.
143. Ibid., p. 39.
144. *Statesman*, 31 January and 13 June 1885.
145. Ibid., 9 May 1886; Ram Gopal Sanyal, ed., *Reminiscences and Anecdotes of Great Men of India* (Calcutta: Sen Press, 1895), vol. 2, pp. 146–7.
146. *Statesman*, 9 May 1886.
147. Sanyal, ed., *Reminiscences and Anecdotes*, p. 147.
148. Ibid.
149. Knight to Sanyal, 3 August, 1886, reprinted in ibid.
150. Banerjea, *A Nation in the Making*, p. 78.
151. India, *Reports on Native Papers*, Bengal, week ending 21 August 1886, p. 935.
152. Ibid., F.H. Skrine, *An Indian Journalist: Being the Life, Letters, and Correspondence of Dr. Sambhu C. Mookerjee* (Calcutta: Thacker, Spink, 1895), p. 176.
153. *Statesman*, 12 June 1886.
154. 28 January 1890; *Indian Mirror*, as quoted in *Statesman*, 30 January 1890.
155. Skrine, *An Indian Journalist*, p. 194.
156. *Reis and Rayyet* (Calcutta), 1 February 1890.
157. Mookerjee to James Routledge, 18 March 1890, in Skrine, pp. 325–7. Compare with George Birdwood's description of Knight's temperament as a younger man, pp. 78–9.
158. Wallace to Knight, 10 July 1888, Dufferin Papers, MSS Eur. F130, 45, d.

159. Knight to Wallace, 27 July 1888, and Wallace to Knight, 14 September 1888, Dufferin Papers, 46, g, and 45, e.

160. Testimony of Gen. Sir Richard Strachey, a member of the Council of India, Commons, 7, *First and Second Reports from the Select Committee on East India (Hyderabad Deccan Mining Company)* p. 218.

161. Testimony of William Clarence Watson, ibid., pp. x (of the report) and 106–7 (of the testimony).

162. Ibid., pp. xiv (of the report) and 314 (of the testimony).

163. *Times*, 17 April 1888.

164. *Statesman*, 17 May 1888.

165. Ibid.

166. *Reports from the Select Committee*, pp. 295–6 and 278.

167. Ibid., pp. xv, 183, 184, 186, and 196.

168. Ibid., pp. xv and xvi.

169. Buckland, *Bengal*, p. 2; Vasant Kumar Bawa, *The Nizam Between Mughals and British, Hyderabad Under Salar Jung I* (New Delhi: S. Chand, 1986), pp. 216–17.

170. Interview with Hilda (Knight) Kidd, 21 August 1968.

171. *Times*, 25 April 1889. The obituary says the colonel, 'a well-known member of the Hyde Park Lawn Tennis Club,' was stricken while playing against James E. Renshaw, the all-England champion. He was 54.

172. Knight family ledger, held in 1968 by Lady Catherine Peake, a granddaughter of Robert, and interview with Hilda Kidd.

173. Family letter, undated, also held by Lady Peake in 1968.

174. *Reis and Rayyet*, 1 February 1890.

Epilogue
A Prophet without Honour?

'It is so long since he left our paper that our office traditions tell us little or nothing about him,' was the reaction of the *Times of India* to the news of the 1890 death of its founder, the man who had created its expansive name and viewpoint, the man who had been hailed as a Bombay civic hero only twenty-six years earlier. It disparaged 'his politics and his idiosyncrasies, for which, we are bound to say, we have little sympathy'. It said that even after losing his money in London and returning to Calcutta, 'he preferred to be on the losing side, not so much from conviction as from the innate love of singularity....'[1]

After such an appreciation, even the obituary of his Calcutta rival, the *Englishman*, appears warm and generous:

This is no time or place to speak of ... the extremes into which he was carried by an impetuous disposition, but it is only a just tribute to the deceased to say that he was fearless in his advocacy of any cause which he adopted, and that his sympathies were easily enlisted on the side of the weak and suffering. His zeal might at times outrun the bounds of discretion, but when it happened the cause was generally one that appealed strongly to the warm and generous instincts of the man....[2]

Other Anglo-Indian papers also showed a sympathetic understanding. The *Bombay Gazette* ran a detailed and reasonably accurate biography.[3] The *Morning Post* of Allahabad called Knight 'a Radical down to the ground, and regarded himself and his journal as representing "Her Majesty's Opposition in India".'[4]

Most Indian newspapers knew and mourned their loss. Surendranath Banerjea's *Bengalee* called him 'a fearless advocate of truth and justice'.[5] The *Hindoo Patriot* said his life was 'one continuous struggle in the cause of Indian reform.'[6] The *Indian Mirror*, in a long appreciation, spoke of Knight's 'almost affectionate regard for the Indians' but also his furious pursuit of those he disliked. 'This trait became more pronounced toward the close of his life, and the state of his health must be in a large degree responsible for it,' it said.[7]

On the Bombay side, *Rast Goftar*, the leading Parsi Gujarati weekly, said 'his aggressive and masterful personality constantly peeped forth from behind the editorial "we".'[8] B.G. Tilak's *Mahratta* said he was 'as severe in condemning the follies of the rulers as in censuring the absurdities of those who passed off for champions of the people.'[9]

Calcutta's firebrand *Amrita Bazar Patrika*, which rarely had kind words about Englishmen, praised Knight for his steadfast support of Indian causes and grieved: 'Robert Knight was always with us,' although he suffered social persecution 'for siding with justice and protecting the weak. Alas! Alas! that of all men, Robert Knight should die.'[10]

Among the Bengali-language papers, *Samvad Prabhakar* was perhaps most eloquent:

Since the birth of English journalism in India, Mr. Knight was the only English editor who devoted his life to the cause of the natives of this country....It is needless to say that every Indian will ever remain grateful to the memory of the deceased editor.[11]

Finally, *Som Prakash* called him 'India's chief friend and statesman,' and concluded: 'Mr Knight devoted his life to the good of India. And will Indians do nothing to perpetuate his memory?'[12] Despite such talk, nothing was done. The only memorial image of Knight is a marble bust, placed in the board room of the *Statesman* offices.

* * *

After a well-attended funeral, Robert Knight's body was interred in the European cemetery on Calcutta's Lower Circular Road. Hilda (then fourteen) recalled going to her father's grave every evening with her sisters to place flowers on it.[13] That summer, Catherine contracted smallpox. When she recovered, she and the three daughters moved to England, where they occupied a house in Staines, on the Thames above London.[14] The family's misfortunes continued. Alice died, apparently in 1892.[15] Edith and four of her five children attempted to join her husband in Australia in October 1892; their ship, the *S.S. Roumania*, was wrecked off the coast of Portugal, and all were killed.[16]

Meanwhile, Paul and the younger Robert took over the *Statesman* as editor and business manager, respectively. Their brother Phillip joined them in 1897 (until 1911).[17] The sons were more conservative than their father, and the paper dropped its anti-establishment approach. Paul also had the business sense which his father had conspicuously lacked (see pp. 41 and 99). Paul's adroit investments gradually evolved into a family fortune, and the mortgage by the Paikpara Raj was redeemed.[18]

In 1898 Catherine returned to Calcutta with her three surviving daughters for the express purpose of finding them suitable Anglo-Indian husbands. This was accomplished. Imogene and Emily ('Bonnie') were married to Charles W. Peake and George W. ('Jo') Kuchler, respectively, in 1900 and 1901. Hilda married Ralph Kidd, a Bombay accountant and later a bank executive, in 1904.[19]

The brothers appointed an 'acting editor' in 1903, S.K. Ratcliffe, who struck some anti-government sparks reminiscent of the old Robert. He tweaked the egotistical viceroy, Lord Curzon, and then fought the unpopular Bengal Partition of 1905.[20] In 1907, the prospering the *Statesman* installed India's first modern rotary presses. In 1910, Paul and Rob moved to England and tried to superintend the paper from there. They bought a large house, Pinewood Grange, in Camberley, Surrey, where they cared for their widowed mother until her death in 1918. Neither ever married.

They returned to Calcutta in 1921 to an altered political scene, a surging nationalist movement dominated by the Congress, which was then controlled by Mahatma Gandhi. Their brother Phil accompanied them and shared journalistic responsibilities, but after his death in 1923 they again moved to England. Their brother Ray, who had taken early retirement from the Indian Civil Service, became editor until 1926. A year later the Knights sold the *Statesman* to an old family friend, Sir David Yule.[21]

Paul, as the eldest, had already assumed something of a protective and benevolent role for the close-knit Knight family. He funded house purchases for several members. George Kuchler (husband of 'Bonnie') became director of public instruction in Bengal, but he retired in 1913; the couple and their four children then lived at Pinewood Grange until 1921.[22] (Kuchler changed his name to Knight in 1919 because of the anti-German passions of World War I.) One of those children, George, recalled that Paul had given them 'every advantage in education, background and security'; George, his brother Robert ('Ivan'), and his sister Catherine were sent to Cambridge, and the other sister, Meryl, to Lausanne.[23] Another great-niece, Joan (Kirchner) Young, remembered that Uncle Paul financed her major surgery and medical treatments.[24] Another great-nephew, the Rev. Canon Jeremy Peake, said that Paul's generosity enabled him to attend Eton. Meanwhile, Rob had lost his ability to walk or talk, reportedly from Parkinson's disease, and Paul tended to his weakening brother.[25]

Alice, the daughter of B.R. Harrington and Alice Harrington, married A. Wilson Braddock, and around the time of World War I they moved to Vancouver, BC, where they bought a farm at Errington. George and 'Ivan' also moved to Vancouver, in the mid-1930s, and opened a small private school for boys, Qualicum College, with the latter as headmaster. In 1939 George married Evelyn ('Eve'), daughter of Wilson and Alice Braddock, his first cousin once removed.[26] (Within the close-knit Knight family, none knit closer.) Catherine, sister of George and 'Ivan', married Charles B. Peake, later Sir Charles and British ambassador to Yugoslavia and Greece.

Rob died in 1940. Paul died on 12 February 1949, at the age of 90, at his home in Eastbourne. He left an ample estate of £128,000.[27] On his instructions all family papers were burnt after his death, probably by his brother Ray as principal executor.[28]

Though shaped by their shared family and Anglo-Indian experiences, the Knights never lost touch with their English kin. Several of the grandchildren remembered meeting 'old Uncle Henry' Robert's younger brother, and 'Great Aunt Em' his sister, (see pp. 8 and 9) and visits and vacations with their grandmother's Rodyk relatives.[29]

The family was also united by its pride in Robert. Almost eighty years after his death a grandson ('Ivan') remembered that his Uncle Paul 'used to speak to me frequently about his father Robert Knight. My uncle's admiration for his father amounted to almost veneration, indicating that Robert Knight must have been a man of great uprightness and strength of character'.[30] He hung a three-and-a-half-foot portrait of his grandfather in the main hall of Qualicum College and found it a source of inspiration.

Nor was Knight forgotten in Calcutta. Ratcliffe, in his 1914 speech, called him 'the ablest Englishman who has so far devoted himself to the career of journalism in India'. He continued:

In 1902, when I joined the staff of the paper to which he had given— together with the finest character of independence—a tradition of careful writing and editing, I found the name of Robert Knight a vivid memory in Bengal. And we may count it, I think, a particularly regrettable circumstance that no adequate memorial of his career and achievement has been written.[31]

A generation later a young the Statesman reporter, Geoffrey Powell, found Knight still well-remembered by the Indian public, which accounted for his own friendly reception 'even in times of political turmoil'.[32] By the 1930s, the Statesman had bought and absorbed its old rival, the Englishman, and had itself become the establishment paper; Powell said that it was called 'the voice of Clive Street, the business quarter'.[33] In 1932, in an India agitating and fighting for independence, the editor, Alfred Henry Watson, was nearly assassinated twice by extremists.[34]

When India became independent in 1947, the Statesman was the last major newspaper to remain under British ownership, until 1962. Its weekly edition became a network linking Anglo-Indians who remained in India and those who had returned to Britain.

On the other hand, Watson's successor, Arthur Moore, urged the Raj to entrust Indians with fuller measures of self-government, and Moore's successor, Ian Stephens, sharply criticized official ineptness in the Bengal famine of 1943.[35] The paper still fought against governmental disasters angrily, as with the partition of 1947, or oppression, as with Indira Gandhi's police-state measures of 1975-7.[36] Stephens, chastising the Raj for delaying famine relief, recalled that his newspaper's founder had done the exact same thing in 1878. 'Perhaps a newspaper's tradition becomes, to some extent, a living thing,' he wrote.[37]

His the *Statesman*, like his family, remained the lengthened shadow of Robert Knight.

FINAL VERDICT ON THE RAJ

In 1897, seven years after Knight's death, the Congress, growing in strength and popularity, had attracted 'unworthy and mischievous efforts' to misrepresent and smear it. *The Statesman* defended the Congress by reprinting a series of articles which the founder had written, presumably in 1888 or 1889, which included his final judgment on the British Indian empire.[38]

Knight denied indignantly that Congress was trying to subvert British rule or set up a 'Native Parliament' but that 'a wise and healthful government must include the people themselves sharing its labors and responsibilities'.[39] In India, though, the British had set up 'what is perhaps the very worst form of government that the civilized world has yet seen'—rule by foreigners. Britain wanted to rule India justly, but the self-interested bureaucracy had not:

Few of them [in the bureaucracy] find it possible to cultivate any sympathy or intimacy with the people, and as a rule their one desire, from the time they arrive in India, is to save as much money as they can during their service, and retire therefrom as early as possible.... If India is ever to rise in the scale of nations and to make solid and enduring progress, it must be by the people developing capacities to rule themselves.[40]

Knight saw the new Indian nation as a plant which must be nurtured by Britain into 'a gigantic tree' growing and developing through its own vital impulses. 'It is with this conviction full in our view that we have to legislate for India—if her people are ever to look back with gratitude upon the alien rule to which they were subjected.'[41]

Thus, after thirty years of almost constant criticism, Knight's valedictory neither condemned nor condoned the Raj. Instead, he offered a means of expiating all those sins of bullying, plundering, cheating, and insulting the people of India which he had exposed.

In the half-century after that 1897 reprint, the British complied, not entirely willingly or bloodlessly, but probably close enough to satisfy the ghost of Robert Knight, taking that path to which he had pointed, as it were, from his grave.

In conclusion, as Robert Knight had foreseen, it was the Indian-language newspapers which were able to reach the masses of Indians and stir them into political action during the twentieth century. The linguistic states reorganization of the 1950s and the creation of a separate Bangladesh in 1971 opened the way for regional journalistic 'print-capitalisms' of a type not considered by Benedict Anderson.[42]

However, it was the newspapers of the educated elite, usually in English, which created a national political consciousness and implanted the role of the press in the evolving modern state and society of India. It is here that Knight, severe and outspoken critic of the British Raj and creator of great newspapers, contributed greatly.

Does Knight have any memorial? In proud independent India of the twenty-first century, when elected assemblies meet to set public policies, and when newspapers explain world events to villagers, or expose corrupt or exploitive forces in society, or sass local politicians with impunity—all of these are a form of memorial to Robert Knight.

NOTES

1. *Times of India* (Bombay), 28 January 1890.
2. *Englishman*, 28 January 1890.
3. 29 January 1890, as quoted in the *Statesman*, 2 February 1890.
4. Quoted in the *Statesman*, 31 January 1890.
5. *Bengalee*, 1 February 1890.
6. *Hindoo Patriot*, 3 February 1890.
7. As quoted in the *Statesman*, 30 January 1890.
8. 2 February 1890, as quoted in India, *Reports on Native Papers* (hereafter *RNP*), Bombay, week ending 8 February 1890.
9. *RNP*, Bombay, weekending, 8 February 1890.
10. *Amrita Bazar Patrika*, 30 January 1890.
11. 29 January 1890, as quoted in *RNP*, Bengal, 1890, p. 113.
12. 3 February 1890, ibid., p. 133. Other Indian newspapers voiced similar appreciations, perpetuated in the *RNP.*

13. Interview with Hilda (Knight) Kidd, 21 August 1968.
14. Ibid.
15. This is the date shown in a photograph of a family memorial, included in a letter to the author from George Knight of 12 January 1985.
16. Letters of George Knight to the author, 21 December 1984, and 12 January 1985.
17. Interview with Imogen ('Grace') deMorgan, daughter of Phillip Knight, 21 August 1968.
18. Letter of G.E. Powell, a later *Statesman* editor, to the author, 9 April 1986. The exact nature of Paul's investments is not known, but family tradition holds that they included significant shares in the Kolar gold fields, in Hyderabad State. Letters of George Knight to his niece, Deirdre ('Sally') Roskill (now Godwin–Austen), 4 October 1982, and to the author, 28 November 1982.
19. Hilda Kidd to the author, 26 August 1968; interviews with Mrs Kidd, 21 August 1968, and 9 July 1972.
20. S(waminath) Natarajan, *A History of the Press in India* (Bombay: Asia Publishing House, 1962), p. 170; N.A., *A Brief History of the Statesman* (Calcutta: Statesman, 1947), pp. 18–20.
21. *Brief History*, pp. 20–2; Nadig Krishna Murthy, *Indian Journalism: Origin, Growth and Development of Indian Journalism* (Mysore: Prasaranga, 1966), p. 170.
22. Letter of George Knight to the author, 21 December 1984.
23. Letter of George Knight to the author, 5 October 1982.
24. Letter of Joan Young to the author, 27 October 1991.
25. Letter of Canon Peake to the author, 23 June 2005.
26. Letter of George Knight to the author, 5 October 1982. The author is especially grateful to George, 'Ivan', 'Eve', and Jeremy for this detailed information on their family.
27. *Times*, 15 February 1949, p. 7, and 10 May 1949, p. 7.
28. Letters to the author from Mrs deMorgan 29 October 1968, and Joan Young, 10 February 1969.
29. Letters of Mrs deMorgan, 29 October 1968, and 21 January 1975, and 'Eve', Knight, 15 December 1991.
30. Letter to the author, 3 February 1969.
31. 'The Press in India', speech to the East India Assn, London, 17 June 1914, reprinted in *Asiatic Review*, new series, vol. 5, July 1914, p. 200. It was Ratcliffe's praise of Knight that evoked the anecdote of Dr George Birdwood, cited above (pp. 78–9). It is now nearly a century since Ratcliffe's plaint, and this opus might be a belated appreciation.

32. Letter of Powell to the author, 18 May 1987.

33. Ibid., 19 April 1986.

34. *Brief History*, p. 24.

35. Ibid., pp. 32 and 40; Rangaswami Parthasarathy, *Journalism in India, From the Earliest Times to the Present Day*, 4th rev. edn (New Delhi: Sterling Publishers, 1997), p. 232.

36. Parthasarathy, *Journalism in India*, p. 233; *Statesman*, 24 April, and 6 June 1947. Michael Henderson, *Experiment With Untruth, India Under Emergency* (Columbia, Mo.: South Asia Books, 1977), pp. 79 and seq. C.R. Irani, managing director of *Statesman*, received a Freedom House award for leading the fight against censorship and other 'emergency' decrees of 1975–7.

37. *Monsoon Morning* (London: Ernest Benn, 1966), p. 197.

38. Robert Knight, *The Indian National Congress: Its Aims and Justification* (Calcutta: Statesman, 1898).

39. Ibid., p. 1.

40. Ibid., p. 17.

41. Ibid., p. 20.

42. One who did so, however, was Robin Jeffrey, *India's Newspaper Revolution, Capitalism, Politics, and the Indian-Language Press, 1977–99* (New Delhi: Oxford University Press, 2000).

The Role of the Press Under Imperial Rule

The most widely-quoted essay by Robert Knight is one which he wrote, not for publication, but in a letter to Major Owen Tudor Burne, Private Secretary to the Viceroy, Lord Lytton, on 31 July 1876, on the need for an independent press and ways in which the imperial government might fruitfully work with such a press. The original letter may be found in the Burne Papers in the British Library, MSS Eur. D951, vol. 27. Brief excerpts have been quoted in journalism histories (without the full citation). Parts were used above (see pp. 147–8). It was one of Knight's favourite subjects, and this was its fullest exposition.

...The Government of India is necessarily a despotism, tempered only by the character of the men who administer it, their accountability to the House of Commons, and by the right of complete freedom of speech which has been accorded to the people. The State has conferred upon the people all the privileges of free men and, in the conscious integrity of its purpose, has conceded the right of free speech in every part of the empire. In doing this, the State seems to me to have placed in the hands of the newspaper Press a very responsible trust. It is not the place of the newspapers, I think, to be courtiers of the Government, but to represent the interests of all classes. And there is no country in the world, perhaps, in which it is more important that the Press should discharge this duty. But there has been a tendency of late years to less cordiality between Government and the Press than ever existed, and I do not think it has been the fault of the latter.... the Government, as a whole, has come to look with less magnanimity upon the Press, especially upon the communication of its servants therewith, and in particular any criticisms of its proceedings or measures thereby. The change is for the worse altogether. To expect the Indian Press to be 'official' is, I think, to mistake its trust; while if we exclude loyal and well-informed criticism from its columns, we must not complain if they are filled with what is not loyal and is ill-informed....

It seems to me that under the system of administration we have established in India, the only right conception of the office of the Press is that of Her Gracious Majesty's Opposition, and whether that opposition shall be well-informed and loyal or the reverse, depends wholly on the relations established therewith by the Government. If it shows sympathy therewith, admits it as far as possible to its councils, places all the information it properly can at its disposal, shows a readiness to defer to public opinion and wishes when they are reasonable, and instead of regarding the newspapers as a natural enemy, treats the Press as an ally actuated by the same desire as itself for the public welfare, ...the country may patiently endure the want of those representative rights that are so prized and cherished wherever they exist, but that at present are admitted to be out of our reach in India. If, on the other hand, the Government shows no sympathy, is jealous of all appearance of consulting it, shows no deference to public wishes, however reasonable, looks upon the Press as factious and inspired by no real desire for the public good, and gives neither the support nor the encouragement it might reasonably expect—then the want of representative institutions becomes unendurable, and the whole Press guides insensibly into an attitude of hostility to the Government....

APPENDIX B

A.O. Hume's Defences of Robert Knight and His Newspapers

Allan Octavian Hume, Secretary of Revenue, Agriculture, and Commerce, defended the system of official subscriptions to Knight's monthly *Indian Economist*, and he showed a rare appreciation of the editor and the worth of his journal. His memo, dated 3 February 1874, is included in the files of India, General Department, Revenue, Agriculture and Commerce (RAC) Proceedings, June 1874, pp. 1–5. Two excerpts follow.

...It was not that Government by any means agreed with Mr. Knight on even a majority of the subjects discussed, but that his paper was the first, as it is still the only, special organ for the discussion of revenue matters; that it awoke district officers of the several provinces from the somewhat sleepy satisfaction with the arrangements of their own provinces ... and generally, by provoking controversies, some of which were very ably argued, placed at the disposal of both district officers and of Government a vast amount of useful material that could hardly have been otherwise acquired....

As far as I can judge, the influence of the paper has been great, and on the whole entirely for good. True, Knight has at times dashed off rabid Philippics, or broached crude and indefencible theories, but with the poison came the antidote....Interest has been awakened, intelligence stimulated, and...indirectly the paper has in a marked degree contributed to the improvement of the Government revenue. Besides, however, controversial questions, the journal has become a receptacle for all kinds of information on every possible branch of agriculture and statistics laboriously culled by Knight from an infinite variety of sources, official and nonofficial, Indian, European and American.

* * *

Four and a half years later, Hume again tried to explain Knight to his council colleagues and defend a policy of subsidizing one of his papers. This critique, while perhaps overly severe, is probably the most candid evaluation of Knight by a contemporary to survive. It is an official Government of India archive, General Department, RAC Proceedings, 30 July 1878, and was found in the Lytton Papers, E218/142B, pp. 549–61.

...it is necessary to realize Knight's character; and as I have known him well for years, and, despite his faults, like and respect him, I will endeavor to explain briefly what he is.

He is very sharp and clever in a small way, writes well at times, and is far better read and educated than would at first be supposed from either his writings or conversation. But he altogether lacks the faculty of estimating the relative proportion of things. He will slur an important point, make a mountain of a molehill, prefer the unsupported statement of a single...witness to the united testimony of a body of experts, will seize an idea, and run away with it at such a pace that no adverse views can ever catch his mind up.

He is...absolutely honest according to his gifts, so much so, that no considerations of interest or prudence will ever restrain him from taking up one man or denouncing another, if he conceives that he has grounds for doing so. He has about the best intentions and the worst judgment of any man I know.

He is the kindest-hearted man in private life, and would not, I believe, hurt a fly, but he has a vile-tempered pen, and continually oversteps in his writings the most liberal limits of journalistic criticism.

He has, on many occasions, done the country, I believe, good service, by stirring up controversy and disseminating right ideas on important questions; but...he has much more often been entirely wrong, and has notoriously of late years...abused and almost insulted various dignitaries and authorities on absolutely mistaken grounds....

Bibliography

PRIMARY SOURCES

NEWSPAPERS EDITED BY ROBERT KNIGHT
(ARRANGED CHRONOLOGICALLY)

Bombay Times and Journal of Commerce, 1857–9
Bombay Times and Standard, 1859–61
Times of India (Bombay), 1861–4, 1867–9
Indian Economist and Statistical Reporter (Bombay and Calcutta), 1869–75
    (some issues included the *Agricultural Gazette*)
Indian Statesman and Gazette of Asia (Bombay), 1872–3
Indian Statesman (Calcutta), 1875–7
Friend of India (Calcutta), 1875–7.
Indian Agriculturalist (Calcutta), 1876–?
Statesman and Friend of India (Calcutta), 1877–90
Statesman (London), 1879–81

PAMPHLETS, PUBLISHED SPEECHES, AND OPEN LETTERS
BY ROBERT KNIGHT

'The Inam Commission Unmasked'. London: Effingham Wilson, 1859.
'Speech on Indian Affairs, Delivered Before the Manchester Chamber
    of Commerce, on 24th January 1866'. (Printed copy in British
    Libraries.)
'The Indian Empire and Our Financial Relations Therewith'. London:
    Trubner, 1866. (Originally a speech to the London Indian Society,
    25 May 1866.)
'Letter to the Right Hon. Sir Stafford Northcote Upon the Present

Condition of Bombay, With Suggestions For Its Relief'. London: Trubner, 1867.

'India: A Review of England's Financial Relations Therewith'. Speech to the East India Association, London, 3 March 1868, later published in *Journal of the East India Association*, vol. 2, pp. 227–83.

'Speech on Local Taxation and the Constitution of the Bench, Delivered in Town Hall, Bombay, 5th of November 1868'. Bombay: *Times of India*, 1868.

'Fiscal Science in India, as Illustrated by the Income Tax'. Bombay: Oriental Press, 1870. (Originally a lecture delivered in Bombay's Town Hall, 28 February 1870.)

'The Land Revenue of India, Is It Being Sacrificed or Not?' Bombay: Thacker, Vining, approximately (henceforth ap.) 1870. (Found in Yale University Library, Yale College Pamphlets collection, vol. 451, no. 20.)

'A Letter to His Grace the Duke of Argyll, K.G., Upon the Annual Claim Made by the Proprietors of East India Stock Upon the Revenues of India'. Bombay: Oriental Press, 1870. (Found in Yale University Library, College Pamphlets, vol. 451, no. 20.)

'The Speech Which Mr. Knight Was Not Permitted to Deliver at the Bench Meeting, Dedicated Without Permission to "The Twaddlers"'. Bombay. Thacker, Vining, 1871.

'Decentralization of the Finances of India'. Bombay: Perseverence Press, 1871. (Originally read before the Bengal Social Science Congress, 22 April 1871.)

'Manchester and England: A Protest Against Sir John Strachey's Financial Statement in the Legislative Council of India, Dated 15th March 1877'. Calcutta: Thacker, Spink, 1877.

'Egypt: A Protest Against the War, With Suggestions as to the Course The Ministry Should Follow'. London: W.J. Johnson, 1882. (Found in Ryland Library, University of Manchester.)

'The Indian National Congress: Its Aims and Justification'. Calcutta: *The Statesman*, 1898. (Found in London School of Economics library.)

OTHER NEWSPAPERS

Amrita Bazar Patrika (Calcutta)
Bengalee (Calcutta)
Bombay Gazette
Delhi Gazette
Englishman (Calcutta)
Hindoo Patriot (Calcutta)

Indian Mirror (Calcutta)
Morning Post (Allahabad)
Pioneer (Allahabad)
Reis and Rayyet (Calcutta)
Times (London)

DOCUMENTS AND OFFICIAL PUBLICATIONS

Bengal, *Register of Baptisms, Marriages, and Burials* (British Library [hereafter BL]).

Bombay, *Register of Baptisms, Marriages, and Burials* (BL).

——, *Act XI of 1852* ('The Rent-Free Estates Act').

G.B., *55 George III, ch. 155* ('Charter Act of 1813').

——, *3 and 4 William IV, ch. 85* ('Charter Act of 1833').

——, *24 and 25 Vic., ch. 67* ('Indian Councils Act of 1861').

——, *55 and 56 Vic., ch. 14* ('Indian Councils Act of 1892').

——, Death certificates.

——, General Register Office, *Census of 1841, 1851* (Parish of Lambeth), and *1881*.

——, *Hansard's Parliamentary Debates*, 3rd series. London: Cornelius Buck, 1859.

——, Lambeth, Borough of. *Electors' Registry for 1837*.

——, *Poor Rate List for Parish of Lambeth, 1829*.

——, Parliament, *East India (Bengal and Orissa Famine)*, HC Report entry no. 335, 1867.

——, *First and Second Reports of the Select Committee on East India (Hyderabad Deccan Mining Co.)*, London: Eyre and Spottiswoode, 1888.

——, *Minutes of Evidence Taken Before the Select Committee on the Affairs of the East India Company*, 5 of 1831.

——, *Statement of Charges Defrayed in England ... for the Year 1859-60*, 49 of 1860, #305.

——, *Royal and Other Proclamations to the Princes and People of India*, 1858, entry no. 1.

India, Foreign and Political Department, *A Collection of Treaties, Engagements, and Sanads Relating to India and Neighbouring Countries*, comp. Charles U. Aitchison. Calcutta: Supt of Government Printing, 1893.

——, General Department, Public Proceedings.

——, Revenue, Agriculture, and Commerce Proceedings.

——, *General Report on the Administration of the Bombay Presidency for the Year 1872-3*. Bombay: Government Central Press, 1874.

——, *History of Indian Railways, Constructed and In Progress.* Simla: Government of India Press, 1924.

——, Home Department, Judicial Proceedings.

——, Public Proceedings.

——, Legislative Council, Proceedings.

——, Military Records.

——, Political and Secret Letters.

——, *Reports on Native Papers,* Bengal and Bombay series.

——, *Report on the Indo-European Telegraph Dept, 1863–1888.*

Shridharani, Krishnalal, *The Story of Indian Telegraphs, A Century of Progress.* New Delhi: Posts and Telegraphs Deparments, 1958.

PRIVATE PAPERS

Held at British Library (Usually Asian and African Studies Reading Room)

Burne, Owen. T. MSS Eur. D951.

Clerk, Claude. MSS Eur. D538/13.

Dufferin and Ava, first Marquess. MSS Eur. F130

Lawrence, First Baron. MSS Eur. F90.

Lytton, First Earl. MSS Eur. E218.

Northbrook, First Earl. MSS Eur. C144

Place, Francis. Add. MSS 27827.

Ripon, First Marquess. Add MSS 43510–644.

Salisbury, 3rd Marquess. Photocopy, Reel 11682, Bundle XX.

Temple, Richard. MSS Eur. F86.

Terry, Sidney. MSS Eur. C250.

Wallace, D. Mackenzie. MSS Eur. F130.

Wood, Charles (Viscount Halifax). MSS Eur. F78.

Letters Written to the Author and Held by Him

From Members of the Knight Family

Imogen ('Grace') DeMorgan, 29 October 1968 and 21 January 1975.

Hilda (Knight) Kidd, 26 August and 2 September 1968.

Evelyn ('Eve') Knight, 15 December 1991.

George H. Knight, 5 and 31 October and 28 November 1882, and 12 December 1984.

Robert ('Ivan') Knight, 3 February 1969.

Rev. Canon Jeremy Peake, 23 June 2005.

Joan (Kirchner) Young, 10 February 1969.

Others

P.T. Dustoor, business manager of the *Statesman*, 15 June and 15 July 1968.

John G. Entwisle, manager of Reuters Archive, 10 October 1995.

H. St Clair Maidment, retired *Statesman* official, 13 July 1968.

Geoffrey E. Powell, a former *Statesman* editor, 9 April 1986 and 18 May 1987.

Miscellaneous Private Sources

Church of England, St Mary's in Lambeth, baptismal ledger for 1826.

Imogene DeMorgan, and Hilda Kidd, interview at Mrs Kidd's apartment in Eastbourne, 21 August 1968.

European and Anglo-Indian Defence Association, *Proceedings of the Meetings of the Council, Commencing from the 29th March 1883 to 30th June 1887*. Now held by the United Kingdom Citizens' Association of Calcutta (its successor organization).

Catherine Knight, family ledger, held by her granddaughter, Lady Catherine Peake, in 1968.

Salar Jung, Personal Papers, Andhra Pradesh State Archives, Hyderabad.

'Testimonial to Mr. Robert Knight/Meeting at Mazagaon Castle, 10th May 1864'. Transcription of the meeting, photocopy held by author.

Jack Zorn (nephew of Robert Knight), note on family matters attached to a portrait, dated 1915.

OTHER PRIMARY SOURCES

A Brief History of the Statesman, Calcutta: Statesman, 1947.

Baildon, Samuel, *The Tea Industry in India*, London: W.H. Allen, 1882,

Balfour, Betty, ed., *Personal and Literary Letters of Robert, First Earl of Lytton*, London: Longmans, Green, 1906.

Banerjea, Surendranath, *A Nation in the Making, Being the Reminiscences of Fifty Years of Public Life*, London: Oxford University Press, 1927.

Bell, T(homas) Evans, *The Empire in India, Letters From Madras and Other Places*, Madras: G.A. Natesan, 1935 [1864].

Berncastle, J., *A Voyage to China, Including Bombay Presidency*, London: William Shobeil, 1850.

Blunt, Wilfred S., *India Under Ripon, A Private Diary*, London: T. Fisher Unwin, 1909.

Bombay Almanac and Book of Directions for 1850, Bombay: Gazette Press, 1850.

Bombay Almanac and Directory 1851 etc., Bombay: Gazette Press, 1851–7 and 1861.

Bombay Calendar and Almanac for 1856 (and *1858*), Bombay: Bombay Times Press, 1856 and 1858.

Bombay Calendar and General Directory for the Year 1846 (and *1848*), Bombay: Bombay Courier Press, 1846 (and 1848).

Burke, Edmund, *Mr. Burke's Speech on 1 December 1783 on Mr. Fox's East India Bill*, Dublin: L. White, 1784.

Campbell, George, *Memoirs of My Indian Career*, London: Macmillan, 1893.

Collins, Henry M. *From Pigeon Post to Wireless*, London: Hodder and Stoughton, 1925.

Digby, William, 'The Native Newspapers of India and Ceylon', *Calcutta Review*, vol. 65, no. 1877, pp. 356–94.

Dilke, Charles Wentworth, *Greater Britain: A Record of Travel in English-Speaking Countries During 1866 and 1867*, London: Macmillan, 1869.

Douglas, James, *Round About Bombay*. Bombay: Bombay Gazette Steam Press, 1886.

Etheridge, Colonel Alfred Thomas, *Narrative of the Bombay Inam Commission. Selections from the Records of the Bombay Government*, new series, vol. 132, Pune: 1873.

Falkland, Lady [Amelia Cary], *Chow-Chow, A Journal Kept in India, Egypt and Syria*, London: Eric Partridge, 1930.

Gladstone, William E., *Midlothian Speeches, 1879*, Leicester: Leicester University Press, 1971.

Hull, E.G.P., *Coffee Planting in South India and Ceylon*, London: E. and F.N. Spon, 1877.

Macaulay, Thomas B., *Speeches by Lord Macaulay, With His Minute on Indian Education*, London: Oxford University Press, 1935.

Maclean, J. Mackenzie, *Recollections of Westminster and India*, Manchester: Sherratt and Hughes, n.d. (ap. 1900).

Ovington, J., *A Voyage to Surat in the Year 1689*, H.G. Rawlinson, ed., London: Oxford University Press, Humphrey Milford, 1929.

Roberts, Emma, *Notes of an Overland Journey Through France and Egypt to Bombay*, London: W.H. Allen, 1841.

Sanyal, Ram Gopal, ed., *Reminiscences and Anecdotes of Great Men of India*, Calcutta: Sen Press, 1895.

Skrine, F.H., *An Indian Journalist: Being the Life, Letters and Correspondence of Dr Sambhu C. Mookerjee*, Calcutta: Thacker, Spink, 1895.

Stephens, Ian, *Monsoon Morning*, London: Ernest Benn, 1966.

Stocqueler, J.H. [Joachim Siddons], *Memoirs of a Journalist*, Bombay: Times of India, 1873.

Strachey, John, *India, Its Administration and Progress*, 4th edn, London: Macmillan, 1911.

Taylor, Bayard, *A Visit to India, China, and Japan in the Year 1853*, New York: G.P. Putnam's Sons, 1874.

Taylor, (Lt Col) C.P., *A Short Campaign Against the White Borer in the Coffee Districts of Coorg, Munzerabad and Nuggur*, Madras: William Thomas, 1868.

Temple, Richard, *Men and Events of My Time in India*, London: John Murray, 1882.

Thacker's Bengal Directory, 1878.

Thornton, Thomas Henry, *General Sir Richard Meade and the Feudatory States of Central and Southern India*, London: Longmans Green, 1898.

Times of India Calendar and Director, Bombay: Press Exchange, 1864.

Wacha, D(inshaw) E., *The Rise and Growth of Bombay Municipal Government*, Madras: G.A. Natesan, n.d., ap. 1913.

——, *A Financial Chapter in the History of Bombay City*, Bombay: Cambridge Press, 1910.

Wheeler, J. Talboys, *The History of the Imperial Assemblage at Delhi, Held on the 1st January, 1877*, London: Longmans Green Reader and Dyer, 1877.

SECONDARY SOURCES

Alavi, Seema, *The Sepoys and the Company, Tradition and Transition in Northern India, 1770–1830*, New Delhi: Oxford University Press, 1995.

Albuquerque, Teresa, *Urbs Prima in Indis, An Epoch in the History of Bombay, 1840–1865*, New Delhi: Promilla, 1985.

Anderson, Benedict, *Imagined Communities, Reflections on the Origins and Spread of Nationalism*, rev. edn, London: Verso, 2006.

Baden-Powell, B.H., *The Land-Systems of British India*, Delhi; Oriental Publishers, 1974 [1892].

Balfour, Betty, *The History of Lord Lytton 's Indian Administration, 1876 to 1880*, London: Longmans Green , 1899.

Basham, A.L., *The Wonder That Was India*, 3rd rev. edn, New York: Taplinger, 1967.

Bawa, Vasant Kumar, *The Nizam Between Mughals and British, Hyderabad Under Salar Jung I*, New Delhi: S. Chand, 1986.

——, 'Salar Jung and the Nizam's State Railway, 1860–1883', *Indian Economic and Social History Review*, 2 (5), October 1965, pp. 307–40.

Bayley, C.A., *Empire and Information, Intelligence Gathering and Social Communication in India, 1780–1870*, Cambridge: Cambridge University Press, 1996.

Bell, T(homas) Evans, *The Mysore Reversion*, London: Trubner, 1865.

——, *Retrospects and Prospects of Indian Policy*, London: Trubner, 1868.

Besant, (Sir) Walter, *South London*, New York: Frederick Stokes, 1898.

Buchanan, Daniel Houston, *The Development of Capitalistic Enterprise in India*, New York: Macmillan, 1934.

Buckland, C.E., *Dictionary of Indian Biography*, London: Swan Sonnenschein, 1906.

——, *Bengal Under the Lieutenant-Governors*, 2nd edn, Calcutta: Kedernath Bose, 1902.

Cannadine, David, *Ornamentalism, How the British Saw Their Empire*, Oxford: Oxford University Press, 2001.

Chakraborti, Haripada, *Trade and Commerce of Ancient India*, Calcutta: Academic Publishers, 1966.

Charlesworth, Neil, *Peasants and Imperial Rule, Agriculture and Agrarian Society in the Bombay Presidency, 1850–1935*, Cambridge: University Press, 1985.

Chaudhuri, Nani Gopal, *British Relations With Hyderabad (1798–1843)*, Calcutta: University of Calcutta, 1964.

Clunn, Harold P., *The Face of London*, London: Spring Books, ap. 1960.

Cohn, Bernard S., 'Representing Authority in Victorian India', in Eric Hobsbawm and Terrence Ranger, eds, *The Invention of Tradition*, Cambridge: Cambridge University Press, 1983, pp. 165–210.

Dasgupta, Uma, *Rise of an Indian Public, Impact of Official Policy 1870–1880*, Calcutta: Rddhi, 1977.

Davidson, Edward, *The Railways of India, Written With an Account of Their Rise, Progress, and Construction*, London: E. and F.N. Spon, 1868.

Desmond, Robert W., *The Information Process, World News Reporting to the Twentieth Century*, Iowa City: University of Iowa Press, 1978.

Dewar, Douglas, *Bygone Days in India*, London: John Lane The Bodley Head, 1922.

Dhar, Kiran Nath, 'Some Indian Economist', *Calcutta Review*, 127 (253) July 1908, pp. 418–35.

Dictionary of National Biography, London: Oxford University Press, 1937–38 (reprint of the 1921–2 edn).

Dirks, Nicholas D., *Castes of Mind, Colonialism and the Making of Modern India*, Princeton: Princeton University Press, 2001.

Dobbin, Christine, *Urban Leadership in Western India*, London: Oxford University Press, 1972.

Dodwell, H.H., ed., *The Cambridge History of India*, vol. 5, British India. Delhi: S. Chand, 1964 [1932].

Dossal, Mariam, *Imperial Designs and Indian Realities, The Planning of Bombay City, 1845–1875*, Bombay: Oxford University Press, 1991.

Douglas, James, *Bombay and Western India*. London: Sampson Low Marston, 1893.

Dutt, Romesh. *The Economic History of India in the Victorian Age from the Accession of Queen Victoria to the Commencement of the Twentieth Century*, 2nd edn, London: Kegan Paul Trench Trubner, 1906.

———, *The Economic History of India Under Early British Rule*, London: Routledge and Kegan Paul, 1956 [1901].

Dyos, H.J., *Victorian Suburb, A Study of the Growth of Camberwell*, Leicester: University Press, 1977.

Edwardes, S(tephen) M., *District Gazetteer of Bombay City and Island*, Bombay: Times Press, 1909.

———, *The Rise of Bombay, A Retrospect*, Bombay: Times of India Press, 1932.

Famous Parsis, Madras: G.A. Natesan, n.d. (1930).

Finkelstein, David and Douglas M. Peers, eds, *Negotiating India in the Nineteenth Century Media*, Basingstoke: Macmillan, 2000.

Ghose, Benoy, ed., *Selections from English Periodicals of 19th Century Bengal*, vol. 7, 1875–80, *The Statesman*, Calcutta: Papyrus, 1981.

Ghosh, Suresh Chandra, *Dalhousie in India, 1848–5*, New Delhi: Munshiram Manoharlal, 1975.

Gleason, John Howes, *The Genesis of Russophobia in Great Britain, A Study of the Interaction of Policy and Opinion*, Harvard: University Press, 1950.

Gopal, S., *British Policy in India, 1858–1905*, Cambridge: University Press, 1965.

———, *The Viceroyalty of Lord Ripon, 1880–1884*, London: Oxford University Press, 1953.

Gordon, Leonard A., *Bengal: The Nationalist Movement, 1876–1940*, New York: Columbia University Press, 1974.

Gorst, John Eldon, 'The Kingdom of the Nizam', *Fortnightly Review*, vol. 35, new series, January–June, 1884, pp. 522–30.

Headrick, Daniel H., *The Tentacles of Progress, Technology Transfer in the Age of Imperialism, 1850–1940*, New York: Oxford University Press, 1988.

Henderson, Michael, *Experiment With Untruth, India Under Emergency*, Columbia, Mo.: South Asia Books, 1977.

Hibbert, Christopher, *The Great Mutiny, India 1857*, New York: Viking, 1978.

Hill, George, *The Electoral History of the Borough of Lambeth Since the Enfranchisement in 1832*, London: Stanford, 1879.

Hirschmann, Edwin, '*White Mutiny': The Ilbert Bill Crisis in India and the Genesis of the Indian National Congress*, New Delhi: Heritage, 1980.

Hutchins, Francis G., *The Illusion of Permanence, British Imperialism in India*, Princeton: Princeton University Press, 1967.

Hyderabad Affairs, Moulvie Syed Mahdi Ali, comp., Bombay: Times of India Press, 1883–6.

Ilbert, C.P., *The Government of India, Being A Digest of Statute Law Relating Thereto*, 2nd edn, Oxford: Clarendon Press, 1907.

Inden, Ronald, *Imagining India*, Oxford: Blackwell, 1990.

Israel, Milton, *Communications and Power, Propaganda and the Press in the Indian Nationalist Struggle, 1920–1947*, Cambridge: University Press, 1994.

Jeffrey, Robin, *India's Newspaper Revolution, Capitalism, Politics, and the Indian-Language Press, 1977–99*, New Delhi: Oxford University Press, 2000.

Kaul, Chandrika, *Reporting the Raj, The British Press and India, c.1880–1922*, Manchester: Manchester University Press, 2003.

Kaye, John William, *A History of the War in Afghanistan*, London: Richard Bentley, 1851.

——, *History of the Sepoy War in India, 1857–8*, London: W.H. Allen, 1876.

Kerr, Ian J., *Building the Railways of the Raj*, New Delhi: Oxford University Press, 1995.

Klein, Ira, 'Urban Development and Death: Bombay City, 1870–1914', *Modern Area Studies*, vol. 20, October 1986, pp. 725–54.

Kling, Blair B., *Partner in Empire: Dwarkanath Tagore and the Age of Enterprise in Eastern India*, Berkeley: University of California Press, 1976.

——, *The Blue Mutiny, The Indigo Disturbances in Bengal, 1857–60*, Philadelphia: University of Pennsylvania Press, 1966.

Kopf, David, *The Brahmo Samaj and the Shaping of the Modern Indian Mind*, Princeton: Princeton University Press, 1979.

Krishna Murthy, Nadig, *Indian Journalism: Origin, Growth and Development of Indian Journalism*, Mysore: Prasaranga, 1966.

Kumar, Dharma, ed., *The Cambridge Economic History of India*, vol. 2, Hyderabad: Orient Longman, 1984 [1982].

Lingat, Robert (trans. from French by J. Duncan M. Derrett), *The Classical Law of India*, 1st Indian edn, New Delhi: Munshiram Manoharlal, 1993.

Lynton, Harriet Ronken, *My Dear Nawab Sahib*, Hyderabad: Orient Longman, 1991.

MacMillan, Margaret, *Women of the Raj*, New York: Thames and Hudson, 1988.

Majumdar, Bimanbehari, *Indian Political Associations and Reform of Legislature, 1818–1917*, Calcutta: Firma K.L. Mukhopadhyay, 1965.

Majumdar, R.C., *History of the Freedom Movements in India*, Calcutta: Firma K.L. Mukhopadhyay, 1962.

——, *History of Modern Bengal*, Calcutta: G. Baradwaj, 1978.

——, gen. ed., *The History and Culture of the Indian People*, Bombay: Bharatya Vidya Bhavan, 1951–69.

Mallet, Bernard, *Thomas George, Earl of Northbrook, GCSI, A Memoir*, London: Longmans Green, 1908.

Martineau, John, *The Life and Correspondence of the Rt. Hon. Sir Bartle Frere*, London: John Murray, 1892,

Masani, R.P., *Dadabhai Naoroji, The Grand Old Man of India*, London: George Allen and Unwin, 1939.

——, *The Evolution of Local Self-Government in Bombay*, London: Oxford University Press, 1929.

Masselos, J.C., *Toward Nationalism, Group Affiliations and the Politics of Public Associations in Nineteenth Century Western India*, Bombay: Popular Prakashan, 1974.

McAlpin, Michelle Burge, 'Economic Policy and the True Believer: The Use of Ricardian Rent Theory in the Bombay Survey and Settlement System', *Journal of Economic History*, 44 (2), June 1984, pp. 421–7.

Mehrotra, S.R., *The Emergence of the Indian National Congress*, New York: Barnes and Noble, 1971.

Metcalf, Thomas R., *The New Cambridge History of India*, vol. 3.4, *Ideologies of the Raj*, 1st Indian edn, New Delhi: Cambridge University Press/ Foundation Books, 1995.

Mill, James, *The History of British India*, New York: Chelsea House, 1968 [1818].

Moon, Penderel, *The British Conquest and Dominion of India*, London: Duckworth, 1989.

Moore, R.J., *Sir Charles Wood's Indian Policy, 1853–66*, Manchester: University Press, 1966.

Moreno, H.W.B., *The Paikpara and Kandi Raj*, Calcutta: Moreno, 1919.

Motiwala (or Motivala), B.N., *Karsondas Mulji, A Biographical Study*, Bombay: Karsondas Mulji Centenary Celebration Committee, 1936.

Moulton, Edward C., *Lord Northbrook's Indian Administration, 1872–6*, New York: Asia Publishing House, 1968.

Naoroji, Dadabhai, *The Poverty of India*, London: Brooks, Day and Son, 1878.

——, *The Condition of India*, Bombay: Ranina, 1881.

Natarajan, S(waminath), *A Century of Social Reform in India*, Bombay: Asia Publishing House, 1959.

——, *A History of the Press in India*, Bombay: Asia Publishing House, 1962.

Parthasarathy, Rangaswami, *Journalism in India, From the Earliest Times to the Present Day*, 4th rev. edn, New Delhi: Sterling, 1997.

Ramm, Agatha, ed., *The Political Correspondence of Mr. Gladstone and Lord Grenville, 1876–1886,* Oxford: Clarendon Press, 1962.

Ratcliffe, S.K. ,'The Press in India', *Asiatic Review,* new series, vol. 5, July 1914, pp. 181–221.

Rawal, Munni, *Dadabhai Naoroji, A Prophet of Indian Nationalism (1855–1900),* New Delhi: Anmol Publications, 1989.

Ray, Bharati, *Hyderabad and British Paramountcy, 1858–1883,* New Delhi: Oxford University Press, 1988.

Raychaudhuri, Tapan and Irfan Habib, eds, *The Cambridge Economic History of India,* vol. 1. Hyderabad: Orient Longman 1984 [orig. edn, Cambridge: University Press, 1982].

Read, Donald, *The Power of News, The History of Reuters, 1849–1989,* Oxford: Oxford University Press, 1992.

Saletore, R.N., *Early Indian Economic History,* London: Curzon Press, 1973.

Sanial, S. C., 'The History of Journalism in India – V', *Calcutta Review,* vol. 127, July 1908, pp. 351–403.

——,'The History of the Press in India – IX', *Calcutta Review,* 130 (2), April 1910, pp. 264–94.

——, ' The History of the Press in India – X', *Calcutta Review,* 131 (1), July 1910, pp. 352–80.

——, 'Father of Indian Journalism – I', *Calcutta Review,* vol. 19 of 3rd series, May–June 1926, pp. 287–325.

——, 'Father of Indian Journalism – II', *Calcutta Review,* vol. 20 of 3rd series, pt 1, July 1926, pp. 28–63.

——, 'Father of Indian Journalism – III', *Calcutta Review,* vol. 20 of 3rd series, pt 2, August 1926, pp. 305–49.

Seal, Anil, *The Emergence of Indian Nationalism· Competition and Collaboration in the later Nineteenth Century,* Cambridge: University Press, 1968.

Searight, Sarah, *Steaming East,* London: Bodley Head, 1991.

Sethia, Tara, 'Railways, Raj and the Indian States: Policy of Collaboration and Coercion in Hyderabad State', in Clarence B. Davis and Kenneth E. Wilburn, Jr, eds, *Railway Imperialism* with Ronald E. Robinson, New York: Greenwood Press, 1991.

Sheppard, Samuel T., *Bombay,* Bombay: Times of India Press, 1932.

'Sixty Years of the Times of India, A Chapter in the History of the Anglo-Indian Press', *Calcutta Review,* 108 (215), April 1899, pp. 86–104.

Smith, Ronald, 'Indian Magistrates and the Secretary of State for India', *Westminster Review,* vol. 133, January–June 1890, pp. 668–75.

Spangenberg, Bradford, 'Altruism vs Careerism: Motivations of British Bureaucrats in Late Nineteenth Century India', in Robert I. Crane and N. Gerald Barrier, eds, *British Imperial Policy in India and Sri Lanka, 1858–1912*, Columbia, Mo.: South Asia Books, 1981.

Spate, O.H.K. and A.T.A. Learmonth, *India and Pakistan, A General and Regional Geography*, 3rd edn, London: Methuen, 1967.

Spear, (T.G.) Percival, *The Nabobs: A Study of the Social Life of the English in Eighteenth Century India*, London: Oxford University Press, 1963, 1st edn, 1932.

Spellman, John W., *Political Theory in Ancient India*, Oxford: Clarendon Press, 1964.

Stokes Eric, *The Peasant and the Raj, Studies in Agrarian Society and Peasant Rebellion in Colonial India*, Cambridge: Cambridge University Press, 1978.

——, *The English Utilitarians and India*, Oxford: Clarendon Press, 1959.

Storey, Graham, *Reuters' Century, 1851–1951*, London: Max Parrish, 1951.

Subramanian, Lakshmi, *Indigenous Capital and Imperial Expansion in Bombay, Surat and the West Coast*, New Delhi: Oxford University Press, 1996.

Suleri, Sara, *The Rhetoric of English India*, Chicago: University of Chicago Press, 1992.

Sykes, Marjorie, *Quakers in India: A Forgotten Century*, London: George Allen and Unwin, 1980.

The Statesman, An Anthology, Niranjan Majumder, compiled, Calcutta: *The Statesman*, 1975.

Thorner, Daniel, *Investment in Empire, British Railway and Steam Shipping Enterprise in India*, Philadelphia: University of Pennsylvania Press, 1950.

Tikekar, Aroon, 'Dr. George Buist of the *Bombay Times*, A Study of Self-Proclaimed Messianism of an Anglo-Indian Editor, 1840–57', in N.K. Wagle, ed., *Writers, Editors, and Reformers, Social and Political Transformation of Maharashtra, 1830–1930*, New Delhi: Manohar, 1999, pp. 98–113.

Trevelyan, George Macaulay, *The Life of John Bright*, Boston: Houghton Mifflin, 1913.

Waller, John H., *Beyond the Khyber Pass, The Road to British Disaster in the First Afghan War*, New York: Random House, 1990.

Watson, Alfred H., 'The Origin and Growth of Journalism Among Europeans', *The Annals* (of the American Academy of Political and Social Sciences), 145 (2), September 1929, pp. 169–74.

Weber, Max, *The Religion of India*, (trs. from German by Hans H. Gerth and Don Martindale), Glencoe, Ill.: Free Press, 1958.

Wedderburn, William, *Allan Octavian Hume, CB, 'Father of the Indian*

National Congress', 1829–1912, New Delhi: Pegasus (India), 1974, reprint of 1913 edn.

Wolf, Lucien, Life of the First Marquess of Ripon, London: John Murray, 1921.

Woodruff, Philip (Mason), The Men Who Ruled India, London: Jonathan Cape, 1963 [1954].

Index